WHAT DID YOU DO AT SCHOOL TODAY

ABOUT THE AUTHOR

Margaret Kelly (Meg) Carroll is Professor in the School of Education at Saint Xavier University where she teaches courses in special education and elementary and secondary methods. The author of nearly twenty professional journal articles and several other books, Meg is also a frequent presenter at professional conferences, teacher institutes, and parent-teacher organization meetings. Meg is the author of a monthly column in her local newspaper, providing tips to parents on learning and helping their children succeed in school. The mother of nine-year-old twins and a five-year-old as well as the pseudomother of a now-grown nephew, Meg brings her expertise as an education specialist and her experience as a parent of students of various ages to this book. Meg has degrees from Loyola University of Chicago (doctorate), Chicago State University (masters) and University of Illinois—Urbana (baccalaureate) and is a certified teacher in the state of Illinois in the areas of early childhood education, elementary education, secondary education, and special education (mental retardation, learning disabilities, behavior disorders). The author has taught in high school, junior high school, elementary school, preschool and at the college level. Meg is passionate about the learning of learners at all levels.

WHAT DID YOU DO AT SCHOOL TODAY?

A Guide to Schooling and School Success

By

MARGARET KELLY CARROLL, ED.D.

Saint Xavier University
Chicago, Illinois

CHARLES C THOMAS • PUBLISHER, LTD.
Springfield • Illinois • U.S.A.

Published and Distributed Throughout the World by

CHARLES C THOMAS • PUBLISHER, LTD.
2600 South First Street
Springfield, Illinois 62794-9265

©1998 by CHARLES C THOMAS • PUBLISHER, LTD.
ISBN 0-398-06856-9 (cloth)
ISBN 0-398-06857-7 (paper)

Library of Congress Catalog Card Number: 98-11121

*With THOMAS BOOKS careful attention is given to all details of manufacturing
and design. It is the Publisher's desire to present books that are satisfactory as to their
physical qualities and artistic possibilities and appropriate for their particular use.
THOMAS BOOKS will be true to those laws of quality that assure a good name and
good will.*

*Printed in the United States of America
MS-R-3*

Library of Congress Cataloging in Publication Data

Carroll, Margaret Kelly.
    What did you do at school today? : a guide to schooling and school
success / by Margaret Kelly Carroll.
        p.   cm.
    Includes bibliographical references and index.
    ISBN 0-398-06856-9 (cloth) . -- ISBN 0-398-06857-7 (paper)
    1. Learning. 2. Education--Parent participation--United States.
3. Home and school--United States. 4. Inclusive education--United
States. 5. Academic achievement--United States.   I. Title.
LB1060.C369   1998
371--dc21
                                                    98-11121
                                                        CIP

With love for Patrick, Daniel, Hannah and Timothy,
of whom I ask the question:
What did you do at school today?

PREFACE

As any parent with a child over the age of five knows, the universal answer to this question is, "Nothing!" By the time a child is in third grade, parents start to wonder if it might not be true. After all, if the child answers the question with the same word so consistently, and the children of friends and acquaintances answer in the same way, could it be true that nothing was done in school that day?

Picture thirty children, in every classroom in America, sitting in chairs in rows, hands folded, doing absolutely nothing. Could it be true? Of course not. When would they be building the bridge of toothpicks that came home last week? When would that picture of the fat snowman have been colored? When would the miracle of reading have happened to your child? When would the frog have been dissected?

More than nothing happens in school. Yet, what happens in most schools is not exactly what happened in your school when you were a student. *WHAT DID YOU DO AT SCHOOL TODAY* answers the questions about current practice in preschools, elementary schools, and secondary schools. Specific school experiences that may not have been part of your schooling, such as cooperative learning, inclusion, and block scheduling, are explained. The vocabulary necessary to "break the code" of teachers and schools will be yours for the reading. Most importantly, perhaps, suggestions are made to help you help your children make the most of their school experiences so as to increase the likelihood of their school success. Advice on how to face the challenges of parenting is also included.

The Contents, as well as the Index, will help you use the book for specific needs or questions as they arise. There are lists of books for children on most of the topics addressed, indicating, when possible, appropriate grade levels. Your children can learn about the topics as you do. In addition, you will find the book readable and interesting to anyone who raises children and whose children go to school. You'll feel more competent to help your children learn once you know the answer to WHAT DID YOU DO AT SCHOOL TODAY?

M. K. C.

ACKNOWLEDGMENTS

THANKS

To Saint Xavier University, for the sabbatical, during
which I "got this book together";
To Deborah Beasley and Noreen Sullivan,
librarians who offered their time and access in their respective libraries;
To my friend, Holly Mackley,
who thinks I am wonderful and can do anything, for her encouragement;
To Linda Burke and Mary Campbell,
who patiently read and edited portions of this text;
To Marie Czech, an attorney and English major,
who carefully read and responded to a draft and who
kept me going with encouragement;
To my dad, Walter J. Kelly, who thinks having smart kids is great,
and who faithfully drives my mother to care for my
children at my house; and
To my wonderful mother, Eva S. Kelly, who lovingly edited
every word of this text,
and who, because her daughter is a college professor, can
never stop wondering:
What did you do at school today?

CONTENTS

WHAT DID YOU DO AT SCHOOL TODAY

Section One

LEARNING

Chapter 1

WHAT IS LEARNING?

Most people, including most theorists and researchers, have their own definitions for learning (Polloway & Patton, 1993). They also have their definitions for and biases about testing for learning. Learning occurs both through education (which happens personally, at home, in society) and through schooling (the instructed learning students do at school). Therefore, schools, though they represent a formal system, cannot be responsible to account for all learning.

Learning is the acquisition of knowledge, certain agreed-upon facts and principles, everything from the way we have agreed to spell words in English to the number of planets around our sun (Polloway & Patton, 1993). Learning is also the acquisition of methods, ways of going about things, and ways of thinking, from using reference books or negotiating trades to making decisions. It is not possible for each student to acquire all of the knowledge nor all of the methods. Teachers and school boards make decisions about which things will receive attention. Because learning also occurs outside of schooling, it is okay that school boards include some things and exclude others. Students may go on to apply what they have learned in school as well as to find out additional knowledge and methods.

This relieves some of the pressure from school boards who perhaps seek to identify the "perfect" curriculum (written plan of what will be studied and in what order) and from parents who may seek the school that has the "perfect" curriculum. Because students will learn from whatever the school curriculum is AND from other sources, parents still influence what students learn. In addition, a school curriculum does not guarantee that every student learns everything. In fact, we can be reasonably assured that every student fails to learn some of the things in whatever the curriculum is. This may be due to absence, not being ready at the time the concept was taught, poor teaching, other things on the child's mind at the time of instruction, insufficient practice to nail down the concept or skill, etc.

What seems to facilitate both kinds of learning (education and schooling) is what Brandwein (1989) calls the "ecology of achievement." This means that persons in all of the child's environments expect and encourage learning. Not just learning those things that the adult expects or determines, but all kinds of learning. An ecology of achievement puts emphasis on learning as the life work of children, with the kind of energy, attention, and ambition that adults devote to their careers.

Learning of **knowledge** and facts consists of memorization of meaningful or conceptually understood material. This means that students must be taught and directed to understand basic concepts and see where such concepts are usefully applied and then memorize some of the content. For example, students learn that multiplication is repeated addition, and, should they forget a particular fact, they could always figure out the answer by employing repeated addition. Students must also be taught to recognize instances where multiplication can be applied, for instance, determining how much three green peppers will cost if the price for one is known. Then, it is far simpler to memorize all the basic facts than to continually use repeated addition.

Learning of methods or **processes** for accomplishing things is harder to teach and takes longer to master. In this example, teachers might introduce students to scientific method for several years in school before students would feel comfortable with designing and carrying out experiments on their own. A number of facts and pieces of knowledge must be culled from memory and applied at the right time in the process. The problem must be identified, steps prepared to carry out an investigation that may answer the problem or question, the experiment conducted, data collected and analyzed, and data displayed in a way that others can read and interpret. The very number of skills and steps involved in a process demands that students be exposed to numerous examples. Parents know that something simple like showing children how to brush their teeth can take months of modeling and years of practice and occasional reminders. Imagine how much more time and exposure sophisticated skills would require.

Chapter 2

HOW DO WE LEARN BEST?

This is a very tough question. Most learners have definite preferences. Some like bright lights while others prefer dim lighting. Some make good progress while eating and reading, others must be focused only on reading. Soft seating in comfortable chairs is appealing to some while others would simply fall asleep in comfortable seating and prefer to sit in straight-backed chairs at a table. Pencil, pen, marker or crayon—everyone has a utensil preference. There are even preferences for print size. Some readers like supporting pictures, while other readers never look at the pictures anyway.

However, fortunately for teachers, there are some aspects of learning that seem to work for most, if not all, learners. These aspects include: using several kinds of stimulation simultaneously (Armstrong, 1994; Lerner, 1997); varied options for assignments and projects (Winebrenner, 1992); cooperative learning (Sharan, 1990); consistent, structured classroom function (Ausubel, 1968); and hands-on, discovery learning (Johnson & Johnson, 1987).

Teachers employ **several kinds of stimulation** when they write on the chalkboard or overhead projector at the same time they are lecturing or providing oral directions. This also happens when children touch or move the objects they are reading about or touch the letters and words as they read. When students read aloud, they are using their eyes, ears, and mouth muscles. There are several advantages of stimulating several senses at one time. One is that students are more likely to be involved in learning as learning becomes more stimulating. Another advantage is that information is stored in the brain in different places depending on how the information was received. If the information was seen and heard, it will be filed in, and therefore can be retrieved from, two different storage places. Finally, if a student does wander mentally for a few seconds during instruction, a visual clue, such as a key word on the blackboard or overhead screen, can help the student rapidly reconnect with the topic and place in the sequence of learning.

Gardner (1983) proposed that the traditional idea of intelligence as one or two skills was probably in error. He identified at least seven intelligences. Each intelligence has its own site in the brain and its own schedule for development. (If, just for fun, you'd like to identify your strong suits, see Armstrong, 1993.) Each intelligence must be stimulated in order to foster its development. These seven intelligences and persons who are exceptional in that intelligence are: linguistic (words: for example, Dr. Seuss); logical-mathematical (for example, Alan Greenspan); spatial (for example: Frank Lloyd Wright); bodily-kinesthetic (for example: Michael Jordan); musical (for example: Whitney Young); interpersonal (ability to perceive and make distinctions in mood, feelings, motivations, and intentions of others (for example, Oprah Winfrey); and intrapersonal (self-knowledge: for example, Erma Bombeck). Stimulating more than one sense at a time or using a variety of activities and skills throughout the day enhances the likelihood of **multiple intelligences** developing (Armstrong, 1994).

Since the publication of his book, Gardner has identified another intelligence, which he titles naturalistic/perception of the world (Fogarty, in press). This intelligence is exemplified in persons who have a natural affinity with the environment and animals and have an intuitive sense of the place of humans in the larger picture. An example of a fictional person exceptional in this intelligence is Doctor Doolittle; a real-life example is Gunther Goebel-Williams, lion tamer for Ringling Brothers Barnum and Bailey Circus. When someone calls you a half-wit, that could mean four out of eight. "That ain't bad!"

Varied options for assignments have many of the same advantages for learners. One big advantage is that of providing students with challenges to develop many skills. If the assignments on which students are graded ask them alternately to use thinking, writing, speaking, reading, researching, map and globe skills, organizing, computing, building and creating skills, think what has been done to develop multi-talented, multi-capable adults! Another advantage is that every child has a chance to use his or her strong suit. Not every student is a fabulous writer. So if not all assignments ask for written work, this child will have a chance to show off some other skill. Yet, because some of the assignments do require written work, the student is receiving practice in strengthening the writing skill. Finally, giving students some options in assignments ("You must do a book report, but it can be a critique, a summary, or an advertising review") provides students with many opportunities for developing thinking and decision-making skills. It also asks students to engage in some self-evaluation to assess their own strengths and weaknesses.

Cooperative learning has been shown by research to be a highly effective learning tool (Johnson, Johnson, & Johnson-Holubec, 1994). The problem with cooperative learning is that most adults have almost no experience with it in school. This was never or rarely used when we were in school. Remember, however, traditional is not always best. Research suggests that students need much more practice in how to work in teams to face the adult world of work. Students can also grasp some difficult concepts if they are explained in a different way, often by another child. Finally, children need to learn to monitor their own work and move away from only working when the teacher is looking at them or yelling at them.

In cooperative learning, the success of each child depends on the success of all of the members of the group. Children work in teams to accomplish some bigger and, often, more interesting projects. Students discover and rehearse important concepts in activities that teachers have planned for them and they carry out themselves (Johnson & Johnson, 1987).

Hands-on, discovery learning goes "hand in hand" with cooperative learning (Hurst, 1996). Often teachers do not permit children to touch items and conduct experiments because there are "not enough materials for each child" (Abruscato, 1992). In cooperative groups, materials can be given to a group rather than an individual. Because students are working in small groups, they can get a better and more personal view of the experiment or material when it is manipulated close to them, rather than one demonstration conducted by the teacher at the front of the room.

Teachers who use consistent **structure** in their classrooms have much more secure learners, who are not worried about where the teacher is coming from next, but who can use their mental energies to concentrate on the subject of study or topic (Orlich, Harder, Callahan, Kauchak, & Gibson, 1994) . Structure comes from letting the tribe members know where the chief is going. Teachers may give students an agenda of what is to be accomplished in the school day or class period, or may let students in on the goals for the quarter. Research shows that students often respond well to these cues and, as a result, at least some students strain forward to try to help meet the goal or finish the agenda (Ausubel, 1968).

Structure in the classroom also comes from spelling out for students what the assignments are and what is required to compete for certain grades. Teachers can accomplish this with the use of rubrics: a written list of what is expected in an assignment as well as what levels of performance will earn which letter grades or descriptive terms (terrific, poor, adequate) (Burke, 1992). Scheduling and keeping to a schedule may also help structure learning. Indicating where materials are within the room also allows students to get what they need to continue learning rather than having to "go through" the teacher for every little thing. Teachers are annoyed by constant interruptions and lose their train of instructional thought. Students remain teacher-dependent when they must get permission and receive directions for every tiny act in the classroom (Orlich et al., 1994). Putting labels around the room for materials and providing structure breed independence.

Within the structure of a good classroom, then, there is room for individual flexibility. There would be no reason for each child to have an assignment identical to every other child because now the teacher's time is available for finding out what each child needs and for determining appropriate assignments for different children. Do not be surprised or upset about individualization; this is the application of the teacher's best professional judgments about the needs of your children and gives your children the best chance for success.

Chapter 3

MEMORY

Imagine that the brain is a huge warehouse with row after row of four-drawer filing cabinets. Each file cabinet houses numerous files and each file houses millions of individual pieces of information. In order to find information again, once you've learned or experienced it, you have to locate the right row, the right cabinet, the right drawer, the right file, the right paper in the file, and the right bit of information on the paper. Is it any wonder that we say we forget things?

Neurological research suggests that every experience we have leaves a **memory trace** (Schank, 1991). What happens when we forget is that either we have taken the wrong routes to locate the information in the brain or that we have filed it poorly in the first place (like forgetting to label the file, drawer, or row, for instance) so we have too much trouble finding the information again. Sometimes we stumble across the information we thought we had forgotten when we are rummaging through a certain drawer looking for something else (the name of an old flame or a locker combination). We are astonished that the information is still there; not forgotten, just misplaced.

How can we facilitate learning and locating information later? One way is to file the information in such a way that we can locate it again. This includes knowing the names for things that we see and do. The more vocabulary that we have, the more clearly labeled the files, drawers, cabinets, and rows can be. Emphasis on vocabulary development is key. More choices than "nice", such as pleasant, beautiful, delicious, friendly, etc., make the filing more specific and the retrieval more efficient.

Another way to assist **memory** is to learn in a variety of ways (Sylwester, 1995). When you learn something in three or four ways (hear it, see it, say it, write it, for instance), the information is filed in four different drawers. If one drawer is stuck or you can't find the information one way, you still have three more places to look to retrieve the same information.

Still another way to assist memory is to make sure that students have opportunities for using the information again and again. The more times we dip into the same drawer for the same piece of information, the easier it is for us to find it in the future: practice makes perfect. It appears that the routes in the brain for locating information are reused. In this way, repeated retrieval sort of grooves a route, making it easier to reuse.

Learning in more than one way means that memorization is more useful if we use more than one strategy for memorizing. Look at multiplication facts in a table and locate specific facts as needed by repeatedly running your fingers down the chart. Look at flash cards over and over again and learn by using your eyes. Listen to "multiplication rock" or "multiplication rap" or repeat your tables aloud by speaking and hearing your own voice. Use a Speak and Math or computer program and learn the facts by two methods at the same time. By using this variety, memory is strengthened by rehearsal or practice in more than one way.

Practice is also effective if, and only if, what is being practiced is correct. Otherwise, we practice, and therefore learn, the mistake. Imagine getting to the fork in the road on the way to two different rows of file cabinets. One route leads to the right answer; one route has been grooved more frequently but leads to the wrong answer. The more traveled route is the one likely to be taken (Sylwester, 1995).

It is best to practice until things are **"overlearned."** This is the situation in which we can almost "do it in our sleep" (Lewis & Doorlag, 1995). You experience this with toothbrushing, for instance. You would find, if you paid attention or watched a videotape of yourself taken every day for a week, that you always put your toothpaste on your toothbrush in the same way and that you always brush your teeth in the same manner and same order each time you do it. This skill is "overlearned" or automatic. It's a good thing, too. Can you imagine using all of the energy required to DECIDE each of those little steps each time you did such a simple thing?

Memory works in some ways like a kiddy workbench. You know, those wooden or plastic workbenches with perhaps three large wooden or plastic pegs. The child pounds the pegs and makes them go through to the other side, turns the bench over, and begins the process again. The child may hit each peg a little bit several times to get the peg all the way through or may get the peg all they way through the work bench with one mighty whack.

Memory works in much the same way. Short-term memory is housed primarily on the outside of the brain; long term memory is stored deeper into the brain, in rows of file cabinets less near the surface (Sylwester, 1995). Most of our learning requires a number of rehearsals or practices to move into long term storage. This is like hitting the peg several times without much enthusiasm. However, some things are so interesting, important, painful, searing, or otherwise powerful that they go into long term storage immediately. These events are similar to the one mighty whack on the work bench peg.

Children benefit from overlearning, or **automaticity,** too (Lewis & Doorlag, 1995). However, much of what they need to learn may not be compelling, therefore requiring more rehearsal than most children want to do. We must coax and encourage them to do the task "just a few more times" until the answers or information can be retrieved "automatically." Overlearning; multiple methods of rehearsal; frequent, practical application of learning materials; and adequate words to describe items and actions all comprise the kind and amount of practice that result in real learning.

Mnemonic devices (memory enhancers) may also be used to help memorize in the first place and to retain information over time (Mastopieri & Scruggs, 1991). Most teachers report that they support the use of mnemonic devices but know fewer than ten to share with their students (Lundberg, 1990). Some memory devices are really acronyms, using the first letter of each of several words that are to be remembered. HOMES–the first letters of the five Great Lakes–would be an example. Another type of mnemonic is one in which the letters required for memorization are made to stand for words that will make a memorizable sentence. "My Very Educated Mother Just Served Us Nine Pizzas" uses the first letter of each planet in the order of their usual distances from the sun. Another similar one is "George Elm's Old Grandfather Rode A Pony Home Yesterday." The first letters of each of those words spells the word "geography."

Other mnemonic strategies involve peg or key words (Hall, 1991). Learners memorize perhaps ten "peg" words to be used over and over again to "hang" different ideas on. For instance, a child might memorize: "One-sun, two-shoe, three-tree, four-door, five-hive, six-sticks, seven-heaven, eight-gate, nine-line, and ten-hen." When the child needed to memorize a grocery list, he would think of butter melting over the sun, syrup pouring out of the shoe over the laces, toilet paper wrapped around the tree, milk pouring over the door, carrots sticking out of the hive, lunch meat layered on top of heaven's pearly gates, plastic wrap sealing off the gate, bread loaves all in a row on a line, and peanut butter spread over the hen. Once the child got to the store, thinking "one-sun" would trigger the image of the butter melting over the sun and the list could be retrieved in this way.

Some mnemonic devices use a number of strategies in combination, involving rhyming, pictures, color, acronyms, movements in space, writing, peg words, etc. Mnemonic devices may be most effectively employed when they are tied to a child's learning style.

Books to help children understand about memory include:

Bahr, M. (1992). *The memory box*. Morton Grove, IL: *Albert Whitman*. (gr. K-3)

Cleveland, W., & Alvarez, M. (1992). *Yo, Millard Fillmore! (And all those other presidents you don't know)*. Woodbury, CT: Goodwood Press. (gr. 4-8)

Fox, M. (1985). *Wilfrid Gordon McDonald Partridge*. Brooklyn, NY: Kane/Miller. (gr. 2-3)

Chapter 4

LEARNING STYLES

Learning styles is the term used in education to refer to the way in which learners prefer to learn or to the way in which a person learns most efficiently. There are probably as many ways to think about learning styles as there are individual styles for learning (Gregorc, 1979). Here are a few ways to consider learning styles as well as tips for how families can make learning more comfortable and successful at home.

One way to think about learning styles is to look at **learning environment preferences.** Some people like to study or read lying down. As long as your child doesn't end up sleeping, there really is no harm in this practice. However, when writing is required, reclining may make for very sloppy work.

Environmental preferences also may show up in the kind of lighting individuals prefer. Choices include natural lighting from a window, when possible, fluorescent lighting or incandescent lighting (regular light bulb). The degree of light required is also a very individual preference. Some people like bright light and others prefer dim lighting. Contrary to popular opinion, the eyes of every person do not require bright lighting in order to function well (Dunn & Dunn, 1987).

Other environmental preferences have to do with the choice of seating (easy chair or straight-backed chair), choice of surface (lap with a notebook or tabletop, with or without table cloth or table pads), and choice of accompaniment (music, food, silence, etc.). In most cases, going along with your children's preferences in these areas will result in more productive homework sessions. If silence in your home is not possible (it certainly is unattainable in mine!), the child who prefers quiet may find some peace behind earphones—without a radio attached.

Another way to consider learning styles is to think about which **sense** provides you with the most learning (McCarthy, 1990). Some people learn better from reading information, others from hearing it said by someone else, and still others by copying information in their own handwriting or by typing it over. Children may repeat information in their own words (they used to call this recitation) or watch someone else do a task and learn from watching rather than from reading the instructions in a manual, etc. Most of us can learn from any of these methods, with more or less enthusiasm or difficulty. However, persons with very strong preferences may actually be unable to learn through their weak suit or suits (O'Neil, 1990).

Still another way to consider learning styles is to determine **brain hemisphere dominance** (Malfese & Segalowitz, 1988; Springer & Deutsch, 1985). Before you dismiss this as hocus-pocus, consider that tracing electrical activity in the brain actually permits us to determine where more activity takes place while the brain is completing certain tasks. One way to track this is with a PETscan (positive emission topography). A PET scan can determine where the pint-and-a-half blood supply that brings oxygen to the brain is distributed (Sylwester, 1995). In this way, it is possible to determine which areas of the brain are active, using the most oxygen, during certain kinds of tasks. This also makes it possible to determine which sites in the brain have responsibility for which cognitive functions.

The halves of the brain actually have different functions (Sylwester, 1995). It not only appears that each half of the brain has certain responsibilities; it also seems that each individual has a preference for using one hemisphere over the other. Each individual uses both hemispheres; however, each person has a "strong suit" or dominant hemisphere. Using the strengths associated with the half of the brain where an individual has dominance may result in greater learning than if the task were to emphasize use of the non-dominant hemisphere. Dominance can often casually be observed by noticing some of the following "traits" or preferences.

LEFT-BRAIN	RIGHT-BRAIN
• Thinking: logical, linear, sequential	• Thinking: creative, spontaneous
• Prefers quiet while learning	• Prefers sound while learning
• Quiet, well-behaved	• More likely to act out
• Learns best alone	• Learns best with peers
• Is persistent	• Moves on to new projects often
• Is a step-by-step learner	• Is a holistic learner
• Learns music by sight	• Learns music by ear
• Remembers names well	• Remembers faces well
• Depends on words/language for meaning	• Depends on images/illustrations
• Concerned with details, rules, directions and procedures	• Likes general guidelines, variety, alternatives
• Wants to know where a lesson is going	• Can learn by exploration
• Uses scientific process	• Uses intuition
• Appeals to logic	• Appeals to emotion
• Good at mathematical calculations	• Good at mathematical patterns/relationships

For example, right-brained people tend to learn music by ear rather than by sight. Left-brained people tend to be very organized and enjoy word games (crossword puzzles, Scrabble), while right-brained people are less organized and prefer games of space (checkers, chess). Left-brained people can memorize better when there is a verbal connection or if they create a word from the first letter of things in the list to be memorized. Right-brained people might memorize better if the list was set to music or if the items in the list could be made into a picture or pictures.

Learning style differences may also have to do with preferences for the **way new information is received.** Some individuals like to plod along, getting one piece of information at a time until they can put the whole picture together. These are incremental learners. Others want to know the conclusion and then seek facts to support that conclusion. Some learners even seem unable to get the idea or grasp a concept at all and then, suddenly, boom, they "fall off a cliff" and get it.

Social and time preferences may further define learning styles. Some people like to learn or study in groups, using oral quizzes and making up strategies for memorizing information. These folks usually learn well by explaining what they understand to others in the group; some of them may have the "teaching personality," they learn from explaining to others. Others like to study alone. Certain students like to work in small clumps of time and work several times a day. Others like to spend a longer amount of time at one sitting and then be done with the job (Griggs & Dunn, 1984).

You probably already have some ideas about how to accommodate the learning styles of the children who live at your address. Let them eat snacks and have music on while they study. If they are not productive, you can go back to your old policies. But if the children study better, stick with the job longer, and get more done, examining their learning styles will have been worth the time.

Considering learning styles is just another way that parents use to think of their children as individuals. Each way of thinking about learning styles (environmental preferences, sense preferences, social preferences, etc.) generates a number of strategies or options that make learning at home more comfortable, efficient or productive for your children. The following suggestions may help:

1 Use choral reading. You and your child read aloud at the same time in order to improve concentration and comprehension.

2. Make audio cassettes of you reading your child's most difficult text-book. Then, even when you are not home, your child can listen to you reading as she follows along in the text.

3. Use graph paper or turn regular notebook paper sideways to help keep track of columns for mathematics computation.

4. Encourage your child to put fewer problems on a page and enjoy more open space around the problems.

5. Teach your child to use any memory tricks that have helped you learn (HOMES = the first letters of the names of the Great Lakes).

6. Let your child get up and go to the window, get a drink, or sharpen a pencil every ten minutes or so during homework.

7. Provide children with individual work areas, by using notebooks or folders as dividers, or by having children work in the same room but facing different directions.

8. Consider alternative kinds of seating for homework, depending on the nature of the work: easy chair, hard chair at a table, lounging on the couch, bed or floor, or standing at the counter.

9. Try different times of day for homework: right after school, one hour later, two hours later, after supper, in the morning, right before bed. See what works best for your children.

10. Try to include more touching and movement in learning. If the child is having difficulty with a certain problem, encourage illustration of the problem or using actual objects (buttons, coffee stirrers, toothpicks) to represent the problem.

11. Permit the use of headphones to block out distracting sounds.

12. Permit the use of headphones and radio or cassettes as long as work continues and quality does not suffer.

13. Try arranging work in different time blocks. Some children work really well for long periods of time, others can work better in several small stretches.

14. Try running a fan during study times to muffle distracting sounds and create a comforting "white" background noise.

15. Experiment with different lighting. You may find fluorescent lights to be the best for some learners while others seem to prefer regular bulb lighting.

16. Try to give instructions or directions orally and in writing. You can use a little hand-held slate or a dry erase board.

17. Help your child set things that have to be memorized to music and/or rhyme.

18. Listen to your child practice memorized things aloud or have the child dictate onto a reusable tape.

19. Buy plastic overlays and let the children place them over text materials and highlight or circle, underline or otherwise mark important information. This may help focus attention on key ideas and vocabulary words, and the sheets may be easily wiped and reused if you use water color markers. (By not marking on school text books, you risk no fee assessment by your child's school, either!)

20. Many children have a strong need for structure. Consider making a family schedule and sticking to it whenever possible. Try to have homework done in the same place at the same time of day once you have discovered what works for your family.

It's interesting thinking about learning styles and how very different each of us is. Perhaps you have thought some about the way you learn best and what might have helped you when you were a child. Most people can learn relatively well under most circumstances, but what we need is optimal learning under the best circumstances as often as possible.

Chapter 5

STUDY SKILLS

Study skills seem to make or break the success of high school students. John Hoover of the University Colorado at Boulder has identified at least 11 different skills that make up the study skills category (1990). Here is a list of those skills along with suggestions on how to acquire or improve them.

One important skill is that of **reading at different rates.** Good students do not read every kind of text at the same speed. In fact, the topic, type and length of reading assignments causes good readers to change strategies. Think of how quickly you can read your rental lease or mortgage documents. The technical nature of the text, and the seriousness of affixing your signature to whatever is written there, demand a slow rate and possible rereading.

Fun reading, in which failure to understand every concept is of no concern, can occur at a rapid rate. This type of reading can be called skimming. It is fast-paced and may also be used when it is only important to grasp the general idea of the text.

Scanning is also fast-paced and is used to find only a specific piece of information. You probably use scanning when you search for your team's scores in the newspaper or when you search for a particular name in the phone book. Regular score searches in the newspaper, phone number searches in a phone book and dictionary searches actually improve scanning skills.

A normal rate of speed is used when it is necessary to grasp details and when information will likely have to be remembered. A slow rate refers to the way you read your mortgage papers. Suggesting to a teenager that there should be different rates of reading speed may be enough to bring this skill to a conscious level.

Reading rate is also important because of memory and time. When students feel they read slowly, they begin to avoid reading, feeling that it is consuming too much of their time. In addition, reading too slowly may interfere with comprehension, especially if the text being read is lengthy, like a textbook or a novel. By the time very slow readers get to chapter three, they may have difficulty remembering what happened in chapter one. The details that need to "click" to get full meaning from the reading get lost and reading is less informational and less pleasurable.

A way to enhance reading rate is to read materials that are too easy for you. The brain and the eye work together to use a memorized system of how many words the eyes should pick up in a "chunk" or cluster of words (Irwin, 1991) and how fast the eyes move from one chunk to another. When you read materials that are too easy for you, the brain gets bored with the pace and either increases the size of the chunk, the speed with which the eye moves from chunk to chunk, or both. This new rate becomes the memorized pace that the eyes and brain use. When you go back to more difficult materials, the brain balks because too much meaning is being lost at the new speed. The brain and eyes usually compromise on a new rate that is not as fast as the newly learned rate nor as slow as the original rate. Repeated use of these strategies results in slowly increasing rates of reading.

Another important study skill is **listening.** At each higher grade level, the demand for accurate and attentive listening increases. Consider the almost exclusively lecture nature of most college classes. In 1988, one researcher reported that students spend at least 66 percent of their school day in listening-related activities (Orlich et al., 1994). At home, that often means carving out time for listening to only one thing. If you are carrying on a conversation, the radio and television should be off. Children often seem able to follow several things at the same time. While this may be a relatively useful social skill, it doesn't foster listening to anything completely or in any great detail. School success depends on listening both completely and in detail.

Giving an oral presentation is another important study skill. The frequency of giving reports in front of a large group or whole class tends to increase as the child goes up in grade level. Good preparation and even rehearsal of presentations make a marked difference in the likelihood of success. Parents often stop "helping children with their homework" after a certain age. There is still plenty of room for help, but perhaps the help required is of a different nature as children approach their teens. Being a sample audience and talking over the organization of ideas can be most helpful to your high school or college age child.

Managing time is a critical skill for success in school and life. It includes allocating time and organizing the space at home to study. Good modeling and talking to your children about how you deal with time constraints can be very useful. Add to that some written plans, "maps" of time, and even date books (certainly appropriate for adolescent students). The natural appeal of computer software may be useful in this area, too, if your family owns a personal computer. Some spiffy software for date books and other written time planners is available.

Keep up the conversations that you initiated when your children were younger. Sitting at the kitchen table with sharpened pencils to hand your seven-year-old gives way to different supports for your child in the upper grades and high school. Concentrate on how you can add efficient, sophisticated uses of listening, differential reading rates, giving oral reports, and managing time to your adolescent's repertory.

Other study skills include using the library, using reference materials, and note taking or outlining. **Using the library** is a companion skill to reading. Students must be able to effectively use the library in order to find the right sources to read. A key subskill here is that of classification. You began practice with this when your child was an infant. These things are animals, these are food, these are furniture, etc. When your children sorted macaroni or beans by type or classified bolts, screws, buttons, etc., by color, size, shape, they were employing this subskill.

Classification is necessary to find things in the library. If your child needs to find information about elephants and can't locate enough information, he or she may need to go to a larger category that also includes elephants (pachyderms, jungle animals, animal laborers, mammals) to find additional information.

Another important aspect of library use is information about how a library is structured. School librarians usually cover the Dewey Decimal System and how books may be organized, but your child may need a gentle reminder course from you right at the time that information is needed. Does that mean that you should be going to the library with your high school age child and digging around, too? YES! You will not need to go on every fact-finding trip, but one joint experience at the library for each academic year accomplishes several things.

One, if your child needs review of important library information, you are there to provide it. Two, adolescence is often characterized by extreme self-consciousness. Some teenagers simply will not ask for help because it looks too nerdy or might draw attention. Three, you're putting your "money" (time, effort) where your mouth is by showing a physical interest in your child's learning. Do more than "talk the talk" about the value of an education.

Finally, use of the library provides encouragement for lifelong learning. I never needed to know what ants eat until I was an adult. Once I was out of school, where was I to find that information except in, you guessed it, a library. Large-print books, tax information, child-rearing books, medical texts with information about side effects of medication and weird childhood ailments, videotapes, children's books, home repair, children's names—all became of interest to me after I was no longer in school. All of these areas of interest had plenty of information on them in the local public library. The last thing we want to teach our children is that learning is something you have to do while you're in school, but avoid at all costs once you no longer "have to" attend school.

Using reference materials relates to using the library and is another study skill. This includes knowing what types of books might be available on how to look up information. You can help your child know that there are books such as almanacs, encyclopedias, addresses of publishers, lists of faculty at colleges around the world, etc. Knowing about book organization (chapters, subheadings) is also invaluable. Knowing how and when to use an index, table of contents, and bibliography is critical. Things that you feel you have always known (guide words in dictionaries, that entries are usually alphabetical, categorical or both, etc.) were, in fact, unknown to you when you were younger and had to be taught and learned.

Note taking is another useful skill. It is useful in conjunction with the use of reference materials. Many reference books do not circulate, that is, they cannot be out on loan. That means that you must photocopy or take notes on what information you need. Note taking is learned by modeling; perhaps take dictation from your child on the first search, then the child writes part and you write part, and finally, your child can takes notes alone. Be sure to point out the use of boldface words, subheadings, italicized words, and captions. These often carry key points. Noticing organizational markers carries over to good skimming when reading a newspaper or magazine, which are important adult skills.

All study skills rest on the complex interaction of students with their learning environments, based on prior learning and motivation (Hoover, 1990). Lots of practice and using different combinations of the study skills of reading at different rates, listening, note taking, making oral presentations, using the library and using reference materials are required before the skills can be used fluently. Hard work requires plenty of cheerleading and encouragement: another significant role for parents of adolescents!

Report writing is a widely used method of documenting information and expressing ideas. This method of sharing information is common, starting after second grade, and is widely employed in high school and college courses.

Writing a report actually requires a number of subskills, including time management and reading at different rates. Writing reports also includes the use of three other skills already covered: note taking (or outlining), using the library, and using reference materials.

Other aspects of report writing include topic selection, correct use of spelling, punctuation and grammar, and sentence construction. Each aspect requires time and attention, which is why report writing is often difficult for students to master.

Topic selection is something that students, especially younger ones, put off, thereby delaying the work on all of the other aspects. Students should be encouraged to develop ideas and talk through possible topics with other people, especially adults who can be helpful. The "mentors" or helpers may know how much information is available on a certain topic, making it a good or lousy one to pick.

Talking through possible topics can also help students establish whether they really have enough interest in a topic to carry out all of the steps required. If a student starts to whine that the ideas are boring, or to complain that enough conversation has already occurred about a topic, this is a good indication to stop pursuing it.

Skimming at least one source of information about a topic may also help a student to determine whether this topic should be pursued. A one-volume encyclopedia may be worth the purchase for your family to have such a book at your address. There may be those emergency times when information is needed and it is Sunday, or later than 9:00 p.m. or not your week for the book mobile. The entries in a one-volume encyclopedia tend to be brief (unlike the entries in multi-volume sets), but readers can get an idea about the possible topic quickly.

Once a topic is selected, it is important to determine the requirements of the assignment. Is the student to write the assignment in "his own words" or may information be copied directly from sources? How many sources (different books or articles) are required? Does the student have to list the reference books used as sources? Most parents have had the unpleasant experience of working with a child to finish up a report after the library has closed and only then realized that the actual title of a reference work was never recorded or some really important piece of information was lost.

Following a little reading about the topic, students are usually able to identify the main ideas that seem to be available about the topic. An outline is constructed about the topic based on these main ideas. If parents have forgotten how to outline or students have either never learned or forgotten, there are alternatives. The alternatives are called **graphic organizers** or **graphic aids**. Graphic organizers show not only the main ideas but their relationship to each other.   A simple graphic organizer is a concept tower. Here is an example:

Animals
Animals in the southern United States
Snakes
Water snakes
Cottonmouth or water moccasin

In a concept tower, information is related in a linear way; that is, all of the levels, as you go down, are increasingly more specific.

Some school reports are book reports. Students are often required to summarize the plot or information in a book they have read. For this type of report, a graphic organizer like this one may be used for this well-known story:

(B) *A race has been scheduled.*

The race is between a rabbit and a turtle.

(E) *The turtle wins the race.*   *Other animals think they know the outcome.*

The rabbit is too sure of himself.

Slow and steady is better than   (M) *The rabbit and the turtle run the race.*

fast and inconsistent.   *The rabbit taunts the turtle.*

The rabbit is way ahead.

The rabbit stops for a rest.

Here the B—beginning, M—middle, and E—end set up the structure for the main points of the story. It is not difficult to take those main points and write a report that includes all the important information. Most students are not intimidated by the short lists and are pleasantly surprised at how they can make the transition to a full-blown book report from the lists.

Once information has been organized, supporting information must be sought under each heading or outline entry. Note taking may then be employed.

Research on writing suggests that most students worry about grammar, punctuation, and spelling as they write (Calkins, 1985). This slows down the thinking process and detracts from good exploration of ideas. A better plan is just to let information and ideas flow and edit afterward (Graves, 1996).

The use of a word processor is invaluable in this respect. Errors do not result in hours of time cleaning up, erasing, recopying, etc. Simple changes can easily be made on recorded information. If at all possible, students should be given frequent opportunities to "write" by word processor.

Once the editing process has begun, it may be useful to read the report over several times, only looking for one kind of error at a time. On one edit, flow of ideas for sensible links is checked. Here reading aloud could be very useful as well as reading to a real listener. On another edit, spelling could be assessed. On another time through, punctuation corrections can be made, and so on.

Not all reports are the type that you probably wrote as elementary and high school students with an encyclopedia as a source. Some reports are the written results of lab experiments or a report detailing how money was spent from some fundraiser. Each type of report has specific requirements that may require direct instruction from a teacher in that subject area for the fine points of writing in that discipline. There are a number of books on writing for different purposes in the children's section of any public library. Use your reference skills and get additional tips!

Test taking is another study skill necessary for effective and efficient learning. There are a number of study strategies that can be employed when students need to read and study text information. One of the study strategies that parents may have been taught when you were in school is the "SQ3R" method. This one, and a few others, will be presented here. Most high school and college students who simply read about these strategies will be able to use them with a little practice. Younger students may need some interpretation and direction from an adult.

"SQ3R" stands for the steps involved in this study strategy (Hoover, 1990). In the first step the reader **S**urveys the text. This includes reading the title of the chapter, any introductory paragraphs, subtitles, italicized words, boldface words and any graphic aids or organizers. (Remember, graphic aids include boxed information, word in "bullets" and figures or graphs.) Usually this skim provides the reader with almost all of the main ideas that will be presented in the chapter.

Then the reader **Q**uestions. Here the reader forms questions based upon the survey. A reader may also use questions at the back of the chapter to determine what to look for when doing more thorough reading. Questions provided by an instructor may also be useful.

The reader then does what many readers would have done in the first place: **R**ead! Wasn't all that other stuff a waste of time? No. Actually the first two steps tend to make readers more efficient when they read, noticing details that support main headings and finding answers to the questions that were posed.

The next step is to **R**ecite. Students verbally answer questions without looking up the information. Then the reader **R**eviews, checking the accuracy of the answers in the **R**ecite step.

Once readers become familiar with this method, the total time for its use is almost the same as the time it takes just to read the chapter. However, more information is learned in the first place and retained longer over time when this method is employed.

A variation of the SQ3R method is called "PQ4R" (Hoover, 1990). A reader **P**reviews, **Q**uestions, **R**eads, **R**eflects, **R**ecites, and **R**eviews. Especially for some learners, the time to reflect or let ideas percolate may be very important for making connections. Not all readers derive perfect meaning on the first read-through. Washing dishes or doing some other task that is not mind-absorbing leaves the mind free to fiddle around with recently presented ideas. Matching up prior knowledge with the new information is improved by reflection. This method works well for older students.

Another problem that readers may face is running into an unfamiliar vocabulary word. A four-step approach may be helpful. "SSCD" may be especially useful for math vocabulary (Hoover, 1990). As with any method, it should be reviewed periodically to maintain effectiveness.

When an unfamiliar word is encountered, a reader may employ **S**ound clues. Sometimes pronouncing a word helps to identify it when just the way the word looks is unfamiliar. **S**tructure clues may also help: knowledge of particular meanings for prefixes, root words, and suffixes gives hints to the reader for whole word meaning.

A reader can also use **C**ontext clues. The meaning of the words around a particular word can give a reader hints as to the meaning of the unknown word. Finally, a **D**ictionary may be used. This is the last resort because frequently looking up a word is time consuming and interrupts the flow of reading comprehension.

SQ3R, PQ4R and SSCD. These sound like some robots from *Star Wars* or bizarre technologies. Instead they are useful study strategies that may improve your reading comprehension and retrieval of information later.

An important and sometimes overlooked study skill is that of **behavior management.** Older students who are not still monitored by parents as they complete homework, and even adult students, are most at risk for failing to use good behavior management.

Successful, productive and organized adults use behavior management on a regular basis. They make goals and don't let themselves have some "goody" *until* the goal is reached. For example, an adult might not let himself watch his favorite TV news program until the dishes are washed and the bills paid. This adult works efficiently and stays with the job because there is a reward waiting and because he has created his own rule. Perhaps he joins the show at 10:12 instead of 10:00 because the job wasn't done until then. But there is no guilt or worry while he is watching the show because he knows he has set a goal, met it, and earned the reward.

Another adult might not let herself read another chapter in her novel until her homework for a college course is completed and the lunches made for the next day. Again, once the jobs are completed, she can really relax and enjoy the novel because she is in control of her own behavior and time. The transition from adults setting these kinds of goals and delivering these kinds of rewards to children, and the children or adolescents themselves setting the goals and giving the rewards, is gradual. Adults can help by asking children what they most want to do when the homework or household chore is completed. Then when the job is done, the child is allowed to do that preferred activity. Here the child is practicing **reward setting.**

Adults can begin to ask children how they will know when a particular assignment is done. How much will be finished? How good is good enough? Then the adult and the child can set the goal and level for agreeing when the job is well done. Frequent practice with these two activities—goal setting and reward choosing—will help children begin to structure their own thinking in a mature way.

Do the two adults described before ever "cheat"? Might the man watch the TV show even before every bill is paid? Might the woman begin to read the chapter on a homework break before the college assignment is completed? Yes. However, most of the goals set are met when adults are productive. So, another important part of helping children set and meet goals is that they have lots of opportunities to see their parents and other adults doing just that. Narrate to your children what your goals are and how you are going to reward yourself when the goals are met and let them know when you do.

Adolescents often choose to test the limits of situations. Perhaps your pre-adolescent child has been pretty good about monitoring his own homework and household duties for several years. You can expect some lack of self-discipline and failure to monitor behavior a little more often as adolescence evolves. Natural consequences of these choices, such as warning slips from teachers or failure to earn a privilege (use of the family car, for instance) usually helps teens get back on track.

As you know, it is not possible to be perfect. Our goal for the children in our families is to help them develop, grow and be responsible most of the time. Helping your child monitor her own behavior toward goals is a critical step to helping your child become independent.

Chapter 6

HOMEWORK

Homework really serves two major purposes. It teaches students **responsibility** by making them responsible for the daily completion of something outside of the teacher's direction and remembering to return something of importance the following school day (Cooper, 1989). Homework is also an opportunity to **extend the school day** and provide additional practice for students on topics, concepts, and skills (Kelley & Kahle, 1995; Walberg, 1985).

The advice for teachers is: Consider using homework to review more established skills for your students. Once you are teaching trigonometry, you may not find class time to review algebra skills. When students are concentrating on local politics, they may not be remembering their map skills. Homework assignments can be used well to keep those skills fresh. Even rehearsing older skills that will be called upon soon in a new area of learning is a sensible use of homework.

The danger of using homework to rehearse new skills is that those concepts may not yet be adequately learned to insure accurate practice. Consider the student who learns to multiply two digit by two digit figures at 9:30 a.m. in math class. That student has only seen that skill used for several minutes and perhaps has not completed any problems herself during the instructional period. The student then goes to five other subject area classes, walks seven blocks home from school, eats a box of Twinkies, watches television for an hour, does an hour of language arts and social studies homework, plays field hockey for a half an hour, eats dinner, has an argument with her mother, and then sits down to do math homework. What is the likelihood that the student remembers how to do this problem type and will complete one problem after another correctly?

Instead, homework could become a great opportunity for students to practice errors. This is called engaging in negative practice, that is, repeating a mistake until it's good and learned (see the section on memory in this section). Another possibility is that the student will be unable to recall how to

do problems of this type. Here you have a student who is adequately motivated to bring home the book, make time to do homework but then is
thwarted by lack of memory on how to do this new thing.

The advice for parents is: Set aside a place and time that you use for
homework as often as possible. Doctor appointments or special occasions
aside, homework is always done from 4:30-6:00 p.m. daily or whatever location and time works best for your family. The parent's role is to provide the
right environment for learning, to provide help when appropriate and to
being nonjudgmental (Eisenberg & Berkowitz, 1995; Johnson, 1995).

It is important to engage all family members at the same time, and clear
other items and sounds out of the area. No one may take a phone call.
(Parents, this is a perfect time to work on bill paying, letter writing, newspaper reading, etc., and probably not the best time to be wielding a mean
Ginsu a foot away from your little scholar, whacking and jiggling the table).
You may also offer some motivation so that your children complete their
homework (Salend & Gajria, 1995).

The advice for students is: Do your homework. Write down what the
assignments are and make it your business to set aside time and energy in
your schedule to get it done. It's hard to fit in social life, work, home chores,
relaxing time and homework, but you can do it if you choose to . . . and there
is a great satisfaction at the sophistication you have shown by juggling so
many things successfully.

REFERENCES

Abruscato, J. (1992). *Teaching children science*. Boston: Allyn & Bacon.

Armstrong, T. (1993). *7 kinds of smart*. New York: Dutton Signet.

Armstrong, T. (1994). *Multiple intelligences in the classroom*. Alexandria, VA:
    Association for Supervision and Curriculum Development.

Ausubel, D. P. (1968). *Educational psychology: A cognitive view*. New York: Holt,
    Rinehart & Winston.

Brandwein, P. (1989). Toward a permanent agenda for schooling. *Education and
    Urban Society, 22(1)*, 83-94.

Burke, K. (1992). *Authentic assessment: A collection*. Palatine, IL: IRI Skylight.

Calkins, L. M. (1985). I am the one who writes. *American Educator, 9(3)*, 26-29,
    42, 44.

Cooper, H. (1989). Synthesis of research on homework. *Educational Leadership,
    47(3)*, 85-91.

Dunn, R. (1990). Effects of matching and mismatching minority developmental
    college students' hemispheric preferences on mathematics scores. *Journal of
    Educational Research, 83(5)*, 283-288.

Dunn, K., & Dunn, R. (1987). Dispelling outmoded beliefs about student learning. *Educational Leadership, 44(6),* 55-62.

Eisenberg, M. B., & Berkowitz, R. E. (1995). The six study habits of highly effective students: Using the big six to link parents, students, and homework. *School Library Journal, 41(8),* 22-25.

Gardner, H. (1983). *Frames of mind: The theory of multiple intelligences.* New York: Basic Books.

Graves, D. H. (1996). If you write, they will too. *Instructor, 105(5),* 40-41.

Gregorc, A. F. (1979). Learning/teaching styles: Potent forces behind them. *Educational Leadership, 36(4),* 234-236.

Griggs, S., & Dunn, R. (1984). Selected case studies of the style preferences of gifted students. *Gifted Child Quarterly, 28,* 115-119.

Hall, J. W. (1991). More on the utility of the keyword method. *Journal of Educational Psychology, 83,* 171-172.

Hoover, J. J. (1990). *Using study skills and learning strategies in the classroom: A teacher's handbook.* Boulder, CO: Hamilton Publications.

Hurst, C. O. (1996). Mini-learning centers. *Teaching PreK-8, 26(8),* 62-64.

Irwin, J. W. (1991). *Teaching reading comprehension processes* (2nd ed.). Boston: Allyn & Bacon.

Johnson, D. W., & Johnson, R. T. (1987). *Learning together and alone.* Englewood Cliffs, NJ: Prentice-Hall, Inc.

Johnson, S. (1995). Coaching homework: New role for parents. *Gifted Child Today Magazine, 18(4),* 32-33, 41.

Johnson, D. W., Johnson, R. T., & Johnson Holubec, E. (1994). *The new circles of learning: Cooperation in the classroom and school.* Alexandria, VA: Association for Supervision and Curriculum Development.

Kelley, M. L., & Kahle, A. L. (1995). Homework interventions: A review of procedures for improving performance. *Special Services in the Schools, 10(1),* 1-24.

Lerner, J. W. (1997). *Learning disabilities: Theories, diagnosis and teaching strategies.* Boston: Houghton Mifflin.

Lewis, R. B., & Doorlag, D. H. (1995). *Teaching special students in the mainstream.* Columbus, OH: Merrill.

Lundberg, M. H. (1991). *Mnemonic devices in elementary education.* Unpublished master's thesis. Chicago, IL: Saint Xavier University.

Malfese, D., & Segalowitz, S. (1988). *Brain lateralization in children.* New York: Guilford Press.2

Mastropieri, M. A., & Scruggs, T. E. (1991). *Teaching students ways to remember.* Cambridge, MA: Brookline Books.

McCarthy, B. (1990). Using the 4Mat system to bring learning styles to schools. *Educational Leadership, 48,* 31-37.

O'Neil, J. (1990). Making sense of style. *Educational Leadership, 48,* 4-9.

Orlich, D. C., Harder, R. J., Callahan, R. C., Kauchak, D. P., & Gibson, H. W. (1994). *Teaching strategies: A guide to better instruction.* Lexington, MA: D. C. Heath and Company.

Polloway, E. A., & Patton, J. R. (1993). *Strategies for teaching learners with special needs.* New York: Merrill.

Salend, S. J., & Gajria, M. (1995). Increasing the homework completion rates of students with mild disabilities. *Remedial and Special Education, 16(5),* 271-78.

Schank, R. C. (1991). *The connoisseur's guide to the mind: How we think, how we learn, and what it means to be intelligent.* New York: Summit Books.

Sharan, S. (Ed.) (1990). *Cooperative learning: Theory and research.* New York: Praeger Publishers, Inc.

Solorzano, L. (August 31, 1987). Helping kids learn—their way. *U.S. News & World Report.*

Springer, S. P., & Deutsch, G. (1985). *Left brain, right brain.* New York: W. H. Freeman & Co.

Sylwester, R. (1995). *A celebration of neurons: An educator's guide to the human brain.* Alexandria, VA: Association for Supervision and Curriculum Development.

Walberg, H. J., Paschal, R. A., & Weinstein, T. (1985). Homework's powerful effects on learning. *Educational Leadership, 42(7),* 76-79.

Winebrenner, S. (1992). *Teaching gifted kids in the regular classroom: Strategies and techniques every teacher can use to meet the needs of the gifted and talented.* Minneapolis, MN: Free Spirit Press.

Section Two

WHAT GOES ON IN SCHOOLS?

Despite reform movements and a number of initiatives, what goes on in school is actually quite similar to what went on in elementary and high schools when you were enrolled. A few initiatives may have made some differences and these will be addressed here: inclusion of students with special learning needs, cooperative learning, whole language instruction, middle schools, multidisciplinary study, bilingual programs and English as a second language.

There are a number of current issues that are receiving a lot of attention in the media that will also be covered in this section: school testing, school testing results and parents' rights. The more parents know about school, the more comfortable they are about conversations with school personnel and with their children who are attending school. The goal is to refute the answer of "Nothing" in response to the question "What did you do at school today?" The best way to do this is to have some "inside knowledge" that makes it easier to stimulate conversation with those involved in schools, including your children.

Chapter 7

INCLUSION

A supposedly new concept is being gradually implemented in education: the Regular Education Initiative. Madeline Will, who was the undersecretary of the Department of Education when William Bennett was secretary, published several papers and made a number of presentations beginning in 1986, advocating this concept which has been called the **Regular Education Initiative** (REI). As this movement has evolved, it has also been called **inclusion.**

Proponents of REI suggest that more children with mild disabilities should be served in the regular classroom and that some students who don't technically qualify for special education services could certainly benefit from special assistance (Roach, 1993). Will (1986) proposed that the traditional lines between special and regular education should be blurred and that students be served by a set of collaborating teachers, some prepared in regular teacher training and some trained in special education.

The idea of serving children with mild disabilities in the regular classroom is not new in two different ways. Since education has been compulsory in the United States, at least a portion of the students in every classroom has had some difficulty learning (Lewis & Doorlag, 1995) . Although each of those students was not necessarily diagnosed as having special needs, teachers have always recognized a range of student abilities and have noted a few students who truly struggle in school.

Even the idea of placing children who have been formally identified as needing special services in the regular classroom is not new; at least one such program was reported in 1913 (Kirk & Gallagher, 1979). In 1975, the federal government adopted Public Law 94-142, which guaranteed an education to all persons with disabilities (originally, the language used was "handicapped" but that term was changed by additional legislation in October of 1990–Public Law 101-476). Public Law 94-142 stated that students should be served in the **"least restrictive environment"** from which they could benefit and insisted that **"mainstreaming"** (serving children with special needs in the regular classroom at least part of the school day) be emphasized, especially for children whose disabilities were relatively mild (Lewis & Doorlag, 1995).

The "letter of the law" states that "to the maximum extent appropriate, handicapped children including children in public and private institutions or other care facilities [must be] educated with children who are not handicapped" (federal legislation now known as P.L. 105-17). This "maximum extent appropriate" has been referred to as the least restrictive environment clause. When this was interpreted as "mainstreaming," students with disabilities had to be performing at or near grade level to be sent to a regular class for that subject area. This left the decision about each child's placement and education to local teams of teachers, parents and administrators (National Association of State Boards of Education, 1992).

Since the 1975 mandate, mainstreaming has been uneven (Lewis & Doorlag, 1995). Some regular classroom teachers have extended their knowledge base and skills and have accepted students with special needs, helping those students be successful learners. Other regular classroom teachers cite the fact that they do not have specialized training and decline to work with students with disabilities. In some cases, administrators have done little to foster teacher knowledge of disabilities or effective instructional methods for special populations, and have done nothing to alter class size when regular teachers are accommodating learners with special learning needs in addition to teaching typical students simultaneously.

Inclusion, a term, like Regular Education Initiative, that does NOT appear in LEGISLATION, is a state-of-the-art term often accepted to mean:

- All students attend the school they would attend if they were not disabled.

- Age and grade-appropriate school and general education placements are made, with no self-contained special education classes in any school.

- Special education supports are provided within the context of the general education class and in other integrated environments.

Inclusion does not require that a student with disabilities be working at or near grade level to be educated in the regular classroom. Students may experience parallel learning plans, or students with disabilities may just do what they can of the work in regular classrooms. They may experience the same instruction but complete different assignments. In some cases, teacher aides teach students with disabilities in the regular classroom but with related lessons on similar topics.

There are several problems with implementing a plan along the guidelines suggested by the Regular Education Initiative or the more recent Inclusion movement. These problems include:

1. Acquiring knowledge, about disabling conditions and how children with disabilities are like their regular peers (and how they may be dissimilar), by teachers, administrators, classmates, parents, school board members, and other community members;

2. Teacher preparation for new responsibilities, including team teaching, instructional modifications, materials selections and alteration, class member preparations, etc.;

3. Possibility of shifted focus on the learners with disabilities and away from regular students and whether the effects of this might be detrimental to any of those involved;

4. Human inertia, that is, resistance to change, whether the change may be harmful or helpful; and

5. Possible shift in funds, including federal reimbursements, if students with special learning needs are accommodated in the regular classroom and are not labeled, resulting in fewer total educational dollars.

One way to overcome some of these problems is to provide information to the community about various types of disabilities, some suggestions about how to meet the needs of a wide group of individuals simultaneously and some simple suggestions for modifying materials, instructions, and assignments. It seems important to point out that even among typical learners there is little uniformity. As in the chapter on learning styles, it should be noted that each individual learns in a unique way. It is not possible for every student to do the same work as every other student in the classroom at exactly the same time in exactly the same way and take exactly the same amount of time to do it. It seems clear that human diversity demands some variety in effective teaching and learning.

PHYSICAL DISABILITIES

Medical/physical/health disabilities are those in which a person experiences a physical or health deficit that substantially limits one or more of life's activities (Lewis & Doorlag, 1995). Many persons with diabetes, asthma, or cerebral palsy, for instance, who need no modifications or whose health conditions are completely controlled by medication, would not be considered disabled because none of life's activities, for them, are limited as a result of their condition (Lewis & Doorlag, 1995). For some people, however, the deficit is more difficult to overcome or they might need some modifications.

Children with health conditions aren't all said to have a physical and medical disability. If the conditions are completely controlled by medication or if no modifications are required, then a student has no need for services and, therefore, no need for a label. Reynolds and Birch (1988) reported that "for every 20 children with medically significant conditions, perhaps four or five of them will be in need of special educational programming" (p. 301).

Physical or health conditions may be present at birth (congenital) or occur later (adventitious). Children whose health or physical conditions may require special educational services are those who have the following (not exhaustive) conditions:

1. Spinal cord injuries (resulting in paralysis from the point of the injury down);

2. Cystic fibrosis (exocrine gland disorder causing lung damage in part due to excess mucous production);

3. Diabetes (insulin deficiency causing irregular sugar metabolism);

4. Polio (viral infection that can paralyze specific body parts or systems, depending on the parts of the nervous systems that are attacked);

5. Asthma (bronchial restriction resulting in coughing/wheezing, insufficient ability to exhale, buildup of carbon dioxide until little oxygen can be exchanged);

6. Allergies (low tolerance or hypersensitivity to certain substances/foods/materials);

7. Spina bifida (inadequate coverage of the spinal cord);

8. Leukemia (form of cancer, excessive production of white blood cells);

9. Hemophilia (normal clotting is defective);

10. Muscular dystrophy (progressive skeletal muscle deterioration);

11. Arthritis (inflammation of the joints);

12. Amputation (loss of body parts);

13. Scoliosis (curvature of the spine due to inadequately matched back muscle strength);

14. Sickle-cell anemia (hereditary condition in which sickle-shaped cells crystallize and "clog" the bloodstream, resulting in growth problems, kidney malfunction, heart malfunction, etc.);

15. AIDS (acquired immune deficiency syndrome, a condition in which the immune system is weakened so that the body is vulnerable to infections and other assaults); and

16. Traumatic Brain Injury (TBI) (impairments that result from accidents that cause injury to the brain—falls from heights, near-drowning, car accidents).

Some of these conditions also affect cognitive or intellectual function, or what caused the physical deficit also damaged cognitive function. In some cases, although the body may be very severely disabled, the intellect is undamaged. It is not appropriate to draw a conclusion about the mind by simply looking at the body (Lewis & Doorlag, 1995).

Children with physical or medical disabilities are often good candidates for regular class placement because they can benefit from the instruction at their grade level (Lewis & Doorlag, 1995). The challenges for students with these disabilities include using physical space and being able to respond in school (when physical disabilities interfere with communication). Wheelchairs, walkers, canes, and casts may be required for mobility. All of these take up space. Picture change of class time at your local high school and imagine the challenges. Simple modifications like letting children with physical disabilities leave class a little early or arrive a little late (minutes, not hours!) may solve these problems. Sometimes a peer helper who is not disabled can be very helpful for negotiating physical space, too.

Children with physical disabilities may need to type instead of write, write instead of speak, point instead of speak, or need someone else to take notes. In each individual case, solutions can usually be devised. A good writer in the class uses carbon paper as she takes notes and there is an automatic copy for the child who can't write. A nondisabled child turns pages for the child who is paralyzed from the neck down. A music teacher uses several pipe cleaners to make the handle of a triangle bulkier so that a child with fine motor control problems can still play that instrument.

Technology and equipment can help, too. Computers may allow children to use their foreheads to control a scanner through an alphabet listing and make choices that eventually convert to synthesized speech. Pictures or words laid out on a "communication board" allow a child to point to the words or images that can then be "read" in the order pointed to and create a message for communication. Students with illegible handwriting and poor motor control may type on a computer or typewriter keyboard, rigged with a key guard that is placed over the keys so that the child must actually poke a finger through a hole to reach the key intended, therefore avoiding accidental pushing of random letters (keys) that interfere with communication.

Children with medical disabilities can look odd. They may have physical deformity or drool or use tubes for urine drain (catheter) or breathing (tracheotomy). These things must be explained to regular class peers who may naturally be curious. Extra equipment should be explained as well; nondisabled students may even be able to help students with disabilities use the equipment.

Especially in the area of AIDS, it seems that children and adults need more information. Perhaps it is because it is a relatively new disease.

Perhaps it is because it has been associated with contagion due to sexual behavior and drugs, raising moral and social specters for some. In any case, children in school should be taught that AIDS is transmitted by sexual contact, sharing needles, or your blood or body fluids coming into direct contact with contaminated blood or other body fluids. AIDS is not transmitted by shaking hands; hugging or lip kissing; tears, coughs, sneezes; or touching objects like dishes, desks, or telephones. More information can always be obtained through 1-800-AID-AIDS.

Sometimes children in the category of medical disabilities die. The effect on classmates can be profound. Teachers and parents may have to play a supportive role in answering difficult questions (Lewis & Doorlag, 1995). Some children with physical or medical disabilities miss school due to illness often. Regular class peers may keep notes or write down assignments to help the teacher keep up with what has occurred in class and try to keep the ill child as up to speed as possible.

Children without disabilities often need information about disabilities in order to accept and adjust in "included classrooms." Knowing why someone has a disability, knowing more about what it's called, and why all the equipment is used does not change the child's disability. So why should we bother? Human nature is such that when we know more, we are more compassionate and more likely to contribute to the welfare of others than we do when we are ignorant.

Books for adults include:

Eggleston, P. A. (1993). *Childhood asthma: A guide for parents.* The Health Information Network, Inc., 231 Market Place, No. 349, San Ramon, CA 94583 (1-800-HIN-1947).

Jackson, P. L., & Vessey, J. A. (1992). *Primary care of the child with a chronic condition.* St. Louis, MO: Mosby Year Book.

Books that may help children understand about physical and medical disabilities include:

Allen, M. N. (1968). *One, two, three—ah-choo!* New York: Abelard-Schuman. (K-1, allergies)

Amadeo, D. M. (1989). *There's a little bit of me in Jamey.* Morton Grove, IL: Albert Whitman & Company.

Bergman, T. (1994). *Determined to win: Children living with allergies and asthma.* Gareth Stevens Publisher.

Calmenson, S. (1994). *A visiting dog's story.* Boston, MA: Houghton. (gr. 1-4, hospitalized children and seniors)

Carlson, N. L. (1990). *Arnie and the new kid.* New York: Viking. (preschool-K, character in a wheelchair)

Carter, A., & Carter, S. M. (1996). *I'm tougher than asthma.* Morton Grove, IL: Albert Whitman.

Cowen-Fletcher, J. (1993). *Mama zooms.* New York: Scholastic. (preschool-K, mom in a wheelchair)

Damrell, L. (1991). *With the wind.* New York: Orchard. (gr 1-2, kid with a wheelchair rides horses too)

Davis, D. (1991). *My brother has AIDS.* New York: Atheneum.

Getz, D. (1990). *Thin air.* New York: Henry Holt. (gr. 5-6, asthma)

Girard, L. W. (1991). *Alex, the kid with AIDS.* Morton Grove, IL: Albert Whitman & Company. (gr. 2-5)

Gosselin, K. (1995). *Taking asthma to camp.* St. Louis: JoJay Books.

Hoffman, M. (1993). *The four-legged ghosts.* New York: Dial. (gr. 2-3)

Kerby, M. (1989). *Asthma.* New York: Franklin Watts.

Krementz, J. (1992). *How it feels to live with a physical disability.* New York: Simon & Schuster. (gr. 4-8)

Landau, E. (1990). *We have AIDS.* New York: Franklin Watts.

Meyer, D. J., Vadasy, P. F., & Fewell, R. R. (1985). *Living with a brother or sister with special needs.* Seattle: University of Washington Press.

Moutoussamy-Ashe, J. (1993). *A photo story of Arthur Ashe and his daughter Camera.* New York: Knopf. (K-6)

Narado, D. (1994). *The physically challenged.* New York: Chelsea House Publishers.

Nelson, T. (1994). *Earthshine.* New York: Orchard. (AIDS)

Osofsky, A. (1992). *My buddy.* New York: Henry Holt. (gr. 1-2, muscular dystrophy)

Ostrow, W., & Ostrow, V. (1989). *All about asthma.* Morton Grove, IL: Albert Whitman & Company. (gr. 3-5)

Pirner, C. W. (1991). *Even little kids get diabetes.* Morton Grove, IL: Albert Whitman & Company. (gr. 1-3)

Porte, B. A. (1984). *Harry's dog.* New York: Greenwillow Books. (gr. 1-2, allergies)

Porte, B. A. (1994). *Something terrible happened.* New York: Orchard. (AIDS)

Roy, R. (1985). *Move over, wheelchairs coming through!* New York: Clarion Books.

Sanford, D. (1989). *David has AIDS.* Portland, OR: Multnomah.

Springer, N. (1991). *Colt.* New York: Dial. (gr. 4-5)

Ward, B. R. (1988). *Overcoming disability.* New York: Franklin Watts.

White, R. (1991). *Ryan White: My own story.* New York: Dial Books.

Wiener, L., Best, A., & Pizzo, P. (1994). *Be a friend: Children who live with HIV speak.* Morton Grove, IL: Albert Whitman Co.

Books that may help children learn about or cope with death include:

Brown, L. K., & Brown, M. (1996). *When dinosaurs die: A guide to understanding death.* Boston: Little, Brown and Company. (gr. 2-4)

Fry, V. L. (1995). *Part of me died, too: Stories of creative survival among bereaved children and teenagers.* New York: Dutton Children's Books. (gr. 4-8)

LeShan, E. (1976). *Learning to say good-bye: When a parent dies.* New York: Macmillan Publishing Co., Inc. (gr. 4-7)

Marsoli, L. A. (1985). *Look before you leap: Things to know about death and dying.* Morristown, NJ: Silver Burdett Company. (gr. 3-4)

Powell, E. S. (1990). *Geranium morning.* Minneapolis, MN: Carolrhoda Books.
(gr. 2-4)

Rofes, E. E. (Ed.). (1985). *The kids' book about death and dying: By and for kids.*
Boston: Little, Brown and Company.

Rogness, A. N. (1972). *Appointment with death.* Nashville, TN: Thomas Nelson Inc.

Schleifer, J. (1991). *Everything you need to know about teen suicide.* New York:
Rosen Publishing Group., Inc.

Simon, N. (1986). *The saddest time.* Niles, IL: Albert Whitman & Co. (gr. 3-5)

Other resources include:

The Allergy and Asthma Network/Mothers of Asthmatics, Inc.
3554 Chain Bridge Road, Suite 200
Fairfax, VA 22030
1-800-878-4403

American Amputee Foundation
Box 250218, Hillcrest Station
Little Rock, AR 72225
501-666-2523

American Juvenile Arthritis Organization
1314 Spring St. N.W.
Atlanta, GA 30309
404-872-7100

Brain Injury Association
1776 Massachusetts Ave. N.W., Suite 100
Washington, DC 20036-1904
800-444-6443

Children's Leukemia Research Association
585 Stewart Ave., Suite 536
Garden City, NY 11530
516-222-1944

Cystic Fibrosis Foundation
6931 Arlington Road, No. 200
Bethseda, MD 20814
800-344-4823

International Polio Network
4207 Lindall Blvd., No. 110
St. Louis, MO 63108
314-534-0475

Juvenile Diabetes Foundation International
120 Wall St.
New York, NY 10005-3904
800-JDF-CURE

Muscular Dystrophy Association
3300 E. Sunrise Dr.
Tucson, AZ 85718
520-529-2000

National Hemophilia Foundation
110 Greene St., Suite 303
New York, NY 10012
212-219-8180

National Spinal Cord Injury Association
545 Concord Ave., No. 29
Cambridge, MA 02138-1122
800-962-9629

Scoliosis Association
P. O. Box 811705
Boca Raton, FL 33481-1705
800-800-0669

Sickle Cell Disease Association of America
200 Corporate Pointe, Suite 495
Culver, CA 90230-7633
310-216-6363

Spina Bifida Association of America
4590 MacArthur Blvd., Suite 250
Washington, DC 20007-4226
202-944-3285

Teens Teaching AIDS Prevention
3030 Walnut
Kansas City, MO 64108
800-234-8336

American Academy of Pediatrics (just a general good source, not only physical disabilities)—Ask your pediatrician for the titles you are interested in.

Division of Publications
141 Northwest Point Blvd. P.O. Box 927
Elk Grove Village, IL 60009-0927

- *Temper Tantrums: A Normal Part of Growing Up*
- *Sleep Problems in Children*
- *Your Child's Growth: Developmental Milestones*
- *Understanding the ADHD Child*
- *Child Care: What's Best for Your Family*
- *Day Care: Finding the Best Child Care for Your Family*
- *Tips on Selecting the "Right" Day Care Facility*
- *Eating Disorders*
- *Television and the Family*
- *Child Sexual Abuse*
- *Healthy Communication With Your Child*

Epilepsy

Epilepsy is a condition that, for some people, causes fear. This is because there are still lots of misconceptions about epilepsy or seizure disorders. Epilepsy is a set of symptoms, ranging from temporary loss of consciousness to unusual repetitive movements and convulsing. Seizures is a word used for these symptoms, which are very specific to the individual (Epilepsy Foundation of America, n.d.). Seizures are caused by short-circuits in brain electricity or, in some cases, are like electrical storms. These storms or shorts are due to brain damage resulting from injury, illness or fetal formation.

The cells of the nervous system are surrounded by a fluid called brain, synaptic or spinal fluid. This fluid helps conduct the electricity that communicates information, sensations and ideas throughout the nervous system.

Usually, the fluid helps electrical impulses, carrying the information back and forth to avoid any damaged brain cells. Sometimes, especially under conditions of fatigue, illness or stress, the spinal fluid decreases in quality and the electrical impulses go through damaged brain cells, resulting in the electrical storm we call a seizure.

Most seizures are very brief and do not include falling down and shaking all over (grand mal). Even grand mal seizures, however, are not called "spells" or "fits." Such terms imply that the person is crazy or willfully losing control. Neither is true. If you see a person having a seizure, remain calm. As a grand mal seizure appears to be ending, gently turn the person's body on the side to keep the air passage free of saliva and to prevent the tongue from falling back over the trachea or breathing tube.

There are more than 20 kinds of seizures, some only occur during sleep. In some seizures, only a portion of the brain is affected. A few persons stop breathing during seizures and then cardiopulmonary resuscitation is required.

If a seizure lasts more than five minutes and you are not familiar with the person's seizure patterns, call for paramedics. Do not stick anything in the person's mouth. Try to clear the area if it looks like the person may fall (just to avoid injury). Some people are groggy or need to rest after a seizure. One of the ways in which the body responds to a seizure is to produce extra adrenaline. This production may leave the body fatigued afterward. Other persons are able to get right back to the task at hand. Some need help orienting and regaining alertness.

There is no reason to suspect mental illness or drug abuse, just because someone has a seizure. Persons with epilepsy are completely normal when they are not having a seizure. It is important to remember that and respond to the person accordingly.

It is also true that not everyone who has a seizure will have another. Fever (febrile) seizures may occur only once and are a protective response by the body to a high temperature. In addition, about 85 percent of people who have experienced seizures no longer have them due to a variety of medications available and due to technological advances in surgery.

Teachers may help students who have seizures by helping the student keep track of when the seizures occur, how long they last, and whether there is any pattern to the timing (stress-related?). Teachers also help when they explain what is happening to peers and behave in an accepting way toward the child. Classmates who are knowledgeable are often very understanding.

More information may be obtained by contacting:

The Epilepsy Foundation of America
4351 Garden City Drive
Landover, MD 20785.
1-800-EFA-1000

Books for children about epilepsy include:

Anderson, R. (1995). *Black water.* New York: Henry Holt.
Hall, L. (1990). *Halsey's pride.* New York: Scribner.
Howard, E. (1987). *Edith herself.* New York: Atheneum.
McGowan, T. (1995). *Epilepsy.* New York: Franklin Watts.
Young, H. (1980). *What difference does it make, Danny?* New York: Andre Deutsch.

Cerebral Palsy

Cerebral palsy is a motor disability due to brain damage. Cerebral palsy is not a disease but a neurological consequence of prenatal, perinatal, and postnatal factors that have damaged the brain in the motor area or in an area through which motor messages must pass (Lewis & Doorlag, 1995). The muscles themselves are not damaged; rather it is the brain that sends inappropriate messages to various parts of the body.

Because cerebral palsy is not a disease, it is not contagious. Usually a pediatrician identifies cerebral palsy, although a neonatologist may recognize it soon after birth if it is severe enough for eyeball identification. Sometimes, a pediatric neurologist is called in to make the diagnosis. When cerebral palsy is diagnosed, the health professional will name it (tell which kinds appear to be present), tell which body parts are affected, tell the degree of involvement (mild, moderate, severe), describe associated disabilities (hearing impairment, vision impairment, etc.), and review any strengths the child has (intelligence, etc.). Some children who have cerebral palsy have damage to the brain resulting in only motor problems. Some, however, were damaged in other areas of the brain, often by whatever caused the damage to the motor area of the brain (lack of oxygen, significant prematurity, infection, etc.).

There are several kinds of cerebral palsy, each characterized by different problems. While cerebral palsy is not a problem in the muscles per se but rather in the brain, it is true that repeated aberrant messages from the brain can do damage to muscles, bones, tendons, etc. One type is **spasticity** in which the muscles that pull in are directed to do so even when the person has not consciously given the command. Chronic pressure from muscles can cause bones in young developing children to deform. When spasticity affects the legs, a typical "scissors gait" can be observed; as the legs walk forward, the knees appear as the hinge on a scissors and the lower legs look like a scissors opening and closing.

Another kind of cerebral palsy is **athetosis** in which the muscles receive intermittent signals to work, resulting in fluctuating muscle tone. This manifests as uncontrolled jerky movements. **Ataxia,** due to lesions in the brain, causes balance and coordination problems. Children with ataxia may walk on their toes. **Tremors** result in involuntary shaking. **Rigidity** results in locked muscles and diminished motion. Each of these types of cerebral palsy means that a child's body makes motions that he didn't intend or that movements are uncoordinated, making it difficult to carry out behaviors that would be simple for persons without cerebral palsy. You can imagine the frustration of the children who have it. This requires some understanding from adults and peers who interact with these children.

School accommodations may include accepting reduced assignments (it may take much longer to write, produce a picture, read, etc.), using a peer to help keep track of school missed due to physical therapy sessions or hospital stays, or early or late dismissal from class to allow movement in less-crowded hallways and stairwells.

Classmates and teachers may have to adjust to strained speech patterns, although, like listening to someone with an accent, this is usually not too difficult once you "get" it. Nondisabled peers may use their speech to represent the sentences that are made by the child with cerebral palsy pointing to a communication board. Classmates may notice that students with cerebral palsy do assignments in different forms: speech for writing, typing for writing, typing for speech, etc. As with any other physical disability, equipment and specialized instructional materials may be required. Regular class peers may learn how to use these items or just be familiar with them from seeing them in the classroom on a daily basis.

For more information, contact:

United Cerebral Palsy Associations
1522 K. St., N.W., Suite 1112
Washington, DC 20005
800-USA-5UCP

LEARNING DISABILITIES

Five percent of U.S. school children have them; **learning disabilities** comprise the most common form of disability conditions (Lerner, 1997). They are also remarkably diverse. This means that, although a group of people may be said to have learning disabilities, the way in which their learning differs from average learners and from each other is remarkable.

Individuals with learning disabilities are not retarded (slow) learners. They should have normal or better intelligence in order to fit this classification. A specific learning disability is observable as a deficit in the way the person is able to think, speak, write, read, or do mathematical calculations. However, the person does not have learning problems because she is blind, deaf, emotionally disturbed, physically disabled, culturally different or abused. In other words, the senses work fine (or are corrected by glasses, etc.) but the brain fails to correctly interpret information from one or more sense. There may also be deficits in memory, perception and ability to pay attention (Lerner, 1997).

Here's how it might work. Sam is a student who works hard and tries in school. He is an excellent athlete and popular socially and he even does well in most of his school subjects. However, Sam is terrible at math. When he see numbers, his brain flips them around and a 2 looks like an upside down 7. He also does not always get the same answer when he repeats the same problem. This is very frustrating for both Sam and his teachers and is not explainable by lack of effort. Even Sam's dad, who loves Sam very much, gets frustrated when he helps Sam try to do math homework.

Hilda learns very well from watching people do things and from listening to directions or conversations. However, Hilda has a great deal of difficulty learning from print. She reads most of the word correctly, but she does not gain meaning from those words. If someone reads her the same materials aloud, she will comprehend well.

Tim is an avid reader. He reads for fun, not just for assignments. He remembers details of what he reads that other students do not remember and he enjoys linking things he has already learned to new information he reads. But Tim gets fidgety in class as soon as the teacher starts to lecture. He often does not follow oral directions from both his parents and his teachers. Some of the children at school think he's an "airhead" because he doesn't always follow conversation.

What do these students have in common? They all have learning disabilities. There is a breakdown in one or more of the ways of learning or in the forms of presentation. Some students with learning disabilities understand and read well but can't write legibly or cohesively. Others don't interpret facial expressions or tone of voice the way their peers might. Still others have difficulty communicating through speaking and gesture. The most common academic deficit is in the area of reading (Lerner, 1997).

Teachers of students with learning disabilities usually do not "cure" the disability. Instead, they work to help students acquire strategies that can help them get around their disabilities and be successful. Sometimes, this means asking the regular teachers to make modifications in assignments or in how they deliver instruction.

For instance, a student may need a visual outline, handout, or overhead display (providing a visual image relating to the auditory one) in order to follow a lecture. Another student may need to be able to take a test orally. An assignment may be shortened or put on different-colored paper. The student may read aloud or write down what he hears. Another student may need to tape a lecture and listen to it several times in order to comprehend adequately.

Most students with learning disabilities do not look any different than their regular class peers and most are able to get most of their instruction in regular classes. It should be noted that some of the modifications that teachers might make (visual display of lecture information) often help regular class students, too. Students with learning disability have a variety of strengths and talents that should not be overlooked in the evaluation and remediation of their weaknesses.

With any disability, students may need special arrangements in class or with regard to their assignments. Because children are young, they often have a simple view of fairness. If you have more than one child in your family, you know that the child's view of fairness is that everyone gets the same. A more mature view of fairness, and one which families can help children grasp, is that of fairness being everyone getting what he needs (Lavoie, 1990).

It is not fair that certain children have learning disabilities. It is not fair that they study three times as long and get grades that are half as good as those of their peers. It is not fair that they take hours longer to read the chapter in the social studies book. It is important for adults to help children understand the basic unfairness that children with learning disabilities face and then they are less likely to complain about peers who have modifications made in their school days.

Classroom modifications include not only the shortened assignments mentioned above but tape recordings to go along with text materials and manipulatives to go with mathematics. Special writing utensils, color coding, reduced periods of time with expectations for independent work, peer tutoring, and more frequent teacher attention, or any combination of these may be needed.

More information about learning disabilities may be obtained from:

Council for Exceptional Children
Divisions of Learning Disabilities
1920 Association Drive
Reston, VA 22091
703-362-3660

Council for Learning Disabilities
P.O. Box 40303
Overland Park, KS 66204
913-492-8755

Learning Disabilities Association of America
4156 Library Road
Pittsburgh, PA 15234
412-341-1515

These organizations have state and local chapters for your convenience. Just write to the national organizations and they will identify local groups for you.

For books about learning disabilities to help your child understand, try:

Hansen, J. (1986). *Yellow bird and me.* New York: Ticknor. (gr. 4-6)

Marek, M. (1985). *Different not dumb.* New York: Franklin Watts. (gr. 1-3)

Gehret, J. (1990). *The-don't-give-up-kid and learning differences.* Fairport, NY: Verbal Images Press.

For books about learning disabilities for you and your child with LD, try:

Fisher, G., & Cummings, R. (1995). *When your child has LD: A survival guide for parents.* Minneapolis, MN: Free Spirit Press.

Cummings, R., & Fisher, G. (1991). *The school survival guide for kids with LD: Ways to make learning easier and more fun.* Minneapolis, MN: Free Spirit Press.

Fisher, G., & Cummings, R. (1990). *The survival guide for kids with LD.* Minneapolis, MN: Free Spirit Press.

MENTAL RETARDATION AND DEVELOPMENTAL DISABILITIES

Probably the exceptionality that people feel they know the most about is **mental retardation.** However, persons with Down Sdyndrome (it used to be inappropriately called mongolism) are not the only people who may be called retarded. There are many individuals with very low ability. Numerous syndromes as well as unknown causes have resulted in limited intelligence.

Mental retardation is not the only term used for persons with delayed development and difficulty acquiring adaptive behavior (behavior that is expected for a given age). Some prefer the term developmental disabilities, although other exceptional groups are included in this term. It is preferred because it suggests that development follows normal patterns but is just delayed.

Most persons who are labeled retarded (80%-85%) fit into the mildly retarded range (Lewis & Doorlag, 1995). In the schools, the terms mild mental impairment (MMI), educably mentally retarded (EMR), mildly developmentally delayed (MDD) or educably mentally handicapped (EMH) may be used. Most students in this range do not look different from their peers. These children are certainly capable of academic learning and are usually only a few years behind their peers in test scores. Youngsters with EMH require more meaningful repetition and more concrete presentations in order to learn. They benefit from seeing the practical application of what they learn as they go along. Many curriculums for learners with EMH include shopping trips, cost comparisons, reading bus schedules and menus, and other daily living skills.

Students with EMH are usually not identified as needing special help until school age. Remember they usually do not look different and in areas of development like crawling and walking often have no delays. They may have been late in starting to talk but some children just start later and their parents may not have suspected retardation because the delays were so mild. However, the tasks demanded in school (remembering facts, recognizing letters, learning about things the child has never seen, touched or heard of before—kangaroos, photosynthesis, mixed numerals, etc.) often cause teachers to notice learning weaknesses or delays. Besides, teachers have 30 other students of the same age to whom they can compare a student with disabilities, a comparison point that parents and families do not have.

Because students with retardation learn at a slower rate, it takes them more years to accomplish the basics. For this reason, the law that governs special education, Public Law 105-17, guarantees students with disabilities an education up to age 21, if they choose not to graduate from high school. This gives special educators more time to help students develop additional skills. By age 21, most students with EMH are functioning at about fifth-grade level, good enough for filling out job applications and reading most newspaper articles, but probably not for filling out a long-form tax return. Most students with EMH are capable of work in factories, offices, and construction. Employers might have to explain things more clearly or give more examples when teaching a new skill, but folks with EMH are often excellent workers who are responsible and conscientious.

For more information about mental retardation, you may contact:

The ARC (a national organization on mental retardation)
>500 E. Border St., Suite 300
>Arlington, TX 76010

Mental Retardation Association of America
>211 East 300South, Suite 212
>Salt Lake City, UT 84111

For books about retardation to help your child understand, try:
Conly, J. L. (1993). *Crazy lady!* New York: HarperCollins. (gr. 5-6)
Dodds, B. (1993). *My sister Annie.* Honesdale, PA: Boyds Mills. (gr. 4-5)
Dunbar, R. E. (1978). *Mental retardation.* New York: Franklin Watts. (gr. 5-8)
Fleming, V. (1993). *Be good to Eddie Lee.* New York: Philomel. (gr. K-2)
Slepian, J. (1990). *Risk 'N' roses.* New York: Philomel.

SENSORY DISABILITIES

Visual and hearing impairments, sometimes called **sensory disabilities,** are "low incidence" disabilities. About 0.2 percent of the school age population has these disabilities at such a level of severity that modifications would be necessary in the regular classroom.

Sensory losses result in the lack of certain experiences and differences in other experiences. These differences may require some understanding as students with sensory losses participate in class discussion. As much as possible, students with sensory losses should be encouraged to encounter classroom experiences and have help interpreting what they experience. Being able to articulate a visual or auditory perception for someone who does not experience one of these can be a really enlightening experience for the students without disabilities.

It may be most difficult for hearing and sighted people to imagine what life is like without the experience of hearing and seeing. There have been some excellent commercial movies that can help with these concepts. Parents can really help children understand and be accepting and supportive of children who are different when they provide explanations and give their children enriching experiences.

For older children, the films *Mask* with Cher and *Children of a Lesser God* deal with the concepts of what it is like to be different. These films also show what it is like to communicate visual and auditory things to those who cannot experience them.

Despite sensory differences, it is most important to help children see how much human similarity there is among people and how little difference the dissimilarities make when humans strive to form relationships with each other. Promoting acceptance is certainly a reasonable goal for parents to set for their hopes with their children. Viva la difference!

Vision Impaired

Vision impaired students include students who are **blind** (no vision or only awareness of light and dark) or **partially sighted** (also called low vision or legally blind). Persons who are partially sighted can see things at close range but have difficulty seeing things more than three feet away. Of course, lots of people have myopia (nearsightedness) or hyperopia (farsightedness), but these people are usually said to have limited vision because, although they have difficulty seeing by themselves, when they wear corrective lenses, they are considered fully sighted. In cases of near- or farsightedness, the cause is usually hereditary. It is also true that most eyes become slightly farsighted as they age, causing people who never wore glasses to need them at around age 40. Some people who have worn glasses since childhood for nearsightedness actually experience a mild vision correction and need less powerful prescriptions as they age.

Students who are blind and those who have low vision may need to learn Braille (a system of dots that can be felt rather than seen) and may need mobility training (figuring out how to get around, use a cane, cross streets unassisted, etc.). Sighted people should feel comfortable around people who don't see. Use all of the regular words you would ordinarily use. It's okay to ask a blind person if she has seen a movie lately. Once a blind person uses a cane or a dog, has had formal mobility training, and is skilled at reading Braille and using a Braille typewriter and computer keyboard, regular class placement is often very appropriate (Lewis & Doorlag, 1995).

If you have an opportunity to help a blind person get somewhere, always ask if your assistance is welcome. Don't just grab someone and start dragging him around. If the person is interested, provide as much information as possible. For instance, if you are coming up to stairs, say so AND tell the person whether they go up or down. Tell the person how many steps it will be until she reaches the curb.

Provide information about a chair and help the person feel both the back and the seat before you expect the person to judge how to sit down. If you are leading a blind person, just let her hold your arm right behind the elbow. You will actually be about a half-step ahead of the person you are leading and, in this way, she can feel when you are starting to change direction or move more quickly or slowly, etc.

Students who are blind may need a sighted classmate to make a carbon copy of lecture notes which can then be read by a sighted person at home. Blind students sometimes take notes using a stylus to make Braille or with a Braille typewriter. Many students who are blind also carry a regular typewriter or need a laptop computer at school in order to type the words for a spelling test or answer the chapter questions at the end of the geography book.

Students who are blind may also use a Kurzweil reader which converts type to mechanically produced speech or an Optacon which converts English print to vibrations. They may also have textbooks and other print necessary for school put on tapes. On short notice, without enough time to have a tape made, such as a newspaper article that coincides with the topic of study, a sighted classmate may need to read aloud to a student who is blind.

Students with low vision often use magnifying devices. They, too, may use tape recordings for the blind. They may also use enlarged text or bold-faced text. These enlarged textbooks often have to be larger than regular textbooks to include the same amount of print or come in multiple volumes (Torres & Corn, 1990). A good resource is:

American Council of the Blind
1155 15th St. NW, Suite 720
Washington, DC 20005

American Printing House for the Blind (hands-on materials, Braille equipment, etc.; catalog in print, in Braille, or on **tape!**)
PO Box 6085
1839 Frankfort Ave.
Louisville, KY 40206
502-895-2405

For books to help your child understand, try:

Alexander, S. H. (1990). *Mom can't see me.* New York: Macmillan.
Alexander, S. H. (1992). *Mom's best friend.* New York: Macmillan.
Garfield, J. B. (1994). *Follow my leader.* New York: Puffin Books. (gr. 4-5)
Keats, E. J. (1986). *Apartment 3.* Old Tappon, NJ: Simon and Schuster. (gr. 2-3)
Little, J. (1991). *Little by little: A writer's education.* New York: Puffin. (gr. 5-6)
Rosenberg, M. B. (1983). *My friend Leslie.* New York: Lothrop, Lee and Shepard Books. (gr. K-3)
Whelan, G. (1993). *Hannah.* New York: Random Books for Young Readers. (gr. 2-3)

Hearing Impaired

Students who are **deaf** (no ability to hear speech sounds) or **hard of hearing** (may benefit from a hearing aid or increased clarity in speech) may need specialized training in sign language and speechreading and the use of devices. The devices include telephone adapters and special alarm clocks that flash light instead of buzzing or ringing.

Once students who are deaf are taught to sign and use specialized devices, they may often benefit from instruction in the regular classroom (Lewis & Doorlag, 1995). Of course, in order to "speech read" (formerly called lipreading), the speakers must face the student who does not hear. Covering your mouth with your hand, wearing a long mustache, or holding a paper in front of your face impedes speechreading.

Other methods to help deaf students be successful in school include the following. Speak naturally and talk in full sentences. Utilize captioned films and other technologies. Use visual examples whenever possible, perhaps supply a written version as well as a spoken version of assignment directions, and allow only one other student to speak at a time.

There is a relatively militant segment of the deaf community of adults that objects to their classification as hearing impaired. They assert that there is nothing *wrong* with them as impairment or deficit implies. They contend that they are simply language and culturally different, as is someone who speaks a language other than English. These deaf adults reject the idea of cochlear implants, which, for certain kinds of hearing losses, can restore hearing by replacing the cochlea with an artificial version. They view themselves as having only a language barrier to cross (Signs Media, 1994). Therefore, the only educational need would be for an interpreter. A helpful agency is:

International Hearing Society
20361 Middlebelt Rd.
Lwonia, MI 48152

Books to help children understand include:

Booth, B. D. (1992). *Mandy.* New York: Lothrop. (gr. 1-2 fiction, deaf child character)
Greenberg, J. E. (1985). *What is the sign for friend?* New York: Franklin Watts.
Hesse, K. (1993). *Lester's dog.* New York: Crown. (gr. 2-3, deaf character)
Levi, D. H. (1989). *A very special friend.* Washington, D.C.: Gallaudet University.
Rosenberg, M. B. (1983). *My friend Leslie.* New York: Lothrop, Lee and Shepard Books. (gr. K-3)

SPEECH AND LANGUAGE DISABILITIES

School age children with **speech and language disabilities** make up about 20 percent of the students served in special education (U.S. Department of Education, 1993). Most school districts have a speech/language pathologist or clinical specialist on staff. These specialists may help by providing direct services to children with speech and language disabilities or by coordinating with classroom teachers, providing consultation regarding appropriate modifications in the classroom. Speech or language is disordered when it draws attention to itself, adversely affects the speaker or the listener, or interferes with communication.

Some problems are really just in speech production. These might be articulation difficulties. One articulation problem is substitution. In this case, the child knows the sound, hears it correctly, and may even produce the sound in certain positions in words. However, in some positions in words or with all production of the sound, the child substitutes another sound. An example would be the child who says "wabbit" for "rabbit."

Another articulation error is omission. Here the child fails to make a certain sound at all where it should appear in a word ("pactice" for "practice"). Some children also make additions; that is, they add sounds that do not really appear in the word ("silily" for "'silly"). In these cases, substitution and addition, the sound that is added or substituted really is used in English words; those sounds just don't belong where the child places them in certain words.

A fourth articulation error is distortion. Here the child substitutes or adds a sound that isn't used in English. You can hear these kind of sounds, for instance, one made at the back of the mouth near the jaw that Carol Channing uses for "s."

Many articulation errors are developmental. This means that they are errors that lots of children make as they begin to speak. Most children work out sounds in a certain developmental order. The last sounds to become clear, usually "l," "r" and "s," are settled by age eight. Children beyond the age of eight who continue with articulation errors can be candidates for intervention.

Other speech errors include volume problems. Here it is most important to determine that the child hears well before any other intervention is attempted. Children may speak too softly or loudly when they cannot hear their own production. Self-esteem should also be checked. Sometimes when children are unsure of themselves, they speak softly just in case they are saying something wrong. Perhaps if it is said softly no one will notice an error. If the hearing and self-esteem check out okay, then the speech mechanism (body parts that produce speech) and the way it is used is investigated.

Other speech problems include phonation and resonance difficulties. In phonation problems, the speech sounds breathy or hoarse. (However, Marlene Dietrich, Stevie Nicks and Brenda Vacarro have parlayed their breathy voices into big money with the designations of sultry and sexy.) Usually phonation errors are due to problems in the larynx. Surgery or changing the way that the voice is used (with therapy) are common solutions.

Resonance errors usually make the voice too nasal (hypernasal) or lacking nasal quality (denasal). The pharynx may require surgery, allergies can be treated, or people can learn new ways to use the speech mechanism to produce speech.

Finally, problems in fluency may cause speech disorders. Most commonly called stuttering (or in the United Kingdom, stammering), this disorder is manifested as repetitions, hesitations or prolongations of sounds, syllables, words, or phrases. All of us stutter on occasion. To determine whether therapy is required, frequency is usually assessed. The degree of difficulty that the speaker or listeners experience is also assessed.

The rest of the disorders in this category would most appropriately be deemed language disorders. These are harder to address in therapy and may have more profound effects in learning. The way the brain handles and interprets language information is usually the culprit for language disorders. They are manifested by immature construction ("baba" for "bottle"), misuses of words by their meanings (although Norm Crosby makes a living with those little "missteps"), misuses of the syntax (order, grammatical construction) of words, or misuses of the practical meanings or intent of words (termed by speech/language pathologists as pragmatics).

Speech/language therapists use self-talk. In this way, they provide children with an ongoing model for language by narrating their own behavior. In parallel talk, teachers narrate what they think that children are thinking and doing, to provide children with words to represent their thought processes. Children are also provided with peer models to imitate. In role playing, children can practice what to say and how to get attention and request what they want. All of these methods work toward giving the child enough mastery of language to be clearly understood and express ideas. For more information:

American Speech-Language-Hearing Association
10801 Rockville Pk.
Rockville, MD 20852
800-638-8255

Speech Communication Association
5105 Blacklick Rd., Bldg. E
Annandale, VA 22003
703-750-0533

Stuttering Foundation of America
P.O. Box 11749
Memphis, TN 38111-0749
901-750-0533

Books to help children understand include:

Kemp, G. (1986). *The turbulent term of Tyke Tiler.* Bath, England: Chivers.
Kline, S. (1992). *Mary Marony and the snake.* New York: Putnam. (gr. 1-2)
Kline, S. (1993). *Mary Marony hides out.* New York: Putnam. (gr. 1-2)

BEHAVIOR DISORDERS AND EMOTIONAL DISTURBANCES

Another group of students identified by school districts as having special learning needs are students who are said to have **behavior disorders** or **emotional disturbances.** The federal term is seriously emotionally disturbed (SED), but even the same acronym means different things in different states. In Illinois, for instance, SED stands for social and emotional disorders. National groups of educators who work with these students have tried a variety of acronyms as well, the Council for Children with Behavior Disorders going so far as to recommend BED (behavior and emotional disorders) so that T-shirts could read: I am good in BED!

Children in this category may have overt behaviors, such as fighting, failing to obey, or bullying other children. Others are more withdrawn and may fail to communicate, cry often, or appear sullen and unwilling to participate (Lewis & Doorlag, 1995).

Children in this category pose a special problem for schools and for parents. Some of these children have been abused or neglected in their homes and are now living in foster homes. These children have suffered in several ways, losing trust with the parents who harmed them, needing to heal, having to live in a new location, and having to start over with a new family.

Other children in this category are well loved and cared for within their families but still demonstrate troubling behavior that is difficult for parents and teachers to cope with. Some have a very high need for attention and will do negative things to get the attention to meet that need. Others appear to have almost no fear and poor sense of possible consequences.

In any case, children in this group need what children in every other group, including "normal" children, need (Kersey, 1994). They need to feel accepted, worthy, significant, and powerful. If the child has been abused, greater needs are presented. As you can imagine, a child who has been violated by the very person whom she loves and trusts, and must depend upon for food, clothing, shelter and love, has a lot of healing to do. This child may be angry, resentful or withdrawn. This child may react fearfully when a teacher or other adult reaches out.

Research on self-esteem suggests that self-esteem is a relatively stable thing, not easily altered by a few experiences. This is good for most of us because it means we can withstand a few bad days or insults or criticisms from others and still feel reasonably good about ourselves. But for children who have poor self-esteem, a few experiences with success are insufficient. Adults may think that what they are doing to bolster a child's self-esteem isn't working because they see no improvement. As long as what the adults are doing does no harm, persistence is the key. It takes countless successful, positive experiences, perhaps over one or two YEARS, to help a child recover from low self-esteem.

Even temporary problems in children's lives that adults feel do not directly involve the children (divorce discussions, parental arguments, strain over the care of a sick family member, etc.) may result in "disordered" behavior in children (Kersey, 1986). Children may not have the coping mechanism of "talking things out" as adults do; they lack a certain sophistication to see when problems may be temporary. They tend to respond very emotionally. Emotional behavior is sometimes interpreted as bad behavior; schools seem not to tolerate extreme or intense behaviors.

For community members, it is important to know that children labeled as behavior disordered can improve. Supportive teachers who use structured programs and provide needed attention and success make a difference. Extra attention or special contracts or reward systems may rub other students in the classroom the wrong way. Again, the child's perception of fairness, that every person should have the same thing, is raised. Adults must continue to work with children to help them see that everyone doesn't start at the same point and doesn't have the same needs or skills to get to the same conclusion.

It is important for community members to be aware of the need to report abuse that is ongoing. In most states, there is an 800 number for anonymous reporting of suspected abuse. Suspicions do not have to be proven by the caller, but, of course, good judgment should be used. Observation over time often helps to determine whether there is a long-standing problem.

As parents of children, who go to school with children who may receive special services under the title of behavior disorders or emotional disturbance, it is important to explain to your children about tolerance and to help them understand what some other children have been through that influences their behavior.

It is also critical to note that all children engage in behavior that is thought of as naughty or unacceptable. No one is perfect and children need to see that they are loved despite occasional mishaps so that the mishaps don't become the persistent view that children have of themselves.

Information from the following professional and informational organization may be useful:

Council for Children with Behavioral Disorders
c/o Council for Exceptional Children
1920 Association Drive
Reston, VA 22091-1589
703-620-3660

Books to help your child understand include:

Anderson, D., & Finne, M. (1986). *Jason's story: Going to a foster home.* Minneapolis, MN: Dillon Press, Inc.
Anderson, D., & Finne, M. (1986). *Liza's story: Neglect and the police.* Minneapolis, MN: Dillon Press, Inc.
Anderson, D., & Finne, M. (1986). *Margaret's story: Sexual abuse and going to court.* Minneapolis, MN: Dillon Press, Inc.
Anderson, D., & Finne, M. (1986). *Michael's story: Emotional abuse and working with a counselor.* Minneapolis, MN: Dillon Press, Inc.
Anderson, D., & Finne, M. (1986). *Robin's story: Physical abuse and seeing a doctor.* Minneapolis, MN: Dillon Press, Inc.

Bernstein, S. C. (1991). *A family that fights*. Morton Grove, IL: Albert Whitman and Co.

Bottner, B. (1992). *Bootsie Barker bites*. New York: Putnam. (K-1)

Check, W. A. (1989). *Child abuse*. New York: Chelsea House Publishers.

Cooney, N. E. (1993). *Chatterbox Jamie*. New York: Putnam. (Pre-K)

Falke, J. (1995). *Everything you need to know about living in a foster home*. New York: Rosen Group.

Gordon, S., & Gordon, J. (1984). *A better safe than sorry book*. Fayetteville, NY: Ed-U Press, Inc.

Hurwitz, J. (1991). *Class clown*. Orlando, FL: Harcourt Brace Jovanovich. (gr. 2-3)

Ito, T. (1995). *Child abuse*. San Diego, CA: Lucent Books Inc.

Mufson, S., & Kranz, R. (1991). *Straight talk about child abuse*. New York: Facts on File.

Myers, A. (1992). *Red-dirt Jessie*. New York: Walker. (gr. 4-5 on mental illness)

Spinelli, J. (1991). *Fourth grade rats*. New York: Scholastic. (gr. 3-4)

Tate, J. (1973). *Wild boy*. New York: Harper.

Taylor, C. (1992). *The house that crack built*. San Francisco: Chronicle Books.

GIFTED AND TALENTED

Another exceptional group in the classroom is comprised of students who are said to have unusual **gifts** or **talents.** The gifted and talented are those who by virtue of their outstanding potential are capable of high performance (Heward & Orlansky, 1992). Notice that the child does not have to be performing at a high level but rather has the potential for such performance (Gifted and Talented Children's Act of 1978). Realistically, most students are noticed and referred for evaluation for gifts because of the high performance they exhibit.

These individuals are likely to demonstrate their gifts in six areas. The first and most common is general intellectual functioning. These students excel in almost every school subject, often are socially very active, and have talents in music, athletics, etc. Another type of gifted child is the one who has specific academic aptitude. This is the child who (like Einstein) has special traits in only one or two areas and may, in fact, have difficulty functioning in other areas.

A third type of giftedness is the child who demonstrates unusual creative or productive thinking, who writes, invents, composes and creates brand new objects, ideas, music, art, and combinations. Still other gifted children show their gifts with regard to the visual and performing arts, in everything from dance to sculpture to oboe playing.

A fifth area of giftedness is that of psychomotor ability. This would be a

Michael Jordan, where physical size, strength or agility alone fail to explain the achievement. A quickness of thought and a genius of opportunity must also be present for this gift. The last type of giftedness is that of leadership ability. Here, examples are Martin Luther King or John F. Kennedy. Persons in this category possess both unusual communication skills and a charisma that makes them attractive to followers. These individuals have the "E. F. Hutton" quality that causes them to attract listeners even when they are not particularly trying to drum up an audience.

The Council for Exceptional Children maintains that gifted children REQUIRE differentiated educational services beyond those normally provided by the school program in order to realize their potential to self and society. This exceptionality is not covered in the federal legislation on handicapping conditions or disabilities. Students with gifts are not universally accorded special education services. Some educators believe that these students will succeed despite regular education, that they will fend for themselves and turn out "all right."

Interestingly, while statistically only 2 percent of the school population is identified as having I.Q.'s above 130, 16 percent of high school dropouts have I.Q.'s higher than 130! There certainly is reason to suspect that regular programs may be insufficient for at least some gifted students (Winebrenner, 1992).

Gifted youngsters pose special challenges for the adults in their lives. Precocious vocabularies and ideas can be threatening to adults. Children who are unusually independent and want to share in decision making do not fit the "children should be seen and not heard" expectation. Gifted children are more likely to question authority, although they are no more likely to be criminals or disregard rules, etc. Gifted children may demonstrate an unusual sense of humor, keen curiosity, acute moral sense of justice, and be equally at ease with children and adults. These traits may rub some adults the wrong way.

Gifted children can be accommodated in the regular classroom (Winebrenner, 1992). Alternative assignments may be offered. Perhaps a pretest on material in a unit could be offered and if a student demonstrates competence, the student could substitute a more appropriate activity for the traditional instruction on that subject. Teachers worry a lot about differentiating experiences for students partly because it can be time-consuming, but also because they are unsure how to address the inevitable questions from other students. It wouldn't hurt to let every student take a pretest. All those who demonstrate competence could substitute another activity by contract with the teacher. Besides, a teacher would gain a better idea of which areas of the topic should receive greater attention and which areas almost every child in the class already knows.

Parents of gifted children have the challenge of helping their youngsters avoid showing off and bragging, at the same time not "hiding their lights under a bushel basket." It is also critical to remember the actual age of the child. Gifted children are still children and, despite some adult tendencies in some areas, need to be treated like children, who are permitted to make mistakes, have bad days, etc.

Gifted children do pose challenges for adults, but they also offer real hope for solving the problems of the world. Not many adults understand solar power enough to develop a cheap, efficient machine for capturing solar power. However, a gifted child who is encouraged to grow in self-esteem and knowledge may one day develop just such a device. Isn't the variety a delight? Resources about giftedness include:

National Association for Gifted Children
    1707 L St. NW 550
    Washington, DC 20036
    202-785-4268

The Association for the Gifted
    c/o Council for Exceptional Children
    1920 Association Dr.
    Reston, VA 22091
    703-620-3660

Books that may help children (even gifted children) understand about gifts include:

Delisle, J., & Gailbraith, J. (1987). *The gifted kids' survival guide II: A sequel to the original the gifted kids' survival guide.* Minneapolis, MN: Free Spirit Press. (gr. 2-8)

Gilbert, S. (1984). *Using your head: The many ways of being smart.* New York: Macmillan.

Books in which the main character is gifted, although giftedness is not the only focus of the books, include:

Bell, W. (1986). *Crabbe's journey.* New York: Little, Brown and Co. (gr. 7-12)

Keyes, D. (1966). *Flowers for Algernon.* New York: Bantam Books. (gr. 7-12)

L'Engle, M. (1962). *A wrinkle in time.* New York: Farrar, Straus and Giroux. (gr. 5-9)

Montgomery, L. M. (1909). *Anne of Green Gables.* New York: Grosset and Dunlap. (gr. 5-9)

Ure, J. (1985). *The most important thing.* New York: Wm. Morrow. (gr. 5-7)

Williams, V. B. (1986). *Cherries and the cherry pits.* New York: Greenwillow Books. (gr. K-3)

Books and articles for adults on giftedness include:

Clark, B. (1992). *Growing up gifted*. New York: Merrill/Macmillan.

Parke, B. N. (1990). *Gifted students in regular classrooms*. Boston: Allyn & Bacon.

Schlichter, C. L. (1989). Literature for children who are gifted. *Teaching Exceptional Children, 21(3),* 34-36.

ATTENTION DEFICIT DISORDER (ADD)/ATTENTION DEFICIT HYPERACTIVITY DISORDER (ADHD)

Attention Deficit Disorder. Why do we hear so much about this "new" disorder lately? What is happening to our nation's youth? Is there really a higher incidence of this condition?

Attention Deficit Hyperactivity Disorder is a new name (only since 1987) for a condition that has been educationally identified for at least 50 years and medically observed for at least a century. Most recently, these children were said to be simply **hyperactive.** Hyperactive refers to too much motor activity—children who were restless, sitting on their knees, wiggling, up and out of their seats in school, etc. However, as research about these youngsters became more thorough, it became apparent that the biggest problem faced by those children in school was not extra motor activity. The biggest problem was a **difficulty in paying attention,** exercising control over impulses and concentrating in school. For this reason, first in 1980 with the term "attention deficit disorder" (with or without hyperactivity) and then in 1987 with ADHD, the American Psychiatric Association tried to use a name that better described what really troubled teachers and parents about the abilities of these youngsters (1989).

For many parents, getting the diagnosis of ADHD is actually the first step to dealing effectively with their children who have ADHD. Most parents report excessive activity (even in utero!), difficulty in establishing routines and patterns, and children who exert constant pressure on their parents with seemingly acute demands from infancy. Parents may feel inadequate and may blame themselves for the difficulty in establishing a relationship with the child. Having a diagnosis helps parents choose from an array of treatment combinations and get on with helping the child instead of feeling shame or blame (Phelan, 1989).

The essential features of ADHD according to the *Diagnostic and Statistical Manual of Mental Disorders* (DSM-IV, 1996) are inappropriate degrees of inattention (not paying attention), impulsivity (leaping before you look) and hyperactivity that are not acceptable for the child's mental age. This would mean that, for learners with retardation, for instance, that comparisons would be made to others at the same level of development, not those of the same age.

Myth has it that inattention, impulsivity, and hyperactivity are always present. Research has indicated, however, that even children with ADHD can pay attention normally with lots of reinforcement (one-to-one instruction or a doctor's office visit) or when an activity is very engaging (video game playing). The conditions that allow children with ADHD to pay attention are those that are one-on-one, novel, intimidating, or interesting to the child. For bright children with ADHD, many things are interesting and they seem to be paying attention a larger percentage of the time (Phelan, 1989).

Children with ADHD are more likely to have temper outbursts, experience variable moods, have poor academic achievement, and present poor self-esteem. They are also three times more likely to be boys. Often, there are relatives who were thought to be inattentive, impulsive or overactive in school. The children with ADHD have difficulty waiting their turn, often blurt out answers even before the question is completed, have trouble sustaining attention in play or other activities, interrupt or intrude on others, seem not to listen to what is said to them, frequently lose objects at home and at school, and have difficulty remaining in their seats when they are supposed to do so (Reeve, 1990).

Many children who are learning disabled, perhaps a third of all children with LD, also have ADHD. Children who have both emotional disturbance and ADHD account for as many as two-thirds of those with emotional disturbances (Reeve, 1990).

There is no known cause of ADHD and there is no definitive test (medical, biological, or laboratory) to diagnose ADHD. The disorder is diagnosed by paying careful attention to symptoms, in much the same way as colds or flu are diagnosed.

Two nationally known experts in ADHD are Sam Goldstein, a psychologist, and Michael Goldstein, a neurologist. They suggest a complete physical exam to rule out other causes for behavior, such as ear infections or allergies. Seeing a pediatrician or family physician may be a good place to start, but it is important to work with individuals who have had experience with ADD and can provide in-depth evaluation (Goldstein & Goldstein, 1990).

Assessment information should come from a variety of sources: medical personnel, parents, teachers, even the students themselves. Reeve (1990), from the University of Virginia, notes that "children can often give surprisingly accurate descriptions of their own behaviors, including those that others may not have observed."

Once children have been diagnosed as having ADHD, a whole variety of treatments may be used. A very common component of treatment may be the use of medical interventions. Generally, it is now believed that children with ADHD have a biochemical imbalance affecting the way in which electrical impulses are carried through the brain. The drugs that are used appear to stimulate the parts of the brain that transfer information so that the brain functions more efficiently.

Ritalin is, by far, the most commonly prescribed drug. Two others, Dexedrine (similar to the active ingredient in adult diet stimulants) and Cylert, are also frequently used. Improvements in a child's mood, ability to concentrate, goal directedness, and reduction in activity levels are signs of the drug's effectiveness. Side effects, including loss of appetite and difficulty sleeping, can often be eliminated by altering the dose, changing the time of administration, or trying one of the other drugs available (Phelan, 1989).

Caution should be observed with regard to medication to control behavior. Side effects can be serious and we should guard against the idea of creating conforming children who exhibit very little diversity from each other. There should be a RANGE of normal behavior, not just a narrow band, or worse yet, one model of what normal is or should be. Children may be more or less quick to acquire spoken language, younger or older when they learn to crawl or walk, and more able or less able to learn to read at a particular age. A relatively large band of acceptability should include most children. When a first grade teacher says that 75 percent of her students are hyperactive, this teacher has forgotten what the normal activity level of six-year-olds is. If that many children are considered abnormal with regard to their activity level, the adult expectations are inappropriate. Medication on that large a scale (75% of the class members) would also be inappropriate.

Medicating children for any physical condition is a big responsibility for parents. It is also a big responsibility for physicians. The challenge for physicians is to observe, in a relatively short period of time, enough information to make a diagnosis and decide whether to medicate. Some indicators are clearer than others. Ear infections, for instance, usually have clearly observable symptoms. The medication most often prescribed, one of a family of antibiotics, has relatively rare side effects, except for those allergic to the medication, so the danger in misdiagnosis or inaccurately identified medication is relatively low. Because the duration of the prescription is often two weeks or less, there is also less danger for long-term ill effects.

Imagine instead that the symptoms exhibited by the child don't show up in the 15-minute visit. Imagine that the doctor only hears about the symptoms and isn't sure of the accuracy of the report. Imagine that the symptoms could be associated with at least dozens of problems, ranging from food allergies to school anxiety to brain tumors. You can see the difficulty in reaching an accurate diagnosis and prescribing appropriate medication.

Probably the greatest weakness in the whole realm of prescription medication is follow-up. Sometimes parents see an improvement and they are so delighted they forget the instructions of the doctor to come back for frequent reevaluation. Sometimes doctors are so busy that they don't clearly enough identify for parents how frequently checkups should occur while on long-term medication. In one study, 55 percent of children on long-term prescription medication were not seen by the doctors even once again before the time of prescription renewal (Lerner, 1997).

Why is follow-up so critical? It must be determined whether the effect of the medication is beneficial. It is also important, sometimes by trial and error, to find the exact right dosage for an individual child. Side effects ranging from nausea to headaches to insomnia, swelling, dizziness, and appetite increases/decreases can often be reduced or eliminated by lowering the dosage or altering the time that the medication is taken. However, these decisions have to be made in conjunction with the physician.

In addition, if the medication is having no effect or ill effect, continuing to take it may be pointless or detrimental. More to the point, some children experience behavior and personality changes which have been described as "zombie-like." This is certainly not what the doctor intended. Communication between home and doctor is the best way to alleviate these concerns.

Some people object to medicating any children with ADHD symptoms. They argue that it is far better to teach children to control their own behavior than treating symptoms with medication that can have adverse side effects. While this may seem true on the surface, there are some children who are so disorganized and exhibit such poor attention that they seem unable to benefit from instruction on controlling their own behavior. For these children, the purposes of medication therapy are to improve goal-directedness, improve ability to pay attention, control interfering mood swings, and permit the child to focus productively on specific activities. If these purposes are met, when no other intervention appeared to be successful and there are few side effects, treatment was warranted.

If a child required insulin for diabetes or chemotherapy for leukemia, most adults would not object. For some children, especially those with severe ADHD symptoms, it may be just as important for them to receive the right medication as it is for any other physical illness. However, few doctors or researchers in the field recommend exclusively drug therapy. Most advocate a combination of treatments including medication and the kinds of interventions identified below.

The Goldsteins (1990) recommend that a child be reinforced for doing his work. Sometimes parents or teachers are so glad to see a child sticking with a task that they don't want to interrupt with praise. Praise is important, however, especially to a child who often hears criticism. A number of work periods are more beneficial than one long period. Variety in tasks may help, too.

Children with ADHD also benefit from structure and consistency. Adults should strive to make directions clear and to keep to a minimum distractions in the area where the child is working. Try to tell the child what you expect rather than what is not acceptable.

Create situations in which the child can have success. If the child must be punished, provide an opportunity to try again, succeed, and get praise instead of punishment. Many of these suggestions also work for teachers in the classroom setting. Having a student repeat directions back and tell how the assignment should be begun may be helpful. Make frequent eye contact with the child and be sure that you have the child's attention before speaking.

Adapt worksheets so that less work is on a page. Try to break all assignments into smaller chunks. Provide extra time to work without drawing special attention if possible. Use tools such as computers, calculators, or tape recorders when they seem to help. This may help routine activities provide some novelty or appeal to an innate interest to the child. Phelan (1989) advocated the use of behavioral strategies for pre-adolescent children.

Again, it may seem that a lot of teacher time could be consumed with the accommodations recommended here. At the outset of work with a child who has ADHD, this is probably the case. However, many of the practices will become more automatic as teachers more routinely engage in the practices. In addition, it cannot be overemphasized that many of the classroom modifications so essential to the success of students with ADHD also benefit students who do not have ADHD or any other disability.

For more information, contact:

Attention Deficit Disorder Association
> 8901 S. Ireland Way
> Aurora, CO 80016
> 303-690-7548

Attention Deficit Disorder Association of Virginia
(for information on organizing an ADHD support group)
> 106 South Street, Suite 207
> Charlottesville, VA 22901

Books to use that may help your child understand peers who have ADHD include:

Galvin, M. (1988). *Otto learns about his medicine: A story about medication for hyperactive children.* New York: Magination Press.

Gehret, J. (1991). *Eagle eyes: A child's view of attention deficit disorder.* Fairport, NY: Verbal Images Press.

Moss, D. M. (1989). *Shelley, the hyperactive turtle.* Kensington, MD: Woodbine House.

Silver, L. (1984). *The misunderstood child.* New York: McGraw-Hill.

Videos for parents about ADD:
> *1, 2, 3, Magic*   Thomas W. Phelan
> *All About Attention Deficit Disorder*   Child Management, Inc.
> *Treatment for ADD*   1-800-44-CHILD

Adults with Attention Deficit Disorder
Medication for Attention Deficit Disorder

Books for parents include:

Adkins, L., & Cady, J. (1986). *Help! This kid's driving me crazy! (The young child with Attention Deficit Disorder)*. Danville, IL: The Interstate.

Bender, W. N. (1997). *Understanding ADHD: A practical guide for teachers and parents*. Upper Saddle River, NJ: Prentice-Hall, Inc.

Friedman, R. J., & Doyal, G. T. (1992). *Management of children and adolescents with attention deficit-hyperactivity disorder*. (3rd ed.). Austin, TX: Pro-Ed.

Hafner, C. (1987). *Learning to parent a hyperactive child*. Wilmington, DE: G. P. King.

Ingersoll, B. D., & Goldstein, S. (1993). *Attention deficit disorder and learning disabilities: Realities, myths, and controversial treatments*. New York: Doubleday.

Jordan, D. R. (1992). *Attention deficit disorder: ADHD and ADD syndromes*. Austin, TX: Pro-Ed.

MEDICATION

There are a number of **medications** that children routinely take, administered by their parents in an over-the-counter form. There are also a number of additives that children encounter in food and drink products, for instance, caffeine. In addition, doctors prescribe medication for children. Finally, parents often supplement the diets of picky eaters or children too busy to eat (lots of two-year-olds and adolescents) with vitamins.

How can parents know enough to coordinate all of the elements appropriately for their children? What are good sources of information?

One source of information is your child's pediatrician. Sometimes parents get so involved in getting the diagnosis or keeping track of height and weight gains during a doctor's visit that they forget to ask questions about the medication a doctor has prescribed or the medications they have been administering at home. This is unfortunate. Not only do doctors possess a lot of "on the spot" information, they also often have a set of informational reference books on hand in which to look up additional topics. Doctors also may have pamphlets from the drug companies that can be given to you for free. Besides, your doctor should know what other elements you are providing to your child as part of the information the doctor uses to adequately prescribe for your child and advise you about your child's health.

It is also possible that doctors fail to provide information because the schedule is so hectic and they see so many patients they honestly can't remember which patients have had this particular medication explained before and which haven't. The onus is on the parents to ask questions to get the information they need to insure the child's health. Questions should include those about the proposed improvement expected by use of a drug.

Other questions should revolve around possible side effects and what to do if any of the common side effects show up, especially at night or on a weekend. Another question is when to discontinue use. Still another question has to do with additives. Is the child allergic to something (grape flavoring, for instance) in the medicine that could be avoided with an alternative prescription?

Another good source of information about medication is the Physician's Desk Reference (PDR) available at most public libraries. This reference volume includes pictures of medications so that parents can compare what they got at the pharmacy with the picture. The PDR also contains the purpose of each medication, other names used for the medication and possible side effects.

Books give you a chance to gain information at your own rate whenever you need the knowledge, not just when the doctor is in the office. You can also look information up over and over again until you understand or remember it without having to interrupt the doctor repeatedly and feel embarrassed, knowing you have asked this question before. Other books that may be useful:

> *The People's Pharmacy*
> *The Parent's Guide to Drugs*
> *Hazards of Medication*
> *The Essential Guide to Nonprescription Drugs*
> *Drug Interactions and Side Effects Index*
> *The Pediatric Guide to Drugs and Vitamins*

You may even choose to read the books first so that your questions to the pediatrician are clearer and so that you are familiar with the language used to describe drugs. You may also better understand the answer then provided by the pediatrician.

A terrific source of information, depending on the personality of the professional, can be your pharmacist. This person has advanced training in the names of drugs, their components, their equivalents, their side effects, and their costs. A pharmacist also usually maintains a number of reference books and can look up additional information as needed.

Many parents have seen television shows encouraging them to stop badgering children to eat vegetables, fruit or juice. Parents are told to introduce and make available nutritious foods but not to make meal time a constant battleground. Instead, children should be encouraged to eat well but take a vitamin supplement if they don't end up eating balanced meals.

All vitamins are water-soluble, except A, D, E and K. Water-soluble vitamins cannot be stored in the body and are simply lost as waste if more is consumed than needed. Vitamins A, D, E and K are stored in body fat and only released when fat cells are used by the body. It is possible to build poisonous levels of fat-soluble vitamins, so consult your pediatrician about appropriate amounts of these for your children. Reading the fine print on vitamin products can be very helpful as well.

It is important to identify for the doctor the medications and other chemicals absorbed into the body so that the doctor can make an informed decision about the possible interactions between and among medications. Perhaps sulfa drugs (some antibiotics) should not be taken with caffeine. Perhaps some antibiotics work best on an empty stomach. Using the physician, pharmacist, and respected print sources to get information can be very beneficial for the peace of mind of the parent and the health of the child.

SUMMARY

"Inclusion" is a state-of-the-art term, not defined in special education legislation. Instead, it really refers to a movement whose purpose is to serve more and more students with disabilities in the regular classroom. What one district means by inclusion will not necessarily be what another district means by the term. Some researchers speak of full inclusion, presumably meaning that every child, no matter how severe the disability, should be educated in the regular classroom. Or perhaps it may mean that those children with disabilities who are included in the regular classroom are fully included, suggesting that every class and educational experience is taken with regular peers. You can see the difficulty.

Inclusion in its various forms, beginning with the Regular Education Initiative and coming today to mean more than that, has proponents. These proponents assert that inclusion is necessary in order to get ready for the integrated society in which today's school children will find themselves, to provide models of successful behavior and learning for students with disabilities to imitate, to educate and broaden the experiences of regular class peers, and to educate youngsters in their neighborhood schools. Detractors have plenty to say, too. They object to what they observe as cost-cutting antics rather than philosophical agreement. Detractors hold that inclusion robs students with special learning needs of the attention they require to be successful, unfairly stresses out teachers with inappropriate training and way too many students to do what they are being asked to do, and robs regular education students of important teacher attention. It remains to be seen how this latest swing of the pendulum in education will turn out.

Chapter 8

COOPERATIVE LEARNING

Have your children and adolescents been coming home from school and telling you that they've been working in cooperative groups? Has your child complained about having to complete assignments on a team or about receiving a grade based on a group effort? Do you ever think to yourself, "This doesn't sound like what we did when I was in school?"

It's true that some methods and philosophies of what a good education comprises have changed since you were in school. The technique referred to is one of the methods that might not have been used when you were in school. It is called cooperative learning.

What is **cooperative learning?** It might be said that it is we instead of me; students are responsible for their own learning and also for the learning of the other group members. Why should your child be concerned with another child's learning? The answer is: Positive interdependence. Each group member is affected by the actions of other group members. Cooperative learning permits alternative types of stimulation and learning. Your child will speak far more frequently and carry more responsibility for learning in a group of four to six children than in a class of 32 students and only one teacher.

How can students be led to engage in positive interdependence? One way is through goal interdependence. This exists when the group recognizes a mutual goal and they are all trying to accomplish it. This can be done by requiring a single product from the group, by each member "signing off" group progress charts, or when everyone does the project but only one grade is earned and every group member gets that grade.

Another way in which students can be directed to work together is through resource interdependence. This exists when each member of the group has only a portion of what is necessary for the task to be completed. Labor, roles, or materials can all be divided. Then, students have to share the materials or each do part of the work to get the job accomplished (Johnson, Johnson & Johnson Holubec, 1994).

71

A final way to help students work together is to employ reward interdependence. In this form, each member of the group receives the same reward for completing the task. Rewards include: bonus points, teacher praise, extra reading time, free time, grades, stickers, stars, food, etc.

What can your child get out of this? The opportunity to speak more often in class, to learn less often from teacher lecture and more often by self or peer discovery, to get more immediate feedback, to determine that there is sometimes more than one right answer, and to gain esteem and to give esteem to others.

It is difficult to think of an adult job that does not require teamwork. Cooperative learning gives children opportunities to practice good team skills. In addition, it is not possible to think of a major world problem that could be solved by an individual. The need to work together, perhaps even for world survival, causes educators to consider the importance of team efforts and early practice with team skills.

Will teachers still be providing direct instruction? Absolutely. Cooperative learning expands a teacher's repertory of teaching methods, rather than limits it. Teachers may choose certain methods for certain subjects or certain goals of instruction.

Teachers may use some of the following activities to give students practice in cooperative learning. A reinforcement technique that requires classroom cooperation to achieve the desired result may be used. This could include anything from completing a certain amount of group work, to earning a field trip, to individual students adding points together, to earn a chance to review for a test in a game format instead of studying alone.

Students might cooperate to plan field trips, plays or presentations, or even contests for classroom decorations. Students may teach other students in small groups in student areas of expertise. Auto mechanics, jewelry making, stamp collecting, double-Dutch rope jumping, and other hobbies might provide topics.

Teachers may assign peer tutors. Children can help each other learn when one is an expert and the other a beginner. Teachers should be careful that every child has a chance to be the tutor, not always be the one receiving help, over the course of an academic year.

When there is a choice of assignments, teachers may group students by interest. Several facets of a current topic under study may be identified and groups may be assigned to each subtopic. Students may use the kind of team learning or rehearsal (drill) activities that were used when you were in school such as "baseball," "spelling bees," "bingo," with questions designed for particular subjects. Students gain points in teams rather than as individuals.

Research on cooperative learning suggests that not only does it result in persons who make better team players in the work world but provides other benefits as well. Students tend to understand more of what they learn active-ly, retain the information for a longer period of time, and improve in self-esteem. Children may be more highly motivated to learn and feel more con-trol and, therefore more investment in, their learning.

When teachers set up cooperative learning, there are a number of guide-lines they will probably use. Groups of two or three are effective for most projects. Larger groups result in more independent work. Heterogeneous groups work for most topics and types of assignments. These groups include students of high, medium and low performance levels in the subject of study.

Groups should be kept together until they work successfully. Groups that work together successfully after six to eight weeks can be switched. This usu-ally means changing groups every academic quarter. Boys and girls should be mixed in groups. Movement should be cut down to a minimum. Therefore, group members will probably be seated near each other even during whole group instruction. Groups should be spread out as much as possible from other groups. All students within each group should be able to see materials and have face-to-face interaction when talking in the group. This often means that two desks will be used for four students.

Teachers often employ special rules when having students work in coop-erative groups:

1. Move to and from groups quietly.
2. Use quiet voices.
3. Encourage everyone to participate.
4. Stay with your group.
5. Use the names of the students in your group.
6. Do not use put-downs.
7. Ask a question only when everyone else has the same question or your question moves the work of the group forward.

There are a number of other cooperative learning activities or methods. Here are some of them so that you will be familiar with the designs your chil-dren talk about at home.

Group retelling is a method in which students are grouped in threes. Each student reads materials about the same topic from different sources and is prepared to retell what they have read to the group. At any point, the oth-ers may add to the retelling from something they have read from in their source.

In dyadic learning, students work in pairs. They begin by reading the two pages from the text. One partner is designated as the "recaller" responsible for summarizing from memory what has been read. The other partner "lis-tener/facilitator" corrects errors, clarifies concepts, and elaborates on the material. For the next two pages, the roles reverse. This can also work for younger children or less sophisticated readers. One child reads aloud a paragraph and then the other child tells what it was mainly about, then the two children reverse roles.

In the buddy system, students work in groups of three. Students are responsible for each other's learning. They provide assistance, read and edit each other's work.

Parents and teachers sometims have questions about cooperative learning. Some of the most common questions will receive answers here.

Q: Do students resent getting a group grade?

A: Usually when students have worked together on a single project or assignment, a single grade for all group members seems the only logical way to evaluate their efforts. If teachers observe that groups are not very effective together, with a few students or a single student doing all the work, the teacher should intervene during the work session. Students may receive an individual grade for work and a group grade for group cohesion; this often solves the problem.

Q: What about cooperative group assignments outside of school?

A: There is no way for the teacher to be assured that students are working well together or distributing work fairly, as a teacher can when students work at school. Cooperative assignments outside of school may place an unfair burden on families and on children for time and location coordination.

Q: Does cooperative learning require bright students to sacrifice in order to help others in their groups?

A: Considerable research demonstrates that high achievers in heterogeneous cooperative groups do no worse than their counterparts working individually or competitively and often do better (Johnson, Johnson & Johnson Holubec, 1994). It is important to remember that cooperative groups are only one instructional strategy. At other times, bright students may be "cluster grouped" for intensive study or work alone on in-depth projects (Winebrenner, 1992).

Q: What is the best size for a learning group?

A: That depends on the difficulty of the assignment and how experienced students are at working together. A more complex task might use as many as six students, but no more. Optimal group size is usually two to four.

Q: What are the basic elements of cooperative learning?
A: There are four basic elements:

1. Positive interdependence (do this by having mutual goals; dividing labor; dividing materials, information or resources among group members; assigning students roles; and giving group rewards).
2. Face-to-face interactions.
3. Individual accountability (determine by teacher assessing each student for knowledge and skills gained).
4. Interpersonal small group skills (students must be taught these skills via modeling, direct instruction and reinforcement from their teachers).

Understanding cooperative learning can help your children understand and benefit more from the learning opportunities that are afforded them. Even young children can work cooperatively and love to learn in a game format. Childswork Childsplay has a game for children aged four to ten, *You and Me: A Game of Social Skills,* and a book titled *Getting Along* (dealing with being bossy, playing too rough and making fun of other children). Send for a catalog from:

Childswork Childsplay
Center for Applied Psychology
P.O. Box 1586
King of Prussia, PA 19406
1-800-962-1141.

Chapter 9

WHOLE LANGUAGE

A growing number of teachers in elementary schools and a few teachers in high schools believe in a **whole language philosophy for teaching reading and writing.** There are also a number of detractors, including, recently, the California legislature. The whole language philosophy suggests that reading, writing, spelling, listening, speaking and every other aspect of language are intertwined (Manning & Manning, 1994). Breaking them into separate subjects to be taught separately is probably not sensible.

Perhaps you remember your elementary school days. You had reading instruction. Then you had spelling where you studied a self-contained list of words (more in each unit each academic year) that had nothing to do with what you were reading about in any other subject area, and some were words you didn't even recognize to read, let alone spell. Then, you had writing class in which you learned about grammar on a different day than you actually wrote.

The idea behind the whole language movement is that various aspects of language can be linked. This makes good sense to students who see the connections and benefits from growth in one area as it improves growth in another.

A balanced whole language program typically includes the following ten elements:

1. Reading to children (even when they are old enough to read to themselves);
2. Shared book experiences;
3. Sustained silent reading (SSR) or drop everything and read (DEAR);
4. Guided reading;
5. Individualized reading;
6. Language experience;

7. Children's writing;
8. Modeled writing;
9. Opportunities for sharing; and
10. Content area reading and writing (Butler, 1988).

Children will like to spend varying amounts of time in each of the activities as they move through the grades, depending on their ages and the needs of that developmental learning level. Often, younger children will be read to more often and engage in more shared book experiences, while older children will spend more time reading alone.

All ten elements are necessary because they develop and emphasize different features of language; together they make "whole" language. Many of the elements were not consistently present in our own education. Each one will receive emphasis here.

READING ALOUD

Reading aloud to children may be the single best activity for developing children's listening and speaking vocabularies. Children can understand at a more advanced level than they can independently read, so reading aloud by an adult or more experienced reader gives them access to more ideas (Butler, 1998).

Reading aloud is also something easy for parents to do with children. A parent does not have to have special training to read to children. Even adults read to other adults. Have you ever called to your spouse or parent or even picked up the phone and said, "Listen to this..."? You read aloud not just because the person is too young to read independently but also to share ideas and information, or to have several children experience the same book at the same time.

Reading aloud to young children can develop other aspects of your relationship with the child as well. Physical closeness with the child right next to you or on your lap enhances the experience. Without realizing it, as you and your child face the book, your body also sets the stage for later independent learning. You turn your head from left to right after you've turned the page, reading first the left side of the book and then the right. Eventually, children begin to imitate that left, then right motion. When you point or follow along the words with your finger, the child begins to notice over time that reading is a top-down, left-to-right sweep thing. Books are handled from front to back, with pages systematically turned toward the left. Children notice that print has constancy; that is, every time you read the same book or passage, you say exactly the same words. Unconscious knowledge such as this lays the foundation for reading for your child.

SHARED BOOK EXPERIENCES

Shared book experiences are most often conducted with younger learners and involve the use of books that are big enough for a large number of children to see at the same time. These are usually called **big books,** just because they are big.

Big books can be made from any book content and there are big books that are large editions of favorite books of regular size. However, books that have particular features are most appropriate for big book use.

Big books should be books in which illustrations help predict the meaning of the text. In this way, young learners who are just beginning to read can predict words from an initial consonant and by looking at the pictures. Large illustrations aren't big so that they can have more detail. In a large group of children, some may be seated relatively far from the book, so good big book illustrations are easily seen and comprehended even from a distance of six feet or so. Big books are also useful if the story line is predictable and uses repetition. In this way, young learners can begin to join in the reading of the book after just a few times of hearing the book read aloud. For instance, *The Gingerbread Man* lends itself to big book delivery because the gingerbread man always says the same thing and the illustrations make it easy to tell which character the Gingerbread Man is talking to at each point of the story.

When the book for a shared book experience is introduced, the teacher calls attention to the title, author, illustrator, cover illustration and the main idea that seems to be expressed by the cover illustration and the title. The teacher reads the story, encouraging participation and prediction, but not to the detriment of the flow of the story (Butler, 1991).

After several times of hearing the story read aloud and looking at the pictures, children begin to read along chorally with the teacher. Teachers will often point to the words as they read. With repetition, children learn a number of things. First, they begin to notice that every word the teacher reads is represented by a printed cluster of letters. Second, as they do when they are read to by an adult in a smaller setting (parent to child), they notice that every time the text is read, the adult says the exact same words. Children begin to conclude that text is reliable.

Sometimes individual children take their turns being the group leader, pointing to the words as other children read aloud. Big book titles are rotated. After several sessions with a book, a new book is used and so on until, some weeks or months later, one of the first books studied returns. Students find that they easily remember many of the words or can reconstruct the words from the pictures, familiarity with the book, and the predictable plot.

Big books are unwieldy, so teachers usually let them stand on an easel or chalkboard ledge for support. Sometimes children create their own big books with their own illustrations. Sometimes teachers make their own big books, too. All of the features of big books and their uses with early readers are based on the premise that fun and empowering shared experiences with books will lead to competent, confident readers.

SUSTAINED SILENT READING

The next component in whole language instruction is **sustained silent reading** (SSR), sometimes called uninterrupted sustained silent reading (USSR). Sustained silent reading is important in order to develop fluency in reading. Fluency means that we read without stumbling, easily flowing from word to word. Fluency also implies reading at a reasonable rate, not slowly sounding out each word or dragging through the text.

Another term used for this activity is **drop everything and read** (DEAR). These periods of time may be for an entire classroom. Then, every person in the class, including teachers and teacher assistants, read individually and silently. These periods of time are usually at least 15 minutes in length, sometimes longer (Butler, 1988).

Sometimes sustained silent reading periods are school wide. Principals, custodians, social workers, secretaries—all school personnel—and students engage in some period of sustained silent reading.

For sustained silent reading, readers select their own reading materials. Comic books, readers, poetry books, how-to books, novels, joke books, newspapers, any reading material is fair game. Young children may simply look at pictures or pick out as many words or letters as they are familiar with to read. Sometimes teachers have smaller versions of big books that they have read, and young readers can begin to "read" by reviewing a book that they actually know almost by heart, as one that was used for shared book experience (Butler, 1991). In fact, many big books come in sets with multiple copies of the book in a smaller individual version.

Students do not have to come to the teacher to find out what each word says. Students should enjoy the printed materials in any way they can independently. During periods of instruction, students may ask about words that were unfamiliar. Teachers may make suggestions during instructional times about the books or print materials that might be well suited to the next sustained silent reading session.

There are many advantages to the inclusion of sustained silent reading in a comprehensive or whole literacy program. One advantage is the fluency already mentioned. Students are empowered to select their own reading materials and enjoy them in any way they can.

In addition, students can spend some of the time observing adults read. They see that adults may not always sit and read in a straight chair at a table. Students see that adults may laugh or look worried or stop and think for a moment when they read. This is wonderful modeling for reading.

Most children assume that reading is something that they are forced to do in school and for homework, but that no one else reads. When you think about it, do your children see you read very often? Perhaps you read in places where your children are not with you and, therefore, do not observe you reading: the bathroom, on the train on the way to work, late at night in bed. Perhaps you are so busy caring for your children when you are with them that you don't read until they are in bed or away from the house.

Children need to believe that grown-ups read for information and that reading is something people do for a lifetime. Sustained silent reading, when every person in the setting is reading, accomplishes this goal.

Sustained silent reading also convinces children that reading is not just for completing assignments and preparing for workbook pages or writing a report. Reading can be for one's own purposes, too. Text can be self-select-ed. A reader can skip parts, read every word, look only at the pictures, or use a table of contents and read specific sections. What a powerful lesson to learn about reading!

GUIDED READING

The heart of the teacher's work with reading in a whole language model is **guided reading**. Guided reading allows teachers to make children aware of the "why and how and the knowledge that you know" of reading (Mooney, 1995).

Teachers use guided reading to provide direct instruction for students on the skills of reading. Teachers may show children how to use resources from the book to gain meaning. This might include the table of contents or the index. It might mean locating and using the glossary or mini-dictionary at the back of the chapter or book.

Teachers help students note words that are italicized, boldfaced, under-lined, or highlighted in any way. They call attention to the headings, sub-headings, and structure of the way information is presented. All of these features allow students to gain more meaning from print—the essence of reading.

Students may be busy reading continuous text and so forget to read the captions of the pictures or even look over the pictures. In guided reading, class conversation draws attention to these items. Students also discuss information provided in boxed or "bulleted" areas, perhaps shaded and usually containing separate, sort of tangential or more in-depth information.

Good adult readers usually already notice and use all of these aspects of print. New readers and less experienced readers benefit from direct instruction in the use of text features and discussion of their meanings as they illuminate the regular text.

Another resource for deriving meaning is the students themselves. A teacher may use an object or pose a question to stir up student enthusiasm or prior experience with a subject before reading about that subject. In this way, all of the brain cells associated with storage and interpretation of concepts on this topic are already activated when reading begins. This can't help but improve comprehension.

In guided reading, the teacher usually selects the text. Most or all of the students use the same text for reading during guided reading. Students may be in groups for guided reading, smaller groups than the whole class. This allows for more discussion and closer observation of each student by the teacher. Smaller groups also allow the teacher to target the text to the interests or ability levels of the students in that group.

Reading in guided reading groups still is usually done silently, following preparation. Reading aloud, especially in the "you read one paragraph, she'll read the next, and so on" model called round robin reading is not well supported by research. Students who have read recently sometimes stop paying attention, figuring they will not be called on again. Other students count ahead and spend all of their time practicing and worrying over the paragraph they think they will be assigned instead of following the gist of the reading (Butler, 1988).

But if the students read silently, how does the teacher know whether they are getting the content? They know the answers and discussion they engage in after reading. Teachers may still have students read aloud occasionally for diagnostic purposes or even for the fun of hearing an interesting story read aloud. But reading in front of a group best occurs after the entire selection has been read silently. This ensures preparation and the likelihood of successful oral reading.

So guided reading consists of some preparation for the topic, silent reading, occasional oral reading, tips from the teacher about approaching the text for meaning, follow-up discussion and sometimes follow-up activities. Students are helped to see how they came up with an interpretation of the author's intent so that they repeat that skill on independent readings.

Periodically, the teacher will ask the students to stop reading and predict what will happen next. On what is the prediction based? Then more reading goes on to confirm or refute the prediction.

Books chosen for guided reading may reflect the variety of purposes for reading: some may be just for pleasure, others for locating information, still others for content area learning (math, science, social studies, etc.). Students will begin to identify certain conventions (ways of writing) that go with certain types or genres of books. Mystery book writers use certain conventions and even employ certain words to help achieve their purposes. Science fiction writers use different conventions. Once a reader has read several of each different type, the pattern starts to become identifiable.

Guided reading might lead students to discover how different authors explore the same topic. In this case, students within a guided reading group might actually each read a different book, but all of the books would be on the theme of trust, friendship, anger or some other topic.

Rereading is another technique employed during guided reading. Here discussion follows the first reading and students reread the story to confirm certain ideas, develop new understandings, check facts, etc.

The goal of guided reading is to have an expert in reading, child development and children's literature (a teacher) guide a novice (a school child) to more sophisticated comprehension, new integration of prior knowledge and the current text, and reading enjoyment. Seems like good goals for learning!

STORYTELLING

Language develops in a sequential hierarchy beginning with experiences of the senses, leading to concept development, understanding what is heard, expressing oneself in speech, and finally, reading and writing (Davis, 1977) . **Storytelling** is a wonderful way to stimulate a child to understand what is heard and to extend vocabulary (Vivas, 1996). New words in a story are often supported by nearby words for meaning and children can figure out what the new word probably means. Skilled storytellers also use dramatic interpretation to assist the listener with new vocabulary interpretation. Facial expressions and body language and movements may help the listeners know what a new word means.

Storytelling also enhances the child's internal understanding of how stories are arranged (Vivas, 1996). They learn the "story grammar." This means that they begin to pay attention to the order of events. They notice that there are signal words that lots of storytellers tend to use: first, then, next, finally, etc.

Usually at an unconscious level at first, and then at a conscious level with more and more exposure, children become aware that stories often begin with some description: of a character, a place (setting), some background. Then there is some problem, crisis or situation that arises. Usually the crisis or problem is resolved and the story ends. Fairy tales use the conventions (familiar patterns) of "Once upon a time" and "lived happily ever after." These also become part of the child's story grammar (Cooper, 1993).

Once children have heard many stories well told, they begin to devise their own. (See the next step on the language hierarchy.) This demonstrates how they have internalized the rules of story construction. Young children usually don't follow the "rules" very well and their stories don't make much sense to the listener as a result. Kindergarten children, and some younger, of course, can create stories that tickle adults because of how well they use the conventions they have heard so many times.

Watching video movies of stories can enhance the understanding that children have of stories and "how they are supposed to go." Of course, any one way of learning can be overused. Multiple viewing of video stories on a daily basis could stifle other kinds of learning. But appropriate videos can be an effective part of a child's learning experience.

Storytelling enhances concept development as children begin to notice the common themes of good versus evil. Hard work, mannerly behavior, sweet nature, etc. often prove to result in a happy ending for the person who employs them. Storytelling enhances oral language reception, i.e., understanding what is heard. Over time, children can sit for longer and longer stories and do not demand "a picture, like in a book" or a "video" to go with the stories; they can conjure up mental images just by hearing the words.

Storytelling facilitates oral language expression as children begin to tell their own stories, imitating the models they have heard numerous times. Understanding "story grammar" (the way that stories usually "go") facilitates learning to read; children learn to expect and get meaning from stories, arranged in many ways like the ones they have heard many times. Further, storytelling can eventually lead to children writing their own stories, reaching the last level of the language development hierarchy.

Does storytelling have a place in whole language classrooms? Without a doubt! The benefit of whole language instruction over more isolated skill instruction is that the teacher consciously tries to link the various steps on the language hierarchy together, recognizing the natural connection for humans among the various types of language and expression. Inasmuch as storytelling fosters five of the six levels of the language development hierarchy, whole language instruction will include storytelling as part of a balanced and integrated stimulation of language development. Students may also find storytelling very motivating. Children who are paying better attention and finding learning more interesting cannot help but learn more as a result.

PHONICS

Guided reading occurs when teachers help students use specific strategies for comprehension. One of the most basic requirements for reading comprehension is word recognition for most or all of the words in the passage. If, however, a word is unknown, how does a student figure out what the word is? A very effective strategy and one that receives instructional time in good whole language classrooms is the use of **phonics.** Phonics allows a child to sound out a word by letter, /b/, /k/, etc., or letter combinations, /ea/, /th/, /ph/, etc., to hear the word. This works well if the word is in the child's listening/speaking vocabulary. She "sounds out" the word, blends the sounds together on a second try, and then recognizes the word and, usually, its meaning, proceeding through the rest of the sentence, weaving meaning together, and completing the sense that the author intended.

Phonics doesn't help when the word, even correctly sounded out, is not familiar to the child. Phonics is too slow a process to be used over and over in the same passage. The child gets bogged down with all of the sounding out and loses track of the meaning. So, as parents, allow a child to use phonics on a word or two in a passage (wait patiently, the process may take several seconds and two or three passes to get through the word). After that, supply an unknown or "not immediately recognized" word. In this way, the child gets excellent decoding (figuring out) strategy practice but is also able to quickly get enough words to understand the passage.

Sometimes, if systematic instruction on all sound-letter correspondences has not been provided in the classroom or if your child did not pick up the relationships when they were covered in class, it may be necessary to help your child rehearse phonic skills. This includes covering all but one letter or combination at a time and eliciting or providing its sound. Repeat the steps more closely together, blending the sounds nearer together so that they sound like the word.

Phonics instruction should be part of guided reading. Students are taught what each letter or letter combination "says." Teachers in whole language classrooms may not use the heavy drill method of teaching phonics that we may have experienced as students. This method often results in "a letter a week" with worksheets and lots of repetition with sounds. Teachers in a whole language model are more likely to teach phonics skills as part of other learning, in spelling or by teaching word families that employ same sound clusters (man, fan, can, pan, tan, than, van, Dan, ran). The emphasis in whole language instruction is on reading authentic texts for real purposes, not "readers" with artificially constructed sentences and little meaning.

Phonics is not the only decoding strategy. Morphemic analysis, that is, breaking down the word into its components, some of which may be recognizable, works for some words. If your child was unfamiliar with the word "preview," you could elicit the meaning of view and then remind the child of another word that starts with "pre" to determine the meaning of the word part (prepay, preheat, etc.).

There are programs which advocate phonics as a separate area of study which should be employed by beginning readers. *Hooked on Phonics* is an example of a commercial program available to parents and teachers. *Discover Intensive Phonics* is a training program available to teachers to give them a model for providing daily lessons in phonics and immediate application in writing as well as reading with the sounds known up to that lesson. These programs have merit and some children learn to recognize words well after using them. "Phonics only" programs build on the premise that children already know the words they are trying to read and if they could just sound out the word, they would recognize it and will also immediately know the meaning.

Many children seem to need more connectedness for learning to be meaningful. Some children may also need much more language development stimulation because the words they are trying to decode are not in their listening/speaking vocabularies. In whole language classrooms, vocabulary development and decoding strategies are taught in tandem (Butler, 1988).

INDIVIDUALIZED READING

The next component of whole language instruction is that of **individualized reading.** Here students are guided by the teacher to books that are at their appropriate levels and often of direct interest to the children.

Teachers get to know their students during guided reading sessions and throughout the school day in several ways. Through their conversations with children, teachers determine what topics are of interest to them. Teachers also pay attention to the reading skills of children and where their reading strengths lie. With this information in mind, teachers then select books for children to read alone. Sometimes more than one child will read the same book or story. These children may then form a "literature circle" in which they discuss the book they have read.

Literature circles may also be used as part of guided reading. The teacher joins the students in discussing the book. In literature circles, teachers do not usually teach specific skills, such as decoding a new word using its root or base word. Instead, the teacher and the students discuss the ideas in the book. Themes of memories, anger, friendship, community, individual differences, etc., are great for exploring with book characters and their human readers.

Literature circles may also be formed with children who have read different books but can join in a discussion of similar themes of ideas that run through the various books they have read. Children really enjoy noticing what is the same and different about the books they have read.

Literature circles may also be formed around different books by the same author, or even by the same illustrator. Children feel clever when they can pick out the details that clue them in to the author's style or illustrator's way of drawing. Favorite author illustrators like Mercer Mayer (Little Critter books) and Tomie dePaola (*Strega Nona*) are wonderful for young readers. Older readers may enjoy books by Laura Ingalls Wilder (*Little House on the Prairie*) or Roald Dahl (*BFG, Willy Wonka and the Chocolate Factory*) or R. L. Stine (books in the Goosebumps series).

Some educators quarrel over the content of some of the books listed above and other books. They note that some of these books may fail to constitute "good literature." Many educators believe, however, that what is most important is that children read, often and with good comprehension. Young adolescents especially enjoy the communal feeling of having read the same books as others in their group and being "in the know" about certain characters. Some children are inspired to read books by seeing television versions of the books, as with public television's mutt, "Wishbone." Whatever works!

Individualized reading allows children to engage in silent reading in books of a teacher's choice. This is very different from sustained silent reading or drop everything and read. In these programs, students read silently but they read things of their choice. Students might even choose books that are too hard to read and just look at the pictures. With individualized reading, children can employ the skills they've been taught in guided reading in books that are just about right in difficulty level (Butler, 1988).

LANGUAGE EXPERIENCE

Whole language instruction in reading and writing can easily be used with non-readers. The components of reading aloud to children and the idea of children "reading" to themselves by turning the pages of books they've memorized are suitable for non-readers and can be carried over in new forms to older readers.

Another "bridge" activity used by teachers in kindergarten and the primary grades is that of **language experience.** In this component, a class of children, a group of children, or one child has an experience shared with the teacher. The children tell the teacher about the experience later, usually in the classroom. The teacher records what the children say, often following rich discussion of the event(s).

Teachers who employ language experience as a technique usually record the story on a large tablet of paper, supported by an easel. Other teachers may write on the blackboard, on posterboard on the bulletin board, or on an overhead transparency. The idea is that students see their oral words converted to print.

Because the language is generated by the students and driven by their experience, they are highly motivated to "read" back the story. This usually occurs after the teacher has read the story aloud several times. Students may actually have memorized the story by the time they "read" it. But the teacher points to each word as the class or individual students read the story.

When the language experience technique is employed repeatedly, students begin to recognize certain words. Unlike some basal readers (most of the reading books we used as children), the words are not controlled for length or difficulty and sentences are not necessarily simple in construction. In fact, some of the words and sentences are sophisticated, just like the oral language of young children.

This kind of meaningful print is motivating to students and is fun because it is shared with an adult and usually other children. Students enjoy taking turns "being the teacher" and pointing to the words for their classmates on later readings. They also may begin to inform the teacher's writing. If the teacher hesitates while writing what a child has said, that child or another child may tell the teacher that the word begins with a certain letter or remind the teacher that they used the same word recently (Butler, 1988).

Language experience is an important part of a whole language program for young children because they get interesting exposure to print that they themselves initiated. It leads to acquisition of some sight words, words that children know as soon as they see them, because of repeated experience with them.

CHILDREN WRITING

A natural follow-up to language experience is **children writing** themselves. Perhaps you've heard some things about children writing as soon as they begin to recognize letters. Maybe some of these things worry you. After all, most of us didn't do any writing except practicing letter formation until we had plenty of instruction and experience with spelling.

One temporary solution to this problem is "**developmental spelling,**" sometimes called "**invented spelling.**" Young children imitate writing by scribbling and eventually getting the idea of writing their scribbles in lines. They soon learn how the letters of their own names or words they see often look. It's fun to watch young children "read" billboards, etc., when they really are recognizing the logo or the way the print looks.

"Reading" logos leads readily to the desire of children to imitate those letters. Developmental spelling is the next logical step. It relies on children using some of what they are absolutely sure of, mixed with some educated guesses. So the boy named Dale uses the D when he attempts to spell "dog." The other letters may not even be English letters. There may be squiggles and there may not even be the two other letters we expect.

As children have repeated exposure to print in guided reading, shared book experiences, and silent individualized reading, they start to notice that the way other people seem to spell dog is "dog." They gradually absorb these traditional spellings and become more conventional.

Children also ask directly for the spelling of some words. Write the words down so that the children may copy them. Or, call out the letters if the child knows and can produce all of the letters just by hearing the letter names. As children gain experience, you may want to use questions to get them to apply phonics or prior knowledge to guess some of the letters themselves.

Of course, children may need direct instruction to learn the names of each letter and some practice to get used to how letters are formed. Imitation alone may not be sufficient because children will not worry about the most efficient way to form letters, they may just make curves and sticks until the letter looks similar to the one they want.

The reason parents worry is that children seem to make the same errors over and over. In fact, they seem to memorize their mistakes. In these cases, it's fine for the parent to say that the way most people spell the word is DOG or that when book writers spell the word, they use DOG. This is quite different from simply saying that the word has been spelled wrong.

Is there ever a point where spelling is not developmental? Well, most adults continue to make some errors so, in that sense, spelling skills do continue to develop. However, most students spell conventionally by the third grade. This is the result of spelling instruction and practice as well as years of exposure to accurate spelling of words in books.

There is also a rule about spelling. Because it is a courtesy to the reader, whenever a written work "goes public," conventional spelling is required (Butler, 1988). When a paper is going to be hung in the hall, published in the school newspaper, etc., then spelling has to be conventional. Other conventions, such as paragraph indentation, capitalization, and punctuation, also require attention.

Again, direct instruction in these rules as well as comparison with print materials in which the rules have been followed help students learn conventions. Empowering children to be writers, people who think of themselves as capable of writing, is one of the most important things families can do for their children.

MODELED WRITING

Another very important step in developing literacy and language use is **modeled writing.** In modeled writing, an adult writes in the presence of children, large enough for all of the children to see. The writing might be done on an overhead or on the chalkboard or on large newsprint paper.

The adult narrates his thinking as the writing progresses. Perhaps, "Oh, I don't know how to start. Well, that's okay, I'll put a beginning on later" or maybe, "No, 'nice' is too simple a word. I'd rather use 'majestic'." You could say, "Let's see, how do you spell 'through'?," etc.

In this way, students see how adults use self-monitoring to check spelling, grammar, and flow of writing. This is an excellent method for teaching specific kinds of writing as well. It's important to learn how to write science laboratory reports, social studies biographies, and the answers to word or story problems in math. Each new form of writing has its own rules, styles and conventions or traditions. Even certain abbreviations or ways of expressing ideas go with certain disciplines or subject areas. Students require direct instruction in each new type of writing. The best way to do this is with modeled writing.

As students watch adults engage in the writing process, they also realize that writing is not an error-free process. In fact, much of writing is "trial and error." An adult can also model how to edit work that has already been drafted. Listening to a more experienced writer think through the writing process allows less experienced writers the opportunity to imitate the process, based on observation of the adult.

Modeled writing works at all ages and at all levels of sophistication. Beginning readers and writers get a real kick out of "helping" adults write an idea as well as noticing adult errors. Older students also feel empowered when they can locate adult errors.

Parents often wonder how to help their children without actually doing the homework. Modeled writing is one way to be helpful. Pretend that you

were writing a similar paper on a similar topic to the one your child has to
write. Give some tips on construction in this way. Or be a good listener as
your child talks through the process of writing!

OPPORTUNITIES FOR SHARING

Opportunities for sharing is one of the best ways for families to participate in a whole language literacy program. In this step, children are provided with ways to show others what they have written and what they know
how to read.

Parents should not mistakenly think of this as a need only for younger children. All writers need to have their work examined and appreciated. Family
interest and the interest of other community members stimulates young writers and readers to continue their efforts.

In what ways can families create opportunities for sharing reading and
writing? This list will just scratch the surface and stimulate your own additional ideas.

Older children can read to younger children from published books, newspapers, etc., or from their own works. Younger children (even those too
young to officially read) can interpret their artwork and squiggles to any
interested party.

Do you have a baby and can't figure out how to have time for listening to
your toddler, preschooler, or grade schooler? Encourage "public" readings
in which the reader holds the text and reads or interprets. This will free up
your hands to feed or hold the baby and still allow you to use your eyes and
ears as the audience.

Imitate televised events or live events your family has experienced. If you
have been to a concert or a poetry reading, encourage your children to set
their writings to music or deliver their poems while standing up or reading
from a "stage" area in your home. (We've used the bathroom step stool more
than once.)

Some children enjoy using props or costumes as part of their presentations. Use old clothes that have been laundered or purchase clothes inex-
pensively at resale shops for this purpose. (As an extension, you may find
your children dressing in costumes for participation at an interactive level
with a television show or movie you've rented.)

Older children can find their own mistakes (an oral form of proofreading)
by reading aloud to you. Reading aloud is slower than reading silently and
this decreased speed allows children to notice and correct errors.

Alternatively, older students may not be interested in having you read their work until it has been turned in and graded. Don't think to yourself that there's no point in reading a paper because the teacher has already marked it. If your children ask that you read their work, try to take the time. Older children, especially, may find it easier to "speak" to you in writing. It is also likely that, other than noting the grade, children have paid little attention to the comments written on the work by the teacher. Your attention to those comments and a conversation with your child about them will call your child's attention to the comments so that she may benefit.

Family writing for a purpose may be important here too. Write to tell about some product that you loved or with which you find fault. Send for the missing bike part. Write to a government official. Finally, opportunities to share should include lots of positive feedback from family members. If you can't trust a little brother to be respectful of his older sister's work, have her read when he is playing baseball. If two siblings close in age are competitive about their skills, avoid comparison and find good points in the work of each.

Even if you finally read the work of your children after they have gone to sleep for the day (when else?!), be sure to write a quick note on Post-it® notes with your thoughts about their efforts.

Families require communication for strength. There is no rule that the communication must be spoken. Spice up communication in your family with shared opportunities for reading and writing.

CONTENT AREA READING AND WRITING

The last of the ten components of a whole language literacy program is that of **content area reading and writing.** In this component, parents and teachers consider the fact that reading and writing in each discipline or subject area has its own demands and specialty requirements.

Teachers in specific content areas, especially in departmentalized upper grades and high school, are often content specialists, having taken a college major in the subjects they teach. Knowing how to read and having had experience writing does not necessarily mean that the students are ready for the specialty writing of their teachers' disciplines. For this reason, content area teachers provide direct instruction in the reading and writing of each discipline (Butler, 1988).

Consider **vocabulary** first. It is clear that the vocabulary necessary to read Shakespeare or a contemporary poet is quite different from the vocabulary required to read a physics textbook. Each vocabulary must be taught.

Vocabulary can be especially tricky because even the same word takes on

a different meaning in different subjects. An example might be the word
RUN. In physical education, RUN probably means what you do with your
legs; in home economics, a run in a stocking is a long tear or mar; in government, a person might RUN for office; in economics, a RUN on the bank
might have happened in 1929; in humanities, a play may have enjoyed a
really long RUN on Broadway; in English, a RUN-on sentence might spoil
an essay; in science, chemicals may RUN together if not stored separately,
similarly in art, where colors might be said to RUN; in law, a criminal might
have a RUN-in with the police; in a work of literature, an author might
describe how a dog had the RUN of the house while his master was away.
Each of these content-specific uses of the same word require content area
reading and writing.

Different skills are also used to take an educated guess at the meanings of
unfamiliar words. In physics, using Latin root words and prefix or suffix
meanings might help a reader achieve word meaning. In a poem, context
clues or main ideas may be more likely to result in a correct educated guess
on the meaning of a word.

Consider also the **way that texts in that subject are printed.** In a math
textbook, print is often interspersed with numerical expressions. That looks
quite different from a history textbook, in which print may continue on for
several pages without interruptions or may appear more commonly in captions for graphs, charts, or photographs.

The traditional way each subject area lays out text books, uses boxed or
bulleted information, provides indexes and tables of contents, notes refer-
ences, etc., is part of content area reading instruction. Content area writing
instruction is similarly required.

Knowing how to write a short story may not prepare a young writer to
write a lab report. It is important for content area teachers to teach how to
write in their specific disciplines, partly by having students read lots of discipline-specific writing which they can imitate. This may mean duplicating
examples of excellent lab reports and it may also mean using modeled writing, in which the teacher demonstrates at the board or overhead how a lab
report is constructed (Butler, 1988).

Parents can help their children meet the new demands of varied writing
by calling students' attention to details of form and vocabulary that seem specific to the field. Parents can also encourage their children to find models in
textbooks and library resources of appropriate writing forms that can then be
imitated.

Parents of young children can also spend time reading to children from a
variety of print resources. It is common to read stories to children. However,
then they are only aware of how stories are laid out. Many young children
who have been read to can easily answer "How should a story begin?" with

"Once upon a time." They can also say, in unison, at the end of the story "...and they lived happily ever after."

Read nonfiction aloud to children, too, so that they become just as familiar with the conventions or traditions of that kind of reading and writing as well. In history, common markers include time-related clues: first, second, many years later, in the seventeenth century, when the country was born, etc.

Science experiments are marked by the order of procedures: begin with a clear glass and 8 ounces of water, quickly add 4 drops of..., allow the mixture to stand in strong light for 10 minutes, etc. Volume, number, temperature, time and calculations, and mixing numbers with letters characterize science experiment writing and reading. Children need experience in switching gears frequently between characters that may look a great deal alike (1 and l, for instance, that is #1 and letter l). Imagine the message a child who mixes them up receives from what she reads!

Some whole language proponents do not put much stock in reading text books, as they consider these texts less than authentic; they advocate going directly to encyclopedias, medical journals, classical works of literature, etc., to gain content area knowledge. Textbooks are, however, authentic in their own right and do provide opportunities for students to learn to read a variety of print materials. Whichever model the school your child attends uses, you are now aware of the need for your child to "shift gears" for a variety of texts.

Successful content area reading and writing is critical to school success. Recognize the demands, give your children plenty of experience with each type of reading, and help your child notice differences in the writing for each field. Instruction in reading and writing, driven by a whole language philosophy, is comprehensive. It treats all aspects of reading and writing as ports along a continuum, not as discrete skills that students will somehow bring to cohesion on their own. Teachers weave instruction in all aspects of language, perhaps along a unifying theme, and most often employing "authentic" reading materials, ones that people other than school children might use. The intention is to prepare students for using skills in varied combinations, like the variable combinations demanded by adult life.

Chapter 10

MIDDLE SCHOOLS

Perhaps you have been wondering what the difference between **middle schools** and junior high schools is. Maybe you haven't even noticed that different schools use different terms: junior high schools, upper grade centers, middle schools.

Junior high schools typically were given that name not just because that was a name that was in vogue at the time but also because the title described the intended function. Junior high schools are meant to be "training outposts" for high schools. Teachers are most often certified with a secondary teaching certificate and have majored in their teaching subject area in college.

Junior high schools are meant to provide students in grade six, seven and eight (usually) with the watered-down experience of high school. Classes are departmentalized, that is, students change from period to period, attending classes taught by subject area specialists. Teachers have a great deal of autonomy with regard to whether they want to require assignments in pen or pencil, insist on spiral notebooks, require students to take notes, etc. In addition, students do not usually have a space to call home, although they may go to homeroom for several minutes each school day.

Middle schools, as described by the professional group, National Middle School Association, differ first in philosophy from junior high schools. Middle schools are meant to pay attention specifically to the needs of young adolescents and treat the **whole student,** not just treat the student serially, first as a scientist, then as a mathematician, then as a writer, etc. (National Middle School Association, 1995).

Middle schools often emphasize **multidisciplinary learning,** which requires students and teachers to weave several areas of study together for a more comprehensive view of a topic. Middle schools should be more likely to have faculty engaged in **team teaching.** The faculty in middle schools often coordinate the assignments given to students so that there is not a pile-up all on one night. One way to do this, for instance, is to designate certain days of the week for homework from certain areas.

94

Many middle schools are working toward (or already doing) something called **block scheduling.** In block scheduling, the school day might be treated as four longer time periods or "blocks" of time, instead of seven or eight shorter periods of time. In these longer periods, students can study subjects in greater depth and with wider variety of instructional and learning experiences. It may also happen that students then take certain subjects for a semester instead of a year or for one year instead of for two years. The total instructional time often remains quite traditional over the course of all of the middle schools years.

What ties the multidisciplinary work together in these longer blocks of time is often themes. Students will investigate the same theme in several subject areas. Often, in middle schools, the theme is novel-driven, that is, the theme is determined by the novel that students are reading in language arts.

Imagine, for instance, that the theme for the next month is the Civil War. Students read a novel about a person who experienced the war, and several issues of morality, loyalty, economics, slavery and governments are raised. In addition, students read nonfiction accounts of the war and diaries of persons who lived through the time period. In mathematics and science, economic and military issues of battle plans, budgets, ammunition, medical care, etc., are studied. In social studies, the events and characters of history are learned and placed in time. In art and music, period artworks and works of music receive attention, with students exploring why such works would have been composed just at such a time. In physical education, students recreate some of the pastimes employed by soldiers between battles, as well as reenact military physical training routines. An historic reenactment is planned as a final project.

There is obviously more coordinated planning demanded of teachers in a school driven by a middle school philosophy (and, by the way, not all schools have changed their names to reflect the philosophical differences). It is also possible to see how much more relevant students might perceive school learning to be, if it isn't packaged into artificial little bundles called periods where one and only one academic discipline can be used at a time.

Sometimes, schools create joint planning time for teachers by having all of the teachers in one grade have a plan period while all of the students of that grade are having lunch, then stagger the teachers' lunches throughout the day. Other schools have tried other configurations, which may be quite unique to the community or faculty of the school.

Middle school students typically move to all of their classes together as a group. These groups make it possible for students to have a "home," that is, a social cohesion, if not a physical space to call home.

Teachers in a middle school may also coordinate other aspects of the school's "hidden curriculum." Lavoie (1995) asserted that every school has a school culture, created by people who have been there a long time. There are rules that are never written down in the student handbook but are nonetheless true. These things may include where boys stand on the playground, which seats are reserved for students in the "in" crowd, or whether you can or cannot go to the rest room with a pass or whether you must seek permission. Middle school faculty may be very sensitive to the needs of young adolescents who want, more than anything, not to be embarrassed, and they may help by writing down or making explicit some of the hidden curriculum items.

Middle school teachers are likely to be certified in elementary education and have subject area course work in many areas. The National Middle School Association advocates that teachers of middle school have a strong background in child and adolescent development and must have a repertory of methods for working specifically with young adolescents (NMSA, 1995).

Another feature of middle schools may be that teachers in middle schools use what has become known as **alternative assessment.** Some professionals refer to this as authentic assessment. These assessment models differ from traditional models in a few key ways. Traditional assessment emphasizes summative or final evaluation. At the end of a unit of instruction, the teacher needs to find out how much material the students have learned and retained. The means of conducting this evaluation is usually tests. The Friday spelling test, the social studies unit test, and the math chapter test are traditional means of evaluating student progress.

Alternative or authentic assessment emphasizes formative or continuing evaluation, adhering to the philosophy that teachers and students need ongoing information about how learning is progressing. Alternative assessment also uses a variety of means to determine how students have changed as a result of instruction. Students might be asked to give a presentation, build an item, or teach what they know to peers. Students are more likely to be asked to assess their own level of performance as well as that of their peers. Students are also more likely to be asked to demonstrate knowledge and skills in more lifelike or "authentic" situations, hence, the term. The increased focus on self-evaluation as well as performing skills in authentic settings is one that is consistent with the idea of learning not just for school but for life.

Middle schools may also develop **teacher advisory programs.** In a teacher advisory program, students are assigned to teachers who provide personal guidance, mentoring, and an ongoing relationship to students. In this way, students may experience school as a more seamless experience with the rest of their lives. Teacher advisory programs have been demonstrated to help students stay in school and be more successful in their school progress (NMSA, 1995).

The faculty of middle schools may also use a model of helping students write in each discipline (see the content area reading and writing portion of the whole language chapter in this section) called **writing workshop.** In writing workshop, faculty take responsibility for teaching the kind of writing appropriate to the discipline content they teach. In addition, students handle their own editing in a process mode. They keep samples of their writing over the course of an academic year in a portfolio and monitor their own progress toward several objectives.

Middle schools are more likely than other schools to call their after-school activities **co-curricular activities** rather than extracurricular activities. The philosophy of middle schools that concentrates on the whole child recognizes the value of non-academic pursuits as paired with academic pursuits, not extra or beyond, as extra implies.

Of course, some middle schools are really junior high schools in middle school clothing; some teachers hew to a high school model even though they teach at "middle schools" and everything about any particular model is not always rosy. Whenever something that is not the way things have been done forever is tried, it is not easy. Middle schools as described here constitute a relatively new movement in education. We await the results.

For more information about middle schools:

National Middle School Association
2600 Corporate Exchange Drive, Suite 370
Columbus, OH 43231
800-528-NMSA

Chapter 11

MULTIDISCIPLINARY STUDY

Sometimes thought of as a new trend, **multidisciplinary study** has been employed increasingly often, not just in middle schools, but in several levels of education throughout the country. It is also not a new trend. When Socrates taught Plato, the conversation and learning was multidisciplinary, that is, all of the topics relevant to certain ideas were discussed, no matter what discipline they came from. These **disciplines** traditionally refer to subject areas: science, social studies, mathematics, philosophy, literature, etc. These can be even more specifically divided. For instance, science can be botany, zoology, biology, physics, chemistry, astonomy, and meteorology. Biology could be divided into anatomy, physiology, microbiology, human biology, etc. In university settings, disciplines have been useful because they allow people to specialize and gain a deeper knowledge in a specialized area or topic. However, developmentally, compartmentalizing knowledge into named bits does not make much sense.

The brain seeks connections; artificially separating out discrete skills does not make sense to the brain (Caine & Caine, 1995). However, for at least several hundred years, elementary and secondary education have imitated university education by teaching in discipline-specific clusters. New problems and a new understanding of how the brain works have resulted in a movement toward more multidisciplinary study.

Imagine that the topic of instruction is recycling. From a science angle, it is important to notice that, when left to its own devices, nature recycles, using dead animals to feed insects, other animals, etc., and then decaying to become part of the soil that grows plants that feed new animals and so on. Science also helps us learn how best to reuse materials: burn, melt, reconstitute, mix with water, etc. Social studies requires us to see the social ramifications of recycling or not recycling. We consider ways to interact with people to persuade them to recycle. In mathematics, measurement for volume receives attention (how many aluminum cans are in a pound, how many tons of newspaper will be required to produce X boxes of stationery, etc.) In

98

language arts, we write to political representatives, practice making speeches to adults or community action groups, etc. In literature, we read Ralph Waldo Emerson about the joys of nature. In art and music, we draw logos and write jingles to persuade people to recycle. We sing rounds that are "recycled" and draw on recycled paper. In this way, the whole curriculum is connecting to provide a sensible linked experience for children. Traditional periods of 40 minutes in length may be inappropriate for this kind of in-depth study; block scheduling may be one solution.

Curriculum that is multidisciplinary is intended to help students make sense out of their life experiences (NMSA, 1995). Various disciplines of the formal school curriculum are used to examine the same theme. In addition, teachers identify the connections among ideas and fields of knowledge. Reading, writing, critical thinking, computing, and other skills are taught in the context of the theme of study, not as discrete and isolated bits of information and skills (NMSA, 1995). Not only can students better learn the skills and information in the first place but also the stage is set for lifelong learning. There are educators who worry about whether all of the items in the traditional curriculum will be "covered" when multidisciplinary units are taught. It seems unlikely. However, with the volume of knowledge now available and the daily explosion of ever more knowledge, it is impossible, given any curriculum and design of implementation, to learn all of the knowledge and skills possible. The assertion of advocates for multidisciplinary teaching and learning is that whatever is learned is connected and more likely to be retained. More importantly, the emphasis is on the skills of acquisition and connection, which allow students to continue to seek additional knowledge and skills long after school graduation.

Chapter 12

BILINGUAL PROGRAMS/
ENGLISH AS A SECOND LANGUAGE

The United States has as its motto on its coins and elsewhere the Latin phrase: *E Pluribus Unum.* This phrase means "one from many." While we do not really become one in a melting pot like crayons in hot sun, we do become one in the sense that we comprise one political and geographic unit, the United States.

It has always been true that persons in the United States came from somewhere else. We are primarily a nation of immigrants. Each immigrant family brought with it a **culture,** composed of a pattern of communication or language, a diet and method of preparing food, a style of dress, common socialization patterns including age and gender roles, and a common set of values (Aragon, 1973).

There are two major approaches to the education of culturally different groups. One is **assimilation,** the goal being to move away from individual culture and toward skills to compete in a macroculture (the dominant culture). Another is **pluralism,** where persons are encouraged to retain their original culture, and schools make accommodations to enhance school success (Kitano, 1991).

For centuries, the United States leaned toward assimilation. Your immigrant parents, grandparents, or great-grandparents probably assimilated. This was partly necessitated by the huge number of immigrants coming in at one time and to just a few locations. Today, immigrants are likely to be from many different cultures and may be scattered all over the map. The philosophy of schooling has also changed, shifting more toward pluralism. Even established groups, the Irish, for instance, are now re-embracing their cultural roots, by taking up step dancing.

In **bilingual education,** students are taught first in their native tongue. Gradually, students are taught English and enter the regular grades as reasonably competent readers, speakers and writers of English. They may

100

enroll in kindergarten as non-English speakers but be integrated into regular classrooms by third grade. It sounds feasible. However, remember that not all students with limited English proficiency (LEP) come to school as kindergartners. They may move to the United States in seventh grade. Thus, bilingual education is challenged to take children at different ages and provide continuous and increasingly English instruction with students who are at various stages of English acquisition (Donato & Garcia, 1992). Further, not all students of different cultures speak another language; some speak dialects of English. Should they receive bilingual education? This is what has spawned the current Ebonics debate, over black English or a dialect of English. Even when it seems appropriate to use bilingual education, it should be noted that skill on the teacher's part in speaking both languages is required. What happens when, as it does in one north side high school in Chicago, sixty-five languages are spoken by the students? It seems near to impossible to have truly bilingual education for each of the limited English proficient students enrolled there (Donato & Garcia, 1992). On the other hand, it does seem clear that it would be foolish to talk all day long to children, trying to teach in a language they do not understand. However, the natural variables of learning rate, age at entry, differing ages of "new" learners, wide variety of languages spoken, etc., makes bilingual education difficult to implement.

Further, research (Lewis & Doorlag, 1995) suggests that persons learning a new language may have conversational skills within a few years; however, academic competency in English, given the sophisticated vocabulary of disciplinary study, may take up to seven years to acquire. Intensive, long-term immersion experiences appear to be necessary for adequate learning to occur (Whitmore, 1994).

There are at least two versions of bilingual education. One, **transitional bilingual education,** uses the student's native language and culture to assist in the acquisition of English. The goal here is to achieve English competency as quickly as possible and integrate students into the general education classroom as quickly as possible. The other, **maintenance bilingual education,** is designed to teach children about their native culture and language as well as to learn English (Cummins, 1989).

In order for bilingual programs to be successful, Cummins (1989) recommended the use of volunteers, cooperative learning methods, books written in various languages available in the classroom and library, groupings which allow children of the same language to communicate, and inclusion of various languages in greetings and school information.

Books to help children understand about immigrant children include:

Bogard, L. (1989). *The fourth grade dinosaur club.* New York: Delacorte.
Howlett, B. (1993). *I'm new here.* Boston: Houghton Mifflin.
Leighton, M. R. (1992). *An Ellis Island Christmas.* New York: Viking.

Another solution for students with limited English proficiency is **English as a Second Language (ESL)** instruction. In this method, which has its own difficulties, instruction takes place only in English and no effort is made to develop or maintain proficiency in the native language. This accommodates a diversity of students from varied cultures and language backgrounds but does not mean that students instantly understand English as instruction begins, which can result in content learning failing to occur.

A wide range of methods and techniques may be used in ESL settings (Chamot, 1995; Kitay, 1996; Zucker, 1995). Lots of pictures and other visual aids are used in an ESL classroom to try to bridge the gap caused by language differences. Reduction of emphasis on clock time may also help, including untimed tests. Students are more likely to have hands-on experiences to facilitate comprehension. ESL teachers may also use media in which students are highly motivated to comprehend, such as films; films also have social and visual cues to use to gain meaning.

Cooperative learning may also be used to facilitate direct interaction with English-speaking peer models. It is also true that most nonnative English speakers learn to speak more rapidly than they do to read and write, which makes perfect sense in light of the language hierarchy (see "Whole Language" chapter). In cooperative groups, these students can contribute orally and another student can write down the answer.

Person-to-person interactions help students, as do incorporating real-life tasks and accepting reasonable answers, not just expected ones. Employing singing, rhythm, movement, and more enthused delivery also seem to help LEP students acquire English competence more successfully than if just traditional methods are used (Franklin, 1992).

Chapter 13

CURRENT ISSUES

SCHOOL TESTING

An important aspect of school performance is performance on tests. Teachers certainly use other measures (Burke, 1992) to assess student progress, but students from kindergarten on are exposed to various forms of tests. A number of factors go into determining test performance. One factor is **test anxiety.**

Test anxiety can have roots similar to other anxieties, such as family difficulties, but it is most often related to academic learning problems or problems in self-esteem. Sometimes very competent students think of themselves as less than competent and, therefore, panic before or during tests.

Preparedness is a good way to reduce test anxiety. Pretend to be the teacher as you preview material to be covered by a test and create questions. To what type of questions does this information lend itself?

Definitions show up in matching items or fill-in-the-blanks. Factual statements appear in true/false formats. Applications or conceptual information lends itself to short answer or essay items.

Second-guessing the teacher by writing sample items is helpful. Discussing test anxiety with a teacher may also do a lot of good. Teachers may be able to make some or all of the following responses.

Teachers may permit students to take a test orally, giving answers on tape, to another student, to a tutor, or to the teacher directly. If the person who is hearing the answers records them, there is a record for discussing grade assignments later as well as a record of the ideas to study from or review later.

Teachers may give tests under untimed circumstances. Teachers may decide to have course grades rest on more than just tests. Assignments can have varied targets: reading, writing, speaking, creating a product, synthesizing information, memorizing, or analyzing information.

Teachers may permit extra credit work or other demonstrations of content learning. Some teachers will permit retakes of the tests to average into final grades. Teachers can help students see where the main ideas are and help students focus their studying time according to importance.

There are still more things that teachers may do to help with test anxiety. They may allow extra time (if not usually untimed) or design tests that avoid total recall of information, giving a word bank or list of possible choices instead. Teachers may give directions individually to stressed students. Teachers may even eliminate extra choices or "answer not given" as an option in multiple-choice formats.

There are also a number of things you can do to reduce test anxiety. Determine with a quick skim how much time you will need to spend on any one section of a test, and make finishing the whole test a priority. Use information given within the test. Some questions may give you information to answer other questions.

Do not change your answer, unless you suddenly remember specific information. Do not read too much into true/false questions; instead, base your answer just on the information provided. Cross off answers as you use them.

The words **always** and **never** often make true/false statements false. When you approach multiple-choice items, usually two answers are obviously wrong. When you are trying to decide between the remaining two, research suggests that the longer one is often right. Remember the directions are usually to choose the **best** choice.

If you don't know an answer, guess. At least partial credit may be given. Besides, sometimes guessing is really based on some vaguely familiar information. Go back over your work and make sure that you have not accidentally skipped one or more items. This is especially tragic when misplacing one answer in the number-two pencil "bubble"; it throws off every answer thereafter.

Spread out your studying. Research suggests that you may double your performance on tests if you regularly review materials instead of reviewing only right before a test. Time is short? Review whenever you eat alone. Prop up your notes on the handlebars of the exercise bike. Read while you wait for trains. Take your study materials with you anywhere you expect to wait: a doctor's office, dentist's office, pharmacy, ticket window, restaurant, etc.

If you are not the student and your child is, try giving this advice to your children. Improving test performance and reducing test anxiety gives a terrific boost to self-esteem.

Another factor that influences test performance is prior experience with tests. Students that have had good experiences with tests usually do not fear them. Using the advice given here may help your child experience some success with tests. In addition, when students have never had to fill in bubbles with number-two pencils before, their attention may be so much on completely filling in the bubbles that the information takes a back seat.

Test format may also influence test performance. Students often have preferences for certain types of questions. Health and rest are major influences on test performance. In the case of health, illness negatively affects test performance by reducing tenacity and concentration. Insufficient sleep has the same effect.

Test performance may also be influenced by whether students have ever been exposed to material. It is not possible for students to correctly answer questions, except by guessing randomly, unless they have been exposed to the content, either at home or at school. When a large number of students in a class fail a certain test item, there is a strong possibility that they have never been taught that content.

The outcome of tests is test scores. All test scores, as all tests, are influenced by a number of variables which include the health or motivation of the child on the days of testing and all of the other factors listed above.

It is to be remembered that a test score represents one sample taken at one point in time. The test score does not equal the child. Children are far more complex than the sum of the test scores. Adults who read the test scores and worry about their meaning would do well to remember that.

There are several things that parents can do to assist children in test taking.

1. Teach your child how to follow directions.

2. Play simple games (Simon Says, etc.) that emphasize following directions.

3. Teach your children how to ask questions when they are unsure of directions or expectations.

4. Teach good study habits, particularly how to organize time and how to move on when one question is difficult.

5. Insist on decent meals and adequate sleep on the days of standardized testing. If you have a picky eater or a child who is too nervous to eat well, relax your rules temporarily. M&M's for breakfast may be better than nothing!

6. Encourage your children to think of testing as another way to demonstrate what they know, not some big one-time fearful event. Children do projects, complete homework, compete in sports, and take tests. They should do their best in all of these endeavors without being encouraged to worry excessively about only one of these experiences.

There are a number of excellent books for parents explaining test concepts, interpretation and terminology that can be found in your local public library or ordered from a bookstore. Provide the background and nutritional support recommended and then relax and let your child know you have confidence in her ability to do her best!

SCHOOL TEST SCORES

It is easy for parents to be confused by test scores that come home on those peel-off labels and on report cards. There are so many forms that grades and scores can take. Here is a brief scorecard on the types.

A **raw score** reports how many items on a particular subtest or test the child answered correctly. Intuitively, this seems to make sense as a good way to report scores. However, knowing the raw score does not help us know if a child did "well" or not. A raw score gives no information to the teacher, other than how many right; it does not provide insight into which items were correctly answered and which ones were missed. A raw score doesn't help a teacher know whether that number right is common for students of a certain grade or age or whether this score is unusually good or bad.

A **grade equivalent** is a way of reporting that a child's performance on that day on that test is comparable to the performance of an average child in the grade and month of that grade that is reported. One caution is that one more item right or wrong might change a child's grade equivalent into another grade or change the score by several months. Grade equivalent also may falsely communicate to parents that the student has "missed" an aspect of the curriculum (the plan for what to learn and in what sequence) by indicating that a child is, for instance at 2.6 grade level when in March of the third grade. However, there may be no direct match between the test and the curriculum, so the grade equivalent may lack meaning for parents.

Another standardized score is the **percentile rank.** Percentile rank provides a means of thinking about scores on intervals from 1 to 99. A percentile rank of 46 means that the child performed better than did 46 percent of the other children who also took the test.

Stanine is still another form of standardized score. Stanines are reported in equal intervals from 1 to 9 and, therefore, may seem easier to interpret. Because there are fewer scores from 1 to 9 than from 1 to 99, a larger number of students will be assigned the same stanine score and thus indicate less differentiation among students and their performances.

Grade equivalent, percentile rank and stanine scores also do not provide the teacher or family with any information about the topics or skills in which the child demonstrated competence. Some test companies provide schools with an error analysis which can report, for individual students or whole classes of students, areas of strength and areas of weakness. This is important because it sometimes happens that a test includes items on a topic never taught. To discover that every child or most children in the class did not answer those items correctly makes sense. Of course, the standardized test scores reflect performance across the whole test, and the child or class of children in question may not "look as good" because of those missed items.

The school and parents must decide what it is they are trying to accomplish with standardized tests so they can interpret standardized test scores in a meaningful way. One way to use such tests would be to have every teacher teach every topic and skill that was sampled in the test. Then have every student take the test and it can be determined what students "got out of" the instruction. This is still not perfect. What if some children were (inevitably) absent for some of the instruction. If those students failed the items that sampled that instructional content, does it mean that the teacher is at fault? What if some students have difficulty learning, but the teacher had to move on to new skills and topics in order to be through teaching all of the topics by the time the test was administered. If those students did poorly on the test, is anyone at fault? You see how difficult it is to use these tests meaningfully.

You might ask, "Why use these tests at all?" That is a fair question. One reason is for schools or school districts to attempt to rate themselves. This is fraught with the difficulties identified above as well as others. What if some students answered questions correctly because they learned the information at home, on television or through some other method? Is that to the teacher's or school's credit? What if students got some answers right by guessing? Is that to the teacher's or school's credit? What if some students performed poorly because they were ill or distracted or tired the day of the test? Does it mean that the teacher or school has not been successful in teaching that child?

These questions just begin to scratch the surface of standardized testing issues. Parents may demand standardized tests and their attendant scores because it is what parents are familiar with from their own schooling. School boards and administrators may hope to prove effectiveness with test performance. Whatever the reasons why standardized tests are used in your child's school or district, it is important to be aware of the frailties of the standardized test system. It may help you use a "grain of salt" in interpreting results.

Because all standardized scores have been statistically manipulated, they require some interpretation to be able to understand them. Teachers perform a valuable role for parents when they take a few minutes to make an understandable explanation of test scores.

EDUCATIONAL ASSESSMENT

Of course, there is more to determining what students know and how well they are learning than tests and their scores. Terms that are being used more often today are **authentic assessment** or **alternative assessment.**

Alternative assessment simply suggests that teachers and others have alternatives to tests (Johnsen, 1996), but sometimes it is used to be synonymous with authentic assessment. Authentic assessment implies more that students show what they know in meaningful applied ways with real materials and, if possible, in "real world" settings (Jones, 1993). For example, to determine how students have mastered reading graphs, students might read graphs, census reports, business reports, newspapers, weather forecasts, etc., rather than in a simulated workbook activity.

If the skill can be performed, observed and rated for quality, the assessment might be termed **performance-based assessment.** Performance-based assessment is used when teachers or parents desire to know more than whether students understand the hypothetical; in performance-based assessment, students must demonstrate the skill in an applied way to the satisfaction of the observer. How does the observer or the student know what the criteria are and whether criteria have been met? **Rubrics** are commonly used. A sample one, shown here, could be used to evaluate a speech presentation, 3 being the highest score and 1 being the lowest

Rubric for Oral Presentation

3   Obvious preparation
      Observable familiarity with the topic
      Evidence of extensive research
      Eye contact throughout presentation; minimal use of cue cards
      Volume appropriately audible through the presentation
      Animated, dynamic, kept the interest of the audience

2   Adequate preparation
      Reasonable familiarity with the topic
      Evidence of considerable research
      Eye contact through most of presentation; some reliance on cards
      Audible most of the presentation
      Clear, most audience members paying attention

1   Some preparation
      Knew something about the topic
      Mentioned research occasionally
      Occasional eye contact; heavy realiance on cue cards
      Barely audible on occasion
      Low expression, most classmates not paying attention

The teacher, often in conjunction with the class, prepares the rubric ahead of time and issues copies to the class or posts the written version in the classroom. Teachers may then simply use additional copies and circle the text descriptions that best describe student performance in each of the six categories. Students' final ratings are usually the one in which most of their performance was judged or the "average" of the weight of the levels in which the performance was judged. If letter grades are required, the scores could be converted to letter grades, for instance, with a "3" being equivalent to "A."

Finally, **portfolio assessment** is receiving increasing attention, for both teachers and students (Goolsby, 1995). Students keep sample work, along with their comments about their work, as well as the comments of classmates, teachers and parents. Over time, it is possible to see differences in neatness, accuracy, sophistication, etc., in work ranging from calculus to creative writing. Portfolios are sometimes used in place of report cards or in conjunction with the more traditional report cards (Balm, 1995).

Disadvantages to portfolios include additional teacher time required to monitor, help students engage in self-evaluation and explain a new method to parents; storage space for the documentation; and student resistance to such an involved process. Advantages include easing anxiety about grades, facilitating parent-teacher conferences, encouraging independent learning and self-assessment (much of adult life is governed by this kind), and more careful monitoring of progress over time (Collinson, 1995).

Test scores and other information about school as it relates to your child (days of attendance, annual grades, etc.) comprise school records. School records may be called cumulative records or cumulative folder or files or, in teacher's jargon, cum folders. The Family Educational Rights and Privacy Act (Public Law 93-380) was passed in 1974 and is sometimes called the Buckley Amendment. Because of this law, parents must be informed of the nature and location of all files and documents pertaining to their children and can examine all records. Most of these records, in the form of report cards or grade reports and test scores, are shared with parents in a specific format and at certain times of the academic year.

A few records are exempt from this access. Any notes that a teacher or counselor makes for her own use and does not share with other school personnel or place in the cumulative folder does not have to be shared. Another aspect of the legislation is that once a child is 18, the records must be made available directly to the student.

PARENTS' RIGHTS

Parents' rights is a relatively new concept in legal terms but has been in existence since the beginning of United States history. The educational term, "parents' rights," suggests that parents have a right to say what their children will be taught. You can imagine the controversy in modern times, however, as you would probably have as many different lists of things to be taught as there are sets of parents that send their children to a school—and two lists might even come from most pairs of parents who would not totally agree with one another!

Schools have always had some local control in the United States, exerted by school boards composed of local residents, sometimes leaders in the community. In the early days of United States history, these school boards were often composed of religious leaders who determined what would be studied by the offspring of that community. As school districts have grown larger and comprised more diverse student populations, the tensions over what should be taught have increased. A less homogeneous student body may result in a greater tension.

Some parents have turned to home schooling in order to control what their children learn and to what topics they are exposed. A few parents' groups have sued local school boards for the right to determine what their children are taught, hence, the term "parents' rights" (Sendor, 1996). For decades and, in some cases, centuries, parents have exercised their right to control what their children learn by enrolling their children in private schools that match the political thought, religious background or other unifying feature of the parents' choice (Crawford & Freeman, 1996). Parents' rights issues have been identified in several concerns over the years: discipline, curriculum and academic rigor (Crawford & Freeman, 1996); advocacy for services for young children with special needs (Pardeck, 1996); sexual issues, including AIDS, birth control and homosexuality (Bjorklun, 1994; Chalk Talk, 1996; Sendor, 1996); parent access to schools (Burron, 1996); library holdings or books assigned for class work (Gounaud, 1996; Layne, 1995); teaching about the Holocaust or other sensitive topics (Short, 1994); procedural safeguards for children receiving special education services (Osborne, 1995); and moral education (Andrews, 1995).

Parents' rights has also been the name given to rights of minors, safeguarded by their parents or guardians. The Family Educational Rights and Privacy Act (also called FERPA or the Buckley Amendment) is the legislation resulting in "rights" most germane to the schooling of children (Reeback, 1981) . Assured via this legislation are parent rights such as the right to inspect and review their child's educational records and the right to add to or change those records under certain conditions. These same rights are accorded directly to the child once he is 18 years old.

Exerting influence over what their children learn is a tradition for American parents. The current parents' rights movement is only novel in that it seeks to control curriculum content in public schools by a means other than sitting on the school board (boycotting certain school events, demonstrating about books in the school library, etc.).

REFERENCES

Andrews, S. V. (1995). Who should be teaching values to children? Stakeholders in moral education. *Contemporary Education, 66(2),* 106-11.

Aragon, J. (1973). Cultural conflict and cultural diversity in education. In L. A. Bransford, L. M. Baca, & K. Lane (Eds.), *Cultural diversity and the exceptional child* (pp. 24-31). Reston, VA: The Council for Exceptional Children.

Balm, S. S. M. (1995). Using portfolio assessment in a kindergarten classroom. *Teaching and Change, 2(2),* 141-151.

Bjorklun, E. C. (1994). Condom distribution in the public schools: Is parental consent required? *West's Education Law Quarterly, 3(4),* 568-78.

Burke, K. (1992). *Authentic assessment: A collection.* Palatine, IL: IRI Skylight.

Burron, A. (1996). Parents' rights–Society's imperative: A balancing act. *Educational Leadership, 53(7),* 80-82.

Butler, A. (1988). *The elements of a whole language program.* Crystal Lake, IL: Rigby.

Butler, A. (1991). *Shared book experience: An introduction.* Crystal Lake, IL: Rigby.

Caine, R. N., & Caine, G. (1994). *Making connections: Teaching and the human brain.* Menlo Park, CA: Addison-Wesley Publishing Co.

Chalk Talk. (1996). Tolerating tolerance in the classroom. *Journal of Law Education, 25(1),* 181-89.

Chamot, A. U. (1995). Implementing the cognitive academic language learning approach: CALLA in Arlington, Virginia. *Bilingual Research Journal, 19(3-4),* 379-94.

Collinson, V. (1995). Making the most of portfolios. *Learning, 24(1),* 43-46.

Cooper, P. (1993). When stories come to school: Telling, writing, and performing stories in the early childhood classroom. *Teachers and Writers, 24(3),* 1-9.

Crawford, J., & Freeman, S. (1996). Why parents choose private schooling: Implications for public school programs and information campaigns. *ERS Spectrum, 14(3),* 9-16.

Cummins, J. (1989). A theoretical framework for bilingual special education. *Exceptional Children, 56,* 111-119.

Davis, L. W. (1977). *Learning disabilities.* New York: Humanities Films.

Donato, R., & Garcia, H. (1992). Language segregation in desegregated schools: A question of equity. *Equity and Excellence, 25(2-4),* 94-99.

Epilepsy Foundation of America. (n.d.). *Teacher tips about the epilepsy.* Washington, DC: Author.

Franklin, M. E. (1992). Culturally sensitive instructional practices for African-American learners with disabilities. *Exceptional Children, 59,* 115-122.

Goldstein, S., & Goldstein, M. (1990). *Managing attention disorders in children.* New York: Wiley.

Goolsby, T. W. (1995). Portfolio assessment for better evaluation. *Music Educators Journal, 82(3),* 39-44.

Gounaud, K. J. (1996). Family friendly libraries manifesto. *Voice of Youth Advocates, 18(6),* 363-64, 367.

Heward, W. L., & Orlansky, M. D. (1992). *Exceptional children* (4th ed.). New York: Merrill/Macmillan.

Johnsen, S. (1996). What are alternative assessments? *Gifted Child Today Magazine, 19(4),* 12-13, 49-50.

Johnson, D. W., Johnson, R. T., & Johnson Holubec, E. (1994). *The new circles of learning: Cooperation in the classroom and school.* Alexandria, VA: Association for Supervision and Curriculum Development.

Jones, D. H. (1993). Using authentic assessment in elementary social studies. *Social Science Record, 30(2),* 17-24.

Kersey, K. C. (1994). *The art of sensitive parenting: The 10 keys to raising confident, competent and responsible children.* New York: Berkley Books.

Kersey, K. (1986). *Helping your child handle stress: The parent's guide to recognizing and solving childhood problems.* Washington, DC: Acropolis Books, Ltd.

Kirk, S. A., & Gallagher, J. J. (1979). *Educating exceptional children* (3rd ed.). Boston: Houghton Mifflin.

Kitano, M. K. (1991). A multicultural educational perspective on serving the culturally diverse gifted. *Journal for the Education of the Gifted, 15(1),* 4-19.

Kitay, J. F. (1996). Tips from the classroom. *TESOL Journal, 5(4),* 32-40.

Lavoie, R. (1995). *Last one picked...first one picked on.* New York: Public Television.

Layne, S. L. (1995). Censorship: The best defense is a strong offense. *Contemporary Education, 66(2),* 103-05.

Lerner, J. W. (1997). *Learning disabilities: Theories, diagnosis and teaching strategies.* Boston: Houghton Mifflin.

Lewis, R. B., & Doorlag, D. H. (1995). *Teaching special students in the mainstream.* (4th ed.). Columbus, OH: Merrill.

Manning, M., & Manning, G. (1994). Writing: Spelling and Handwriting. *Teaching PreK-8, 25(3),* 103-04.

Mooney, M. (1995). Guided reading beyond the primary grades. *Teaching PreK-8, 26(1),* 75-77.

National Association for State Boards of Education. (1992). *Winners all: A call for inclusive schools.* Alexandria, VA: Author.

National Middle School Association. (1995). *This we believe: Developmentally responsive middle level schools.* Columbus, OH: Author.

Osborne, A. G., Jr. (1995). Procedural due process rights for parents under the IDEA. *Preventing School Failure, 39(2),* 22-26.

Pardeck, J. T. (1996). Advocacy and parents of special needs children. *Early Child Development and Care, 120,* 45-53.

Phelan, T. W. (1989). *All about attention deficit disorder.* Glen Ellyn, IL: Child Management, Inc.

Reeback, R. T. (1981). *Questions about FERPA: The Family Educational Rights and Privacy Act (The Buckley Amendment).* Washington, DC: Bureau of Education for the Handicapped.

Reeve, R. E. (1990). ADHD: Facts and fallacies. *Intervention in School and Clinic, 26(3),* 70-78.

Reynolds, M. C., & Birch, J. W. (1988). *Adaptive mainstreaming: A primer for teachers and principals*. New York: Longman.

Roach, V. (1993, February). Winners all: A call for inclusive schools. *PTA Today*, 13-14.

Sendor, B. (1996). A flawed picture of parents' rights. *American School Board Journal, 183(3)*, 12-13, 39.

Short, G. (1994). Teaching about the Holocaust: A consideration of some ethical and pedagogic issues. *Educational Studies, 20(1)*, 53-67.

Signs Media. (1994). *An introduction to deaf culture. Film*

Torres, I., & Corn, A. L. (1990). *When you have a visually handicapped child in your classroom: Suggestions for teachers*. New York: American Foundation for the Blind.

U. S. Department of Education. (1993). *Fifteenth annual report to Congress on the implementation of the Individuals with Disabilities Education Act*. Washington, D.C.: Author.

Vivas, E. (1996). Effects of story reading on language. *Language Learning, 46(2)*, 189-216.

Whitmore, K. F. (1994). *Inventing a classroom: Life in a bilingual, whole language learning community*. York, ME: Stenhouse Publishers.

Will, M. C. (1986). Educating children with learning problems: A shared responsibility. *Exceptional Children, 52*, 411-415.

Winebrenner, S. (1992). *Teaching gifted kids in the regular classroom: Strategies and techniques every teacher can use to meet the needs of the gifted and talented*. Minneapolis, MN: Free Spirit Press.

Zucker, C. (1995). The role of ESL in a dual language program. *Bilingual Research Journal, 19(3-4)*, 512-23.

Section Three

FAMILY INVOLVEMENT
IN LEARNING

Families are involved in the learning of their children long before enrollment in school, before and after school hours, and during holidays and the summer once children are enrolled in school. Families help their children learn in the community and during every season. Families also face a number of challenges in parenting their children, including those related to preparation for school learning, growth and development, and safety and welfare. In this section, these aspects of **family involvement in learning,** related to school learning, are explored.

Chapter 14

PREPARING CHILDREN FOR SCHOOL

School success is influenced by what children experience long before they ever attend school. Some of the most critical aspects of development that lay the foundation for school success are language development, motor development, and social development, especially increasing independence. Here are some ideas to help parents prepare preschool age children meet their learning needs and **prepare children for school.**

LANGUAGE DEVELOPMENT

Dr. Burton White (1995), a popular pediatrician who has written a number of informational books for parents, suggests that the peak time for language acquisition is nine months of age, before most children even begin speaking. Therefore, early and frequent language stimulation cannot be overemphasized (Stark, 1989). It may make you feel foolish, talking to your infant, when it is obvious that you will not get a full-blown conversation in return, but the stimulation is critical to your baby's **language development.** Early stimulation determines what areas of the brain get enough "exercise" to generate neural connections. These neural connections are necessary for later learning as well as the learning your child does as a baby (Sylwester, 1995).

My own experience with raising children has made this point clearly. One day in the laundromat, I was explaining to my twins, who were barely two, how the washing machine worked, with the coins going in and the soap and the swirling around, when a patron asked me if I really thought that they were understanding what I was saying. I wasn't at all sure, but they were listening and I was talking. The lilt of my voice, the inflection I used, the fact that I thought enough of them to answer their questions, and repeated exposure to words in their environment couldn't hurt.

117

In fact, there are tragic documented cases in which lack of language stimulation decidedly affects children negatively (Sylwester, 1995). Children who are not talked to when they are young are often delayed in school. We do not really know when a child is ready for a word like "evasive" or "ambulate." Instead, if descriptive words are all around them, whenever they are ready, they can reach out and "grab" the word for filing into their listening/speaking vocabularies.

Vocabulary and language development are critical to school success. Yet sometimes little conversation passes between family members because there seems little to say. Perhaps you have overlooked some opportunities.

Tell your children the stories that form the foundation of your faith or of fond memories you have from your childhood, centering on holidays. We spent centuries sharing our history orally; there is a tradition for telling stories and listening. Especially if you avoid competing with the television and wait until the children are in bed, you have more or less a captive audience.

However, be prepared to find out that your children actually enjoy listening to your stories and benefit from the language stimulation that the stories provide. Don't worry about repetition (unless the children complain!). Most children enjoy knowing "what comes next" in a story and may even want to "tell the next part" once a story is sufficiently familiar.

You may find yourself using the same words in the same order when you tell a story over and over. That's fine! Once you develop the "best" choice of words, why not use them? Besides, print is always the same when you read the same book and still there are certain books that we read over and over.

Don't mind interruptions either (if they pertain to the story). Children who look for further information and clarification or detail are really listening and comprehending. They are forming mental pictures that may need to be brought more into focus, so they ask questions. The interaction that you share as you talk together can be every bit as important (maybe more!) as the story you set out to tell.

Whenever possible, explain about new or specialized food to your children. What in the world is mincemeat? Why does it matter whether you eat meat at the same meal with dairy products? Who came up with the tradition of leaving cookies for Santa? These conversations broaden children's cultural experiences and traditions and make the world around them seem more understandable. In general, the informal kinds of things we say to children, waiting for a bus, driving in the car, whirling through the grocery store, have great impact on their development and their learning.

Aside from vocabulary development and language construction, it is important to consider HOW your talk to your child. Children do not think like "little adults" (Phelan, 1989). It takes many repetitions of what is expected before children internalize rules and self-monitor their behavior with regard to the rules. Rather than react with "How many times must I tell you?," assurances that you still are standing by a rule and that the limits are there to protect the child may work much better (National Education Association, 1987a).

Puppets are another great way to stimulate language (Texas Child Care, 1996). Puppets naturally seem to capture the imagination of children. Just think of Pinocchio, Lamb Chop, or Garfield Goose. Puppets can be made of simple materials you have at home or they can be store-bought.

The simplest puppet is your hand. Simply decorate the tip of one finger with a face and you're in the puppet business. Or, if you wish to be fancy, decorate the side of your thumb and the side of your index finger for a mouth-moving puppet. Finger puppets may also be made of fabric and may either cover just one finger or be worn on several fingers. The look of the puppet is not nearly as important as how the puppet sounds. Practicing with different voices can be a lot of fun. Even consider accents to give the characters more flavor (Lindquist, 1996).

So you want to get really sophisticated? Make a paper face and glue it to a popsicle stick. Make a whole family and have them bow, dance and talk. Wrap fabric around your finger for clothing. Hold it on with a twist tie or rubber band. You could even wear a glove to be the clothing of the puppets.

Some puppets that can be bought are a lot like gloves. They may be knit or crocheted or made of fabric, but they fit on the hand and usually the thumb is the lower jaw and the rest of the hand makes the upper jaw. These puppets are usually used with the puppeteer in full view.

Other puppets may be made from milk bottles, toilet paper rolls, cardboard, or any other material that fits your imaginative view of the character you are creating. Think of how the character will move as you create.

Remember the puppets in the *Sound of Music*? Those are marionettes. They are made to move from above by a number of strings. Usually with marionettes, the puppeteer is not seen by the audience.

Commercially made puppets may be purchased at art fairs, teacher stores, craft stores, and toy stores. There are even racks of upright dowels for storing cloth hand-puppets that you can buy.

Children often ask for stories. Develop a few characters and use them over and over; using the same characters can make it easier to come up with story lines. Let your child create puppets and be the puppeteer along with you. Puppets made of paper bags–the folded bottom becomes the movable mouth–are easy for children of almost any age to make.

Sometimes the puppets can talk about things that are too difficult for parents and children to talk about directly. Some children even feel more comfortable, when they first learn to read, to have the puppet read for them so that the puppet is being judged, not the child.

Talking to children as often as they need to hear us in order to stimulate their language development may seem awkward at first, especially when they are still too young to respond in words. Using puppets can help. That's why puppets may help adults feel comfortable as they connect with their children.

Puppets are inexpensive and usually fun. Make or buy a few and warm up with your children!

MOTOR DEVELOPMENT

Young children need time to try **physical activities**, often under the watchful eye of parents and caretakers, as well as the active encouragement of parents and caretakers (Butler, 1996). The kinds of activities can be climbing; running; throwing; catching; rolling; kicking; hitting with a bat, racket, stick, golf club, balloons or broom; dancing; jumping; swinging; sliding; swimming; wiggling; hopping; skipping; and singing. Children should be shown how to do these activities in the adult way and then permitted, within reason and safety, to "do their own thing" with the materials and activities (Zaichkowsky & Larson, 1995).

Building with blocks, cups, twigs, Leggos, pots and pans, rocks, bricks or whatever is handy can be entertaining and good fine motor practice for children. Use of pens, crayons, pencils or markers may also be encouraged but caution exercised. Remember children explore by eating and often don't feel constrained to "write" or draw on paper; they like to branch out to wallpaper, followed by painted walls, floors, counters, tables, checks, etc.

Other physical or motor activities include finger painting and finger plays. Finger painting can be done with traditional finger paints, available in dime stores. Finger painting can also be carried out with edible products so that there is no fear of toxicity—try pudding or yogurt. If you are really into clean surfaces and not worried about tasting, children can finger paint with shaving cream. Your table has never looked so clean!

Finger plays include puppet shadows and (do you remember?) songs with finger actions, such as "Here is thumbkin...." There are probably several books in your library or bookstore with excellent suggestions for finger plays.

SOCIAL DEVELOPMENT

Children need lots of experiences with new people, in the company of adults whom they trust, in order to experience **social development** (Nabors & Edwards, 1996). Take them with you on errands and to church and restaurants whenever appropriate. Increasing exposure to people results in increasing comfort in meeting new people.

Psychologists find that children develop caring behaviors when they are exposed at young ages to caring models. Children tend to approach strangers (store clerks, gas station attendants, etc.) in the way their parents do. If parents do not make eye contact or smile, children will not engage in these behaviors either. Polite words, such as please and thank you, must be used to and in front of the child before they will become part of the child's own repertory.

There is nothing as exciting as watching a young child develop, unless it's watching two or three. Take the time to learn with your child and you will both be delighted with the results.

INDEPENDENCE

One of the things that worries parents most is developing **independence** in their children. What drives the ability of children to be independent is the ability to be dependent (McNamara, 1996). Seems strange, doesn't it? But the logic of this seeming contradiction makes sense. The more fully dependent a child can be, that is, the more secure the child feels in the care of the family, the more confidence the same child will have to face the world and try new things.

Helping children feel that kind of rock-solid security is very difficult. As adults, we find our world to be insecure and unstable. It is tough to provide stability for children. Sometimes the demands of the children for reassurance seem outrageous. Sometimes a child will pass through a stage (sometimes years) with a very real need to know where a parent is, how long the parent will be gone, what the parent is doing—even when the parent is in the next room!

Examine your own level of confidence. Don't you find yourself much more confident and ready to face the world when things are calm in your home life and you feel secure financially? Maslow (1987), a noted researcher in human psychology, suggests an explanation. Maslow contends that humans have basic needs (air, shelter, water, food, belongingness, self-esteem, and esteem by others), and unless basic needs are met, humans are incapable of striving to meet higher needs. Thus, it is important for humans to have their basic needs met—and they are not just physical—to gain independence.

Teachers and schools play a role, too. Three basic needs, as cited by Maslow, are belongingness, self-esteem and esteem by others. Getting picked last for a team, failing a test, being ridiculed or teased, or not being accepted by the "in" crowd can reduce a child's sense of belongingness, self-esteem and esteem by others. This makes it hard to concentrate on learning, which may make failing a test again or being ridiculed again more likely. A failure cycle is difficult to break. Therefore, every opportunity to build a child's self-esteem and facilitate a child's sense of belongingness should be seized and used.

Generally, the actions required to help children meet these needs are simple and easy to deliver. Teachers may: use children's names when addressing them, make eye contact during the time a child speaks, write tiny personal notes to children and model acceptance of diversity of students in the classroom. Classmates may: avoid cliques, encourage and praise each other, work together to learn to be successful, and avoid sarcasm or "put-downs."

Other unmet needs (being hungry, lacking adult supervision, etc.) may also result in poor learning and school achievement. Who can concentrate or even feel confident enough to take risks and try something new under such conditions? In fact, parents who fail to take care of feeding and supervising their children may be guilty of child neglect. Therefore, it is the daily job of parents or families, with no vacation time, to provide for children's basic needs.

The challenge of parenting is to sacrifice your own needs at times to meet the needs of your children. While we certainly cannot always meet the challenge, we raise more confident, capable, independent children when we do.

Chapter 15

LEARNING WHEREVER YOU ARE

The need for ideas that parents can use at home to enhance learning has grown as more parents have the demands of work and home to juggle (Albrecht, 1996). In addition, as more preschool age children enter day-care centers, preschools, nursery schools and other care facilities, parents feel the need to reinforce school learning and link home activities to school learning. Here are some ideas for **"home learning recipes."**

EVERYDAY LEARNING OPPORTUNITIES

These activities will revolve around **everyday** events and realistic home **learning opportunities** (Partridge, 1996). The materials required are commonly available and do not require special trips to a "teacher store."

In the area of food preparation, what about rehearsing and refining a theme? In this case, I recommend muffins. Muffin recipes often have less sugar than cake recipes, and many of the types included here have at least one very nutritious ingredient. Muffins are also at the base of the food pyramid. For each week, you will need muffin tins, muffin papers, a bowl, and a wooden spoon. Other ingredients will vary. Select a day of the week when you will have half an hour to spend before a snack time or mealtime (i.e., Wednesday at 5:30 or Saturday at 9:00). Keeping the same time for the same category gives structure and allows the child to anticipate the event.

On the first time you make muffins together, read the recipe to the child and do most of the work of preparation. Each successive "cook day," do less and less of the work, allowing the child to remember and practice what he has learned.

Most muffins can be cooked in 15-20 minutes and many are delicious when served almost immediately (watch for the heat of steam as you break them open; steam burns, too!). A cooking category with fast results is a good one for young children. Muffins are also a good beginning because one bowl is sufficient and sifting and other tasks are minimal. You don't even need a mixer.

While the muffins are cooking, use the time to share and learn. Read books together, especially if you have any books about cooking, muffins, making a mess or cleaning up. Talk about cleanup and enjoy the aroma as the muffins get closer to being done.

Here are some tips for the first several weeks.

Banana Oatmeal Muffins

1/2 cup oats ***	1/2 tsp. salt (optional)
1 tsp. cinnamon	3/4 tsp. nutmeg
1/4 cup melted margarine	1 egg
1/2 cup milk	1 cup flour
1/2 cup brown sugar	2-1/2 tsp. baking powder
1/2 tsp. baking soda	1 cup crushed banana **
1/2 cup unsalted sunflower seeds (optional)*	

*   Some young children do not like to mix textures; crunchy may not work.
**   Bananas are rich in potassium.
***   Oats are a terrific source of roughage.

Mix everything until moistened. Fill muffin papers in a muffin tin. Bake at 425-degrees in a preheated oven for 15 minutes. Makes 12 muffins.

Hot Cheese Muffins

2 cups flour	3 tbs. sugar
1 tbs. baking powder	3/4 tsp. garlic salt
1 dash Cayenne Pepper	1 cup grated cheddar cheese *
1 egg	
1 cup milk *	
1/4 cup melted margarine.	

*   Cheese and milk are good sources of protein and calcium.

Mix everything except 2 tbs. of cheese. Spoon into muffin papers in a muffin tin. Sprinkle remaining cheese on top of each muffin. Bake in preheated 425-degree oven for 20 minutes. Makes 12 muffins.

Prune Cinnamon Muffins

1/2 cup pitted chopped prunes *   1 1/2 cups flour
1 1/2 tsp. baking powder   1/2 tsp. salt (optional)
1/2 cup sugar   1/2 tsp. cinnamon
1 egg   1/2 cup sour cream
1/3 cup melted margarine

    *   Prunes are an excellent source of iron and roughage.

Mix everything until moist. Spoon into muffin papers (about half full) in a muffin tin. Bake in a preheated 375-degree oven for 12-15 minutes. Makes 12 muffins.

Strawberry Muffins

2 eggs   2/3 cup sugar
1/3 cup vegetable oil   1 tsp. vanilla
1 cup flour   1/2 tsp. cinnamon
1/2 tsp. baking soda   1/2 tsp. salt
2/3 cup crushed ripe strawberries *

    *   Strawberries are an excellent source of vitamin C.

Mix everything together into muffin papers. Spoon into muffin papers in a muffin tin. Bake in a preheated oven at 325-degrees for 25 minutes.

Apple Date Muffins

1/3 cup sugar   1 egg
1/4 tsp. vanilla   1/2 cup chopped dates *
1/3 cup vegetable oil   3/4 cup flour
1/4 tsp. baking soda   3/4 cup chopped fresh apples **
1/4 cup chopped nuts (optional)

    *   Dates provide a reasonable source of calcium and iron.
    **   Apples are naturally sweet and a source of fiber.

Mix everything together. Spoon into muffin paper in a muffin tin. Bake in a preheated oven at 325-degrees for 25 minutes.

Some other categories of foods that you could try after you work with these and other muffin recipes might include: pancakes, fritters, fruit salads, meatballs, fresh vegetables or dips. Get cooking!

LEARNING IN THE COMMUNITY

The school is a child's **learning community**, but the geographic or neighborhood community should also be a child's school. When parent-child learning takes place in the community, it enriches family life in the following ways:

1. Adults personalize learning for children.
2. Children can become independent, self-directed learners.
3. The community provides a forum for children to practice learning strategies they acquired in school.
4. Children can develop relationships which expand school learning and direct children to future study, avocations or careers.

What is needed to have a community in which a child also learns? It means that communities sponsor events that provide children with experiences and learning opportunities (McClure, 1977). Exhibits at the library, plays at the theater, and classes at the park district are examples of these events. Fun events, such as the haunted house, festivals and parades, can also foster learning.

Perhaps you remember from your own childhood or adolescence a special adult who took an interest in you, took you and your interests seriously. Most children look for a relationship with an adult who is not a parent but provides learning experiences (Girard, 1996). Marty McFly (the Michael J. Fox character in the *Back to the Future* movies) has such a relationship with the inventive "Doc Brown." Maybe your own more down-to-earth relationship was with the scout leader who answered your questions about frogs and wildlife or the neighbor who knew a lot about fireworks and told you stories about Fourth of July celebrations.

Children also learn from community members who employ them to cut grass, deliver groceries or shovel snow. Except for one unfortunate incident, George Bailey found a mentor in Mr. Gower, the druggist who employed him in *It's a Wonderful Life*. Children learn about responsibility, the specific activities and requirements of certain jobs, the acquisition of their own money to help out at home or have spending money, the relationship of hard work to earning, and the sense of self-evaluation that finds a job well done because of effort that was expended and care that was taken.

Parents also have a critical role in helping their children learn practical information out in the community. Try some of the following activities.

1. Tour local factories and businesses. Always make arrangements with the sites by phone first.
2. When you go to a merchant to conduct business, describe the objects in the store or the work of the persons in the store to your children.
3. In many stores, there are types of merchandise that are appropriate for children. Consider buying a small item for your child on one of your visits: a cookie from the bakery, a card or bookmark from the

card store, a scarf or hat from the clothing store. Even if the purchase was the object of your visit, the item will personalize learning and foster interest in your child about the function of the store.

4. As you walk in the community with your children, be sure to describe objects that you see. Even very young children understand a great deal of what is said to them. Tell them about the bird's nest in the leafless tree or the colors of the landscaping stones in the neighbor's yard or the way that the traffic lights let trucks and cars go or signals them to stop.

When children complain that "school doesn't have anything to do with the real world," it is possible that they have not had enough experiences in the "real world" to link school learning to real life. Merchants should be open to questions from parents and their children. Parents should provide information regularly to their children.

Children's books about community include:

Brown, L.K., & Brown, M. (1986). *Visiting the art museum.* New York: Dutton.
De Santis, K. (1988). *A dentist's tools.* Northbrook, IL: Dodd.
Getz, A. (1979). *Tar beach.* New York: Dial.
Gibbons, G. (1984). *Department store.* New York: Harper.
Rylant, C. (1988). *All I see.* New York: Franklin Watts. (gr. 1-3)
Van Laan, N. (1992). *People, people, everywhere!* New York: Knopf. (pre-K)

LEARNING AT THE LIBRARY

The world of books is a magical entrance to the universe for family members whatever their age. In addition, reading is an important aspect of most life activities and, therefore, is a critical skill to develop. Family reading programs help support children's academic learning both through reading itself and reading in subject areas, such as social studies. Reading with children helps them become stronger, more independent learners as they develop these skills and capabilities: reading skills, intellectual skills, good speech and language patterns, motivation for learning, independence, listening skills, visual skills, and social and emotional maturity (International Reading Association, 1980).

Have you ever read of a good idea in a book or magazine or heard about it on TV? But...the information you need to follow up on the idea is in a book...and you have the title, author and publisher...and you can't find the book at a local bookstore? The perfect solution is at the **library.** A massive volume with information about publisher's addresses, books in stock, etc., is available to clerks at bookstores. Stop and ask—they may even be willing to special order your book.

You can also write directly to publishers, and in some cases even call 800 numbers. All you need is *Books in Print,* available at your library, and its companion books that list all publishers and their addresses.

If you are looking for books on particular topics or you know the author but aren't sure of the full title, these reference books can help too. Some books are really just pamphlets. These will be listed in *Books in Print,* along with their most recent prices.

Perhaps your child asks a question to which you have no answers. What do lightning bugs eat so that I can put some food in the jar for them? Why do ants dig their homes underground? What really causes thunder? Is a sponge at the paint store really a plant? Where do retired American presidents live?

It's very easy to find answers to some of these questions (and others that your child may ask you) by using the card catalog in the children's section of the library. Other answers can be found in the several sets of encyclopedias in the children's section. You may even use an almanac or encyclopedia that is on the computer to search for the answers.

Even young children may like finding the answers when they can SEE the answer to a question. Besides, imagine what a gift you have given them if they begin to EXPECT to find answers and information in books. If you search four or five times for information in books, watch them ask the sixth time to go to the library to find answers. Eventually, independent searches for information will be routine.

The foundations of expecting meaning from print are essential to good reading. When young children are read to, and some books are read over and over, the children begin to realize that print must be stable and immutable. The letters on the page must be meaningful, because whenever adults confront the same page of letters they read the same words. Children who make this connection then start asking adults, "What does this say?" in response to encounters with print. Expecting print to make sense is a strong motivation for conquering the decoding of that print.

Looking for information and teaching children that information can be found in books, as well as reading aloud to children so that they think print is meaningful, contributes powerfully to helping children be good readers who want to read. Your additional skills at locating particular books through *Books in Print* may make a "reading believer" of your child. There is probably no greater edge for success in school.

Books for children about libraries include:

Bellairs, J., & Brown, J. G. (1978). *The treasure of Alpheus Winterborn.* New York: Harcourt Brace Jovanovich. (gr. 5-6)

Caseley, J. (1993). *Sophie and Sammy's library sleepover.* New York: Greenwillow. (pre-K)

Gibbons, G. (1985). *Check it out.* San Diego, CA: Harcourt Brace Jovanovich. (gr. 1-3)

Huff, B. A. (1990). *Once inside a library.* Boston, MA: Little, Brown. (gr. 1-2)

Knowlton, J. (1991). *Books and libraries.* New York: HarperCollins. (gr. 2-5)

Swallow, P. (1986). *Melvil and Dewey in the chips.* Belvidere, NJ: Shoetree Press. (gr. 2-3)

Chapter 16

LEARNING WHENEVER YOU CAN

Learning can (and should!) happen in any season, at any time of year. Any topic or event offers the opportunity for learning.

LEARNING IN THE SPRING

Spring is a wonderful time for parents to interact with their children in a new environment—the outdoors. Most people, even adults, experience some new energy in the spring and seem to "take on" activities that aren't as appealing at other times of the year. Fortunately, as family attention is turned to zoo trips, zoo inhabitants provide a more spectacular show by presenting the world with new additions. Children are often most interested in younger animals, almost as if they recognize in other species roles similar to their own.

Don't suppress those instincts to go out and do things, from playing ball to watching birds to watching dirt bike races. Almost any shared experience in a family results in learning for the children.

LEARNING DURING SUMMER VACATION

Summer vacation for most elementary and secondary school age students seems to be just around the corner (even on September 2!). Aside from making plans to keep youngsters occupied with jobs, day care, day camp, summer camp, and park district classes, consider summer as an opportunity to rediscover learning in the family (Heyns, 1978). Perhaps you'll find more time for talking at dinner or another meal during the day because parents and children can abandon the arguments about homework. Perhaps parents and children do things together during the summer that they don't do at other times of the year. Whatever your design for summer looks like, sample some activities from those listed below to enhance learning and having fun:

1. Whenever the family undertakes a building or fixing project, let children help take measurements for materials.

2. Take advantage of free fairs, festivals, museums, and library events in your neighborhood. Have you been meaning to see the history exhibit at your town or county museum? Go! (Besides, they're usually air-conditioned in the summer!)

3. Go to events that your children have found in the paper or other places and have expressed an interest in participating in; take along a friend for each older child if you can manage it. Having a friend your child's age along may make a trip more appealing. Besides, then you may be able to trade with that family, gaining some free time for yourself the day your child goes with that family on an adventure.

4. Plan on longer grocery shopping trips in the summer. Don't just consider shopping something to "get over with"—plan together, use a list, have children guess in what aisle items will be. (Besides, most stores are air-conditioned in the summer!)
   a. Have children "comparison shop" in advance with newspaper ads.
   b. Children can collect coupons and pull out appropriate ones. Allow each child a maximum budget of money for "treats" instead of draw ing battle lines in the cereal or candy aisle.

5. Buy school supplies whenever there is a sale instead of breaking the family budget purchasing everything at one time in the fall.

6. Make a family collection place in your home. Collect rocks, pine cones, stickers, buttons, anything that everyone enjoys and you have space to display. Nutty ideas are sometimes the most fun. Put your mini-museum on a bookshelf, end table, or top of a dresser.

7. Get wet! Even sitting on your porch with an ice cube under each foot is fine. Keeping cool is an important idea in the heat of summer, when tempers flare and it is easy to be irritable. The emphasis on keeping cool is good for your comfort and good for family relations. You haven't spent this much time together since last summer vacation, and getting reacquainted is much easier when you're comfortable.

8. Use a cookbook, especially for outdoor cooking or refrigerator dishes. There are a few cookbooks at the library and you may already have some cookbooks that you haven't used lately. Other recipes may appear on the packages of products you usually buy. Think cool as you select items. This is probably not the best season for the Tollhouse chocolate

chip cookie set and having the oven on for an hour and a half.

9. Garden. Using the hose is probably the best part of gardening on hot days. But there are other satisfactions too. Getting dirty and then getting clean afterward is appealing to most children. Beauty refreshes the spirit at all ages and flowers can meet that need. Maybe you can grow food and have fun tasting it or using it in the recipes you gather.

10. Use water. Wash the car, wash the aluminum siding, wash the yard equipment, make designs with water in old dish detergent bottles, making outdoor "soup" (recipe: water, stones, leaves, flowers, dirt and sand in a large bucket or kettle, stir well!). Make ice cube pops (use fruit juice or Kool-Aid and pour it into regular ice cube trays), make slush types of drinks....Water cools and refreshes!

11. Use paper. Fold (origami), draw, paint, arrange pieces of paper or make a collage. Use tissue paper or crepe paper for flowers that won't wilt.

12. Use books. Read, get ideas for things to do, look up information for another activity, look at pictures, write books like the ones you have read, talk about books after you have read them, and read aloud to each other.

13. Listen to music. Talk about who composed the music or who wrote the lyrics. Make up your own songs. Dance to music. Sing along with the radio, record player, compact disc player or tape recorder.

14. Decorate your property. Sidewalk chalk lasts well and can often be found in dollar stores. Choose one square of sidewalk or cover more space. (The spray chalk variety that is available now works well but doesn't clean up as readily as standard chalk.)

Try to keep some routine in your summer to help your children feel more secure, even though they don't have to get up at the same time to go to school, etc. Make sure everyone gets enough sleep; crabbiness from sleeplessness will raise the level of summer tension to an intolerable level when the heat cranks up.

Enjoy some new freedoms with more time outdoors. Always keep safety in mind. However, if you are a beleaguered parent who hears several times a day the summer refrain "there's nothing to do" or "I'm bored," read on.

Summer expectations are among the hardest to combat. They are worse than holiday expectations, probably because the summer goes on and on. It is entirely reasonable to tell children and adolescents what to expect for the summer instead of letting those expectations grow unchecked and be dashed.

Tell them there will only be one "big" fun thing a week—carnival, museum trip, nature walk, park trip, or arcade visit. TV time will be one hour in the morning and up to two hours at night. You get the idea. Picture for yourself and what you can really deliver and then deliver the description to your children.

Another tip is to go to the "big" fun things and expect to take your children's lead. That is, if you go to a museum or art fair, do not expect to stand and read every plaque or notice every brush stroke. Let the children set the pace. If you adjust to their timing, you might just have a good time instead of being totally annoyed that the children lack patience or "just don't know what's good."

If possible, let the children pick some of the family activities. At least, let them pick from a list that you have devised. Get ideas from the newspaper or from friends who have children. Don't be swayed by the opinions and advice of people with whom you don't usually agree. The resulting "vacation" may be disastrous.

Make a list of the things about which your children say, "but, Mom, I was just in the middle of..." or "you never give me enough time to...." Those things will give you and the children ideas for those times when boredom rages.

Consider the "classics" section of your video store. Could you con your teenager into watching *The Music Man* or *Wait Until Dark*? Conduct a genre film study over the summer, watching a mystery or comedy or drama video each week. You could also watch a video produced or directed by the same filmmaker each week and become mini-experts on the talents of that artist. Select an actor (Shirley Temple, Sean Connery, Bob Hope, Richard Pryor, Michelle Pfeiffer, Halle Berry) and every week watch a video in which that person stars. Consider book and video pairs: *Madeline* and her videos, *The Verdict* and its video, etc.

Consider combining the bored with the needy. Could your teens regularly shop for an older person, bring in the paper or mail for an ill neighbor, cut the grass for the working mom with three small children? Could you get them to write a weekly (monthly?) note to Grandma or to a classmate who moved?

Adopt an "I'll scratch your back if you scratch mine" philosophy. Can you trade your teenager some terrible job for the chance to be taken somewhere? A brother-in-law traded his dreaded lawn work to his daughter for permission to attend some concert. A newspaper columnist wrote of retiring some of her guilt over never finishing household jobs with three little words: chores, children, allowance.

If all else fails, take to separate rooms, with a fan or air conditioner if necessary, to cool off. What did you say? You're becoming an advocate of year-round education? ENJOY! Take every opportunity to learn, from people you meet and experiences you have!

SPACING OUT

Space exploration is something that has captured the imagination of humans since the time of the ancients. In the eerie and slow beginning of *2001 Space Odyssey,* the ancestors of humans are shown to be interested in going beyond their limited world as they toss a bone high into the sky. In our generation, space travel has become almost routine. Six to seven shuttle launches are planned for each year. A space station, purchased from the Russians or built for the United States, is a reality. The United States has assigned an astronaut to the space station, replaced her more than once, and will continue assigning Americans to tours of duty in space.

Space shuttle launches are rarely covered on television and receive a footnote in most news coverage (Berger, 1984). But how much do we know about the U.S. space program?

One way to find out is to go to a shuttle launch. See the shuttle leave the ground, see the smoke, observe the brilliant orange flame, feel the slight trembling of the earth nearby. Watch as the shuttle reaches a speed of approximately 10,000 miles per hour in about eight seconds, perhaps feel the breeze created miles away by the force of the launch, and hear the sound barrier broken as the shuttle leaves our atmosphere.

Where does this occur? At the Kennedy Space Center in Florida. How can you get information? Try the World Wide Web page of http://www.hq.nasa.gov. This site will provide you with a number of searching options. One of the options leads you to a listing of the shuttle missions planned through 2001 (uncanny connection?).

Launch dates are subject to change. Not all launches leave on their scheduled dates. If a technical problem is encountered or weather conditions are incompatible with launch guidelines, for instance, a launch can be postponed or even scrapped.

How can you see a launch? You may write directly to NASA and request a car pass which allows you to go to a designated area along the waterfront with excellent viewing vantage. Loudspeakers provide intermittent information about the launch and your hear the countdown. What a thrill!

Do you prefer to study shuttle launches from home? Movies are still to come but books are plentiful. *Flying the Space Shuttles* (Don Dwiggins), *Piloted Space Flight* (Isaac Asimov), *Sally Ride and the New Astronauts* (Karen O'Connor), *Zero Gravity* (Gloria Skurzynski), and *To Space and Back* (Sally Ride) may satisfy family curiosity.

There are even wonderful books for young readers or nonreaders to begin to get the feel of space exploration. *Me and My Flying Machine* (Marianna and Mercer Mayer) is a flight of fancy. *Easy-To-Make Spaceships that Really Fly*

(Mary and Dewey Blocksma) provides great ideas for making a fleet of space-ships from paper plates, straws, cups, tape and staples.

Space exploration may just be something for your family to explore (Lambert, 1983). Dream of what you would send as the payload (cargo) of a shuttle launch. Connect with some of the most exciting travel in human experience.

Chapter 17

HOLIDAY PREPARATION

One of the biggest concerns of parents at various times of the year is how to live through the holidays. Good preparation and laying a foundation will help to make the holidays more meaningful. Holidays also provide a way to integrate learning with family activities.

As we approach the holidays, a common complaint of adults about children is that they expect too much. "His gift list stretches into the next county." "Do they think we're made of money?" Children's expectations are fueled by the media, especially television and catalogs. However, expectations also arise from parents frantically worrying about gifts ("What should I get for Grandpa?" "I hate to buy for Cousin Marie," etc.) and suddenly making locations in the house off limits.

It is entirely within the control of parents to refocus children's attention to some degree. Begin by emphasizing what children can get or do FOR OTHERS, not what they themselves will receive. Most families will find that trying to meet the needs of others will mean that planning must begin early. No one paycheck can support holiday buying, and if you decide to make presents, you will need time. Concentrating on others does not give children much of a chance to be drawn into the "What's for me?" syndrome.

Begin by making a space in your home for storage of the items for family members. Encourage children to make lists of those people who will receive gifts and ideas of what to get or make for them. Then choose a time every week or so to shop, create gifts and wrap. Once a person's gift is complete, wrap it and label it. Store it in the place set aside for this. We use brown paper bags marked for the family and store them in the attic. Then move on to preparing a different person's gift.

Practice skills for learning by making some gifts, following directions from craft books or recipes from cookbooks. There are numerous books available in both the children's and adult's sections of your local public library with lots of suggestions.

136

Conduct some research in the community and find out if there are families who may need assistance or shelters seeking supplies and gifts. (Churches and social service agencies may be great sources.) Add some individuals or agencies to your list. Consider what would be the best kind of gifts—food, hats and gloves, etc.—and arrange for how these gifts will be delivered.

Rehearse budget-making and route-planning as part of your activities. Map skills will get a workout as you decide what route to follow for delivering presents. Making and sticking to a budget will help to bring the economic realities home to children.

Perhaps money is tight in your house and there is little left for gifts or helping others. Simple fund raisers, such as taking aluminum cans to a local recycling plant or clipping coupons and watching for sales on the items you want to buy, may allow you to help others anyway.

Pick a craft project for each week before your special holiday and work together as a family to make an ornament or other decoration. Save these decorations in one place until close to the holiday and then have fun decorating the house. Make these occasions stand out by serving special treats reserved for good times, like hot cider or hot chocolate or Aunt Sue's lemon cookies.

Lots of adults and some children are depressed when the holidays are over, wondering why the actual events didn't live up to their expectations. Taking the time to enjoy the preparation and not saving all of the excitement for one moment or day will help. In addition, knowing that you spent more time planning for and meeting the needs of others will make this holiday exceed expectations in filling you and your children with joy and satisfaction.

CHOOSING PRESENTS

I'd like to give some advice to Santa with regard to presents. You may read this, too, if you like.

Please bring things that stimulate a child's imagination. A toy that does only one thing looks great on the commercial. In fact, the children on the commercial seem near ecstasy as they play with the toy. In real life, five minutes and discard is more likely.

Baby dolls have always been popular because there is more to do than just dress them. Children can pretend they are parents and thus have a whole range of activities for their roles: changing clothes, changing diapers, washing, feeding, holding, singing to, and so on. Bats and balls have the same potential. Balls can be rolled, thrown, bounced, juggled, etc. Bats can hit balls, be used as canes, swords, or nightsticks, and as balancing poles for the tightrope.

A costume box is another wonderful idea, Santa. A plastic box or laundry basket will hold up best. In it, any number of costume materials may be stored. The best source of clothes is yard sales or resale shops. Wash each item carefully and check for pins, tags or other items that should be removed. Wigs are a wonderful addition for young children. Buying a used wig may seem unsanitary. (I bought them for less than 70 cents each and washed them with bleach and hot water in a lingerie bag. If they couldn't take the rough treatment, I figured I hadn't wasted much money; however, they came out fine and I was assured there were no lice or germs.)

Hats are readily purchased. (I also sewed Robin Hood type hats as well as pirate hats out of felt squares.) Occasionally, the squares are on sale at fabric stores (often five for $1). Hats from resale shops should be considered only when it seems possible to wash or clean them thoroughly.

Little girls may be asked to stand up in weddings as junior bridesmaids or flower girls. The fancy dresses required have a short shelf life and so are sometimes available at resale shops. Even if it says dry clean, wash on a delicate setting. If the dress can't hold up to washing, it probably is not a good bet for heavy use with children anyway. Nurses' uniforms, vests, service station shirts, polo shirts, aprons and lots of other items found at resale shops can be easily cleaned and give many ideas for imaginative play. Even shoes (ballet slippers, work boots) may warrant consideration.

Commercial costumes are also available (although they are more expensive), but Christmas only comes once a year, right, Kris Kringle? The nylon costumes for Halloween are really designed for limited use and often cannot tolerate one washing without disintegrating, running, or streaking colors. However, in mail-order catalogs from Lillian Vernon to Miles Kimball, knight sets, cowboy costumes, ballerina outfits, makeup kits, etc., are options. Fortunately, Christmas follows Halloween and, if you intend to create a costume box as a gift, you can stop at local establishments to purchase dress-up items in the first days after Halloween at greatly reduced prices (for really low prices, maybe washability doesn't matter much). Masks provide little room for imagination and are unsafe for play, so please don't bring any masks.

One more item is needed to complete the costume box gift: a full-length mirror. Inexpensive ones (under $10) are available at discount department stores right near home (and near the North Pole, too). Have a good time thinking of clothes and accessories that can be mixed, matched and used for more than one costume. We want to stimulate children to think and play at the same time, to learn to make choices and experiment with different identities and to become the best they can be. Thanks, Santa!

Parents, when selecting gifts, look for toys or other presents that have the possibility of being used more than once. Toys and gifts should help children exercise their imaginations. A good gift is durable, easy to clean, and created of parts that are not easily lost, broken or swallowed. For young children, messy is fun. Gifts of finger paints, play dough, tempera paints, paint-with-water books, and watercolors are good choices. However, accompanying gifts such as second hand shirts, smocks, or leaf bags with the head and arm holes cut out are musts.

Dolls are good choices (including trolls and GI Joe's, if you prefer) if there are clothes or other items to add to the fun. Tough cardboard boxes, like those from Market Day products, make good "homes" and traveling cases. Children can cut out rugs, clothes, refrigerators, etc., from paper to furnish a box home. This means markers, glue sticks, safety scissors and pencil/pens as well.

For children who are a little older, dolls (especially the incredibly persistent Barbies and remarkably resurgent trolls) are still a good bet, with accessories. Be cautious about "one function" dolls that go potty, say a few words, or pose. Children don't usually adapt these dolls imaginatively. They often use the one function several times, get bored and toss the doll aside.

Children of seven or so may be starting collections. A sturdy shelf or bookcase to display the collections is a welcome gift. Books are always wonderful and it's fun to browse in the children's book section of bookstores.

By the age of eight, most children are prolific artists and designers. Tablets of paper or stacks of paper tied up with string or boxed are perfect. Discarded paper from your work or the work of your friends is fine as it is often printed only on one side. Tape and a stand-by-itself tape dispenser are good companions. Subscriptions to children's magazines such as *Ranger Rick, Highlights, Children's National Geographic* and *Turtle Magazine* can provide ongoing pleasure. For older children, *Sports Illustrated* and *Teen Beat* may be more appropriate. Even magazines that you might think of as adult magazines may be appropriate for teens with specific interests: *Civil War, Science Fiction,* etc. Think of things that are novel and interesting and still may help children learn. Look for: a telescope, a microscope, a kaleidoscope, compass, prism, or tool set and wood.

Give a membership in a children's book club. Give tickets to a play or circus. Give a membership to a museum. For junior high or senior high youth, look to personal preference or hobby for guidance. If the child has a pen pal, a gift of stationery or fancy pens or a book of stamps would be welcome. Again, a display shelf for collections would be useful. A fishing tackle box or even a formal jewelry box would be great for the child with lots of pierced earrings, bracelets and necklaces.

School supplies may be worn out or lost by Christmastime—feel free to replenish. Subscriptions to magazines, specialized by hobby (art, fishing, sports, etc.) are terrific. Give concert tickets or public transportation tokens. Give coupons or gift certificates for local restaurants or fast-food joints for date nights. Buy cut-rate movie passes; they make great gifts.

COMMERCIALS AND ADVERTISEMENT

I know it's time for the holidays when the television **commercials** are RIDICULOUS! They are numerous. They are merciless. They are false. Did you ever notice how every child playing with an advertised toy or game is deliriously happy? And every child eating the advertised food is in seventh heaven? Please!

My children beg me to "hurry up" into the room with the TV so I can see the next item they want me to buy them. Their voices whine and their words promise undying commitment to "take care of" and "really play with" the desired thing. Hogwash!

What about the pictures on the games and toys themselves? The children in the pictures are happier than any natural child has a right to be. What loving parent wouldn't want to have a child that happy? But we all know in our heart of hearts that the dolls, computer game, cardboard game or toy will not result in instant and continued happiness or satisfaction.

Children may also be persuaded by the temptation of other children's belongings. "But, Mom every other kid has it!" "When will we get a Nintendo?" "Dad, all of the kids have ---." "Mom, the other Girl Scouts have at least ten ---each; I only have 4." They seem not at all bothered by their lack of facts to back up these claims. Somehow, they are convinced they would be happier and more content if only they had x.

So what is a parent to do? Follow your instincts!

1. Set a spending limit and keep to it.

2. Try to determine if there is more than one way to use whatever it is.

3. Decide whether your child will exercise any brain cells when using this toy.

4. Look for durability. How long will it last? How much wear and tear can it stand?

5. Look for quality in materials and construction.

6. Try to determine if your child will still want to play with this in a month? Six months? A year?

7. Can you make or buy secondhand another one of these that is just as good?

8. Is there anything dangerous about this item (physically or psychologically)?

9. Would you want your mother (aunt? grandmother? dad?) to know that your child has one of these?

10. Would you want your minister or spiritual leader to know that your child has one of these?

Sometimes seeing the value of an item by answering these questions can help parents resist the nagging pleading of their offspring. Many a holiday has been ruined with parents spending too much time, energy and money on presents only to have children tire of the items on the same day and look nothing like the delighted children who were paid to look that way in the commercial.

A few final considerations:

- Colored pencils, fancy scissors (that cut scallops or notches), glue, scissors;
- Books;
- Videos;
- Craft items;
- Models, glue, and paints;
- Watercolor paints and good paper;
- Magnet kits;
- Action gear (roller blades, safety pads, bike and helmet, etc.);
- Musical instruments;
- Puzzles; and
- Simple toys that can be shared (jump ropes, balls, ring toss, etc.)

If you plan, YOU too can have a happy holiday.

Finally, give back and encourage even young children to do the same. Go through the current collection of toys and "stuff" and select some items for the Toys for Tots drive, church collections or neighborhood efforts described in local newspapers. Giving is every bit as wonderful as getting. Maybe you and your children CAN look as happy as families in the commercials!

DEALING WITH STRESS

Adults are often ambivalent about holidays. They have warm memories of holidays from their youth. They look forward to the happy times associated with the holidays of the current year. Adults look forward to initiating their children into family holiday traditions, enjoying the same decorations, anticipation, and celebrations year after year. Yet there is the pressure to get the "right gift" for any of several people, the need to clean the house or prepare special foods for more events with greater expectations, the struggle to get children what is affordable and appropriate without disappointing them, and the occasional blues during the times that (at least according to TV or the movies) should be blissful.

Children sometimes suffer from **stress** as well (NEA, 1987b). Fortunately, some of the same information helps both adults and children. A terrific book published by Free Spirit Publishing (400 First Avenue, North, Suite 616, Minneapolis, MN 55401, 612-338-2068) is *You and Stress*. The authors, Gail Roberts and Lorraine Guttormson, note that different things cause stress for different people. They even distinguish between eustress (caused by happy circumstances) or distress (caused by unhappy circumstances). Most people need no assistance for coping with eustress. But distress can and does make adults and children sick.

Most important is consideration of whether any of the sources of distress can be done away with or reduced. Would it be possible to make fewer commitments, do some of the preparation way ahead of time and thus spread out the work or reduce the number of presents? Can the family choose one night a week to just relax and watch a movie or read together? Could all family members work together to accomplish something more quickly and with less effort?

It may help to label the feelings of your children. Use words to describe what they are feeling. (If you are wrong, they will let you know!) If you don't know, you may have to ask some questions to help determine what is wrong. Children need to be helped to see that whatever feelings they have are feelings that others have too. An adult can help a child see some solutions, instead of thinking that a situation is hopeless (Bauer, 1990). In fact, an adult who just takes the time to listen may be very important to helping a child cope. Finding a good place, paying attention to nonverbal behavior, and avoiding judgmental responses make listening more effective (Landfried, 1989).

There are also activities that tend to minimize distress (Roberts and Guttormson). These include listening to music or radio; taking a walk or walking a dog; calling, visiting or writing a friend; crying; or putting flowers or plants in a place you will see often. You may also eat foods that are good for you; play a sport; punch your pillow or a stuffed animal; avoid caffeine; avoid sugary foods; exercise; write someone a letter telling everything you feel, but tear it up; go to an art gallery, museum, aquarium, plant conservatory, play, concert or arcade. Laugh or make someone else laugh; go window shopping; go to the zoo; visit someone in the hospital or in a home for senior citizens; sing (LOUD!); meditate; paint or sketch something; avoid people who will be negative when you already feel sad or distressed; hug your pillow or stuffed animal or someone you love; or reorganize your stuff. Sleep a little extra; wear some bright or outrageous clothing; play cards; or paint a wall or room or redecorate something.

Albert Ellis has identified some MYTHS that help make the humans who believe them miserable. Try not to buy into these:

1. You must be loved by everyone and everyone must love everything you do.

2. You must be intelligent, competent, and capable in everything you do.

3. The world is over when things don't turn out the way you want them to.

4. You never control your own happiness. Your happiness depends on how others treat you and on the events that happen to you.

5. If you expect the worst or worry about things that are bad, it will keep them from happening.

6. It's easier to run away from problems or ignore them than to solve them.

7. You need someone else to depend on. You can't function independently.

8. There is only one right way to solve any problem. If you don't choose that one right way, the consequences will be terrible.

9. You can't help feeling the way you do.

10. If something bad happened in your past, you must be affected by it forever.

Let go of these myths (or at least some of them!) and you'll probably feel considerably less distressed.

If you choose to solve a problem rather than let it continue to distress you, consider some of the fears people feel that cause them to postpone problem solving: fear of making a mistake; fear of being hurt, losing love or hurting others; fear of change; fear of being held responsible; or fear of resolving the problem. To solve a problem or avoid letting these fears control and distress you, you can team up with someone else to think of solutions; brainstorm (list every possible, even crazy, answer you can think of); laugh; use constructive criticism; talk to yourself and talk yourself through the problem using positive language; or practice a new way of behaving by role playing with a friend.

Time-out is often thought of as a means of punishment. Another way to think of it is to view time-out as a way of coping. This is a strategy in which one determines that the behavior in progress is not working and a respite must be sought. By walking away, sitting down quietly, taking a deep breath, a person gains some space before continuing to act (Bauer, 1990).

Roberts and Guttormson have written their book in the form of a workbook so that you can work through the things that give you trouble. Another good book is: *Helping Your Child Handle Stress: The Parent's Guide to Recognizing and Solving Childhood Problems* (Katharine Kersey, 1996, Washington, DC: Acropolis Books Ltd.). Use these ideas for holiday stress— or any other kind!

WINTER BLUES

Get the **winter blues**? What's there to do?

Did you know that many museums are free at least one day of the week? Some museums are also free for the last hour or so that they are open. It can't hurt to call.

Did you know that most public libraries have some kind of programming? There may be story hours for children, puppet shows for very young children, travel shows for seniors, book fairs to sell older books from the shelves, free paperback trading shelves, you name it.

Did you know that many public libraries have free or inexpensive video loans? Maybe they have *Toy Story, Follow the Drinking Gourd, Rescuers Down Under, Baby-sitters Club,* etc.

Did you know that at some newsstands and in many libraries there are copies of parent magazines? They are full of information about how to be a good parent, fun activities and things to do with your children, stories about real parents, ways to save money, etc.

Did you know that watching television (appropriate for your child) WITH your child is an important way for your child to learn? Answer and ask questions. Wonder about the meaning of new words. Talk about what might happen next. Let your child use "dress-up" clothes to feel more like the characters. Be sure to explain facial expressions, hints, double meaning words, etc., that will help your child get all of the meaning in the show.

Did you know that books from the library cost nothing (as long as you're not late returning them; put a big sign on the refrigerator in red pen!) and you can take out more than one?

Did your know that children can get their own library cards in most communities with proof of residency in the appropriate community? It's worth the excursion.

Did you know that local college and community centers sometimes have free events? Check with your park district office, your community college or the chamber of commerce in your community.

Did you know that fruit and vegetables reduce the risk of cancer, provide important nutrition for growing bodies and actually help improve mood? Well-nourished bodies feel better and allow the mind to have a better attitude!

Did you know that homework can help your children learn? Don't wait until too late, when you and your children are *too* tired, to even ask about homework. Set a routine for reporting homework, a place for doing it, and a time for working on it. Many a dreary night can pass quickly with homework, but adults have to help children have a positive attitude about it. If you wait until you are too tired: you may lose your temper, your child may cry or tantrum, the homework may not be finished giving your child a worry for the next day, and little will be learned. Make homework a priority and try to get the most out of it!

Did you know that hot chocolate with marshmallows is a great winter drink? Especially after homework!

Did you know that exercise can lift the mood and spirit? A walk on crisp afternoons or evenings can be a great idea. If you are too tired or it's not safe to walk in your neighborhood in the evening, try exercise at home. Bending and stretching feels good. Running in place in stocking feet (don't forget about your neighbor downstairs) or dancing can be great exercise—and music helps to lift moods too!

Did you know that the most important influence on your child's mood is YOUR mood? Do the best you can to feel good yourself and you will go a long way to helping your child feel happy!

A book for children about parents and children and moods is:

Winthrop, E. (1979). *Are you sad, Mama?* New York: Harper. (K-2)

HOWL-AWEEN!

Holidays can bring out the best or the worst in children. As the fall inches toward **Halloween,** you may find your children happy and excited at the prospect of costumes, parties and treats. Or you may feel pushed to the brink by the mind changing, hounding and costume searching. And if you don't allow your children to participate in common festivities for religious or cultural reasons, you may begin to feel that you have been cast as the Wicked Witch of the West!

It seems that more and more parents worry about allowing their children to trick-or-treat. Perhaps it is the ideas that our times are more dangerous. Perhaps it is that we as parents are older and our feet hurt! The idea of walking block after block with our youngsters is less than appealing. Perhaps it is of concern to us that the offspring get and then want to eat so much foodstuff that isn't good for them. Perhaps you have a keen memory of Halloween weather that has recently been, well, yucky.

Whatever your concerns, try a change! Becker (1996) suggests the idea of a Halloween reading party. Allow your children to make their own invitations. Guests may be invited to come in costumes. Guests should also bring a copy of their favorite scary or Halloween story. Guests will likely have practiced at home and then take turns reading each story aloud. Listeners may draw pictures of what they think of as they listen. Listeners could decide to act out the story after they hear it.

A crafty Halloween party might also be fun. Clerks in craft stores often have good ideas for craft projects for children of different ages.

Old-fashioned kinds of fun may be just right too. Have you always wanted to have a taffy pull? Get a recipe from a book at the library or from your grandmother. Bobbing for apples sounds fun? Use a clean bucket or tub and try the Gala apples—what a flavor!

If you do decide to trick-or-treat, consider going to the homes of people you know well and staying for a while. Visiting and showing off costumes may give children more satisfaction. Two or three stops may satisfy your children. Choosing hosts wisely, such as older friends who no longer have children of their own or someone who is in the house a great deal for health reasons or limited mobility, means that you are also providing entertainment and fun for someone who no longer trick-or-treats herself.

What about the treats at your own address? Who is distributing and what are you giving? Take pity on the harried parents of young children who hate to hear, "No more candy." Consider giving pennies, Halloween rings, or other tiny gifts.

Have some fun yourself and dress for the occasion of answering the door or accompanying your children on the rounds. Not too scary—remember the very young and very sensitive. Mutual guessing can be funny: Are you another Batman? You think I look like Morticia?

Take a spin around town or even take a walk one of the fall evenings before Halloween. There may be decorations to see or a haunted house at the community house, park district, or local church. These holidays and their specialized activities are the stuff of which memories are made.

Chapter 18

CHALLENGES OF PARENTING

There are more than a few challenges that we face as parents. A number of those challenges will be addressed here, along with suggestions for how to cope with them ourselves and to teach our children to do the same.

DEALING WITH DIFFERENCES

Dealing with **differences** and disabilities of self and also the differences and disabilities of others is a major part of maturing. Self-acceptance can often result from learning to accept others. Parents and teachers alike need to help youngsters understand and accept human imperfections; a good starting point is teaching children to have compassion (not pity) for those with disabilities (Eysenck, 1994).

As children, most of us can remember being fascinated by persons who were obviously different, a person in a wheelchair, a person without a limb, someone talking to himself or a person with a vision impairment with a cane and a dog. We may also recall a variety of parent responses: "Don't stare!" or "Stay away from that man!" These responses do not teach acceptance, nor do they address the natural curiosity about the human condition that children share with adults (National Conference for Human Relations, 1994).

Embark on a disabilities education plan early in the lives of your children (see "Inclusion" chapter). It is not necessary to wait for a chance encounter with an older person who doesn't hear well. Add talk about disabilities with discussion of anatomy or hygiene. For instance, when talking about ears, their proper function and the proper way to clean them, it is appropriate to wonder, "What do you think it would be like if you couldn't hear well?" This speculation and the children's responses that follow can lead to some information about the clues that a person may be hearing impaired and what to do in an encounter with someone who is deaf. These suggestions might include talking louder or more clearly (for someone who hears but not well), enunciating every sound (not more slowly or exaggerated speech) or moving into the person's line of vision so that lips and facial features are available for speechreading.

Minor childhood injuries may also provide appropriate forums for disabilities discussion. At the time of a sprained ankle, some understanding of adapted mobility (wheelchair, crutches, braces, etc.) might be gained. Children stare when they are interested, particularly in something unfamiliar. If parents and teachers make disabilities more familiar, the inclination to stare can be reduced.

Teachers may capitalize on the natural interest of students. What about creating a showcase of objects/equipment invented for the use of persons with disabilities? The inventors, the object/equipment and the persons who may benefit from them could all be included. Reading about disabilities can enlighten children about the experiences, hopes and aspirations of persons who have disabilities.

Parents even have a unique opportunity to help children accept disabilities by close association with family members. Explain grandpa's poor hearing, great-aunt's arthritis and baby sister's speech that is still hard to understand. Ignoring these opportunities for communication deprives children of the chance to be familiar with differences and to be comfortable with their own unique qualities.

People with disabilities function in everyday life and offer special experiences to teach about the human condition and the human spirit, as well as how to deal with living in an imperfect world (National Conference for Human Relations, 1994). If you feel that you don't know enough about disabilities to teach your child, see Section Two information. In addition, the books suggested for young readers there may be very helpful for teaching and learning in your home.

Other differences that children may notice may be differences in appearance, culture, practices, religion, etc. Children are easily influenced in these and other areas of learning by the adult models they live with (National Conference for Human Relations, 1994).

What is prejudice? According to the *American Heritage Dictionary of the English Language,* prejudice is "an adverse judgment or opinion formed beforehand or without knowledge or examination of the facts." Further, prejudice can be "irrational suspicion of a group, race or religion."

It is protective for humans to draw inferences from situations before they get too deep into those situations, before it is too late to extricate themselves or before they are actually in danger. Prejudging, or judging on very little information, is necessary to drive defensively, or to determine quickly how to act, dress or speak in a given situation. Prior experiences as well as "instinct" allow us to draw conclusions quickly. Prejudice, unfortunately, does not allow us to change our views, even once we have been able to test the situation a little longer and "examine" the facts. Common prejudices of race, religion and class are transmitted to our children because of our responses in our children's presence.

Certain prejudices seem to be almost universal. I wonder how they are maintained by persons who have faith, belong to a religion and are instructed by their faith not to hold such views. One way is to give a reason. "I hate *x* group because my grandfather's store was held up by a member of *x* group." "When members of *x* group moved into my neighborhood, I had to move!"

Another way to avoid the discomfort of prejudice juxtaposed with religious teachings is not to notice that they don't match. This is the most common situation. A minister regularly talks in everyday conversation about how "blackies" have ruined the game of basketball with their "jumping and high-fiving." He often speaks of how Jews control the entertainment and money industries and how the rest of the world is at their mercenary mercy. He doesn't hesitate to note how lazy and unclean Hispanics are. I don't think he has ever considered that his frequent remarks are inconsistent with the teachings of the church he represents. He certainly hasn't taken the time to find out that he is inaccurate.

What I wonder while I am noticing these things about him is what prejudices I am showing my children and of which I am unaware. The oft-repeated quote, "The unexamined life is not worth living," gives me pause. Have I adequately examined my own knee-jerk responses? Does my behavior show some underlying prejudices that I carry? Do I give every homeless person, person of color, odd dresser, senior, street beggar, telephone solicitor and others the courtesy and respect that just being a human being demands?

Worse yet, as a parent, do I show my children to respect others or at least not show disrespect to others (Hart, 1995)? Do I wince, roll my eyes, pull my children away, or otherwise diminish the humanity of others? I'm not suggesting that I should put my children in harm's way. I wouldn't leave them alone with an alcoholic or tell them to give a homeless person who might have tuberculosis a hug. But there is no reason to glare, sniff or roll my eyes when we pass such a person.

I had an opportunity to be in a situation with a number of athletic adult males. My first instinct, my prejudice, was to recoil at the "macho" behavior displayed. My prejudice caused me to be very uncomfortable and not to want to stick out this "opportunity." However, by overcoming my prejudice at least a little, I afforded my child an opportunity to participate in something from which he may benefit. I also found the few individuals I dealt with at a personal level to be gracious, informed, and helpful; and I became more comfortable with the males involved.

It seems to me that many prejudices follow this pattern. Some outward behavior or appearances of a group or members of a group are unappealing to us, perhaps because of prior experiences, perhaps because we were taught to hold these views. When we "stick it out" and collect our facts and examine them, it is often true that at least some of the people we were disinclined to know turn out not to be so bad!

It is important, for the sake of our children, to help them determine when to prejudge as a protective and temporary mechanism and when to continue collecting and examining facts so that they make decisions on individuals and not on the groups to which the individuals belong.

It also seems important to do some direct teaching. This can be done in a number of ways, including experimenting with ethnic food via cooking (Gardner, 1988) and attending ethnic fairs. Family vacations offer opportunities to study cultures from a variety of disciplines: art, music, mathematics, language arts, social studies, physical education, and home economics (Kronowitz, 1985). Here's to ALL of us!

Books that may help children include:

Angelou, M. (1996). *Kofi and his magic*. New York: Courtney-Clark.
Ancona, G. (1995). *Earth daughter: Alicia of Acoma Pueblo*. New York: Simon & Schuster.
Bunting, E. (1997). *Going home*. New York: HarperCollins.
Fleming, V. (1993). *Be good to Eddie Lee*. New York: Philomel.
Garland, S. (1993). *The lotus seed*. Orlando, FL: Harcourt Brace & Co.
Hoffman, M. (1991). *Amazing Grace*. New York: Dial.
King, M. (1996). *Granddaddy's gift*. New York: Bridgewater.
Levitan, S. (1995). *A piece of home*. New York: Dial.
Lillegard, D. (1987). *My first Martin Luther King book*. Boston: Houghton Mifflin.
Mendez, P. (1989). *The black snowman*. New York: Scholastic.
Polacco, P. (1990). *Just plain fancy*. New York: Bantam.
Rattigan, J. K. (1993). *Dumpling soup*. Boston: Little, Brown.
Swope, S. (1989). *The Araboolies of Liberty Street*. New York: Clarkson N. Potter.

TEACHING ABOUT WAR

"This troubled world of ours is like a puzzle with a peace missing." Coming across anonymous quotes like this may get you wondering about what to tell your children about the Persian Gulf War or any other violent event that they hear about or see pictures of in the newspaper or news magazine. Even very young children have questions about the colored ribbons they may see everywhere and about the dramatic, and often frightening, pictures they see on television or on the cover of a news magazine.

First, it is important to let children know that their feelings are all right. Even "bad" feelings, like fear and anger, are okay. Second, it is important to remember that children experience the world in a different way than adults do. They personalize experiences and worry that a **war** will result in an immediate loss for them, such as a parent dying. Parents should reassure the child, saying that the child is cared for and protected. Demonstrating on a map (some of which are made available as pullout sections in local papers) just how far away the war is may help. (Hopefully, every war will be far away so that your child can be reassured.)

Some children are extremely sensitive to suffering or seem to have an acute sense of what others may be experiencing. For these children, personal reassurances may be inadequate. Limiting time spent watching television or listening to the radio would be appropriate for a very sensitive child.

In general, take the lead from your child. Sometimes, children ask questions that seem very sophisticated and it is easy to give them more information than they can digest. Try not to lie, use language they can understand, and provide a little information at a time. If children want to know more, they can always ask again.

Often children will want to alleviate suffering or otherwise feel some control over what is happening. Writing letters or sending drawings to soldiers could be a good idea. Praying for peace or doing a good deed for someone in need here in the United States can provide some sense of influence or acceptance.

Children who are worried about war or dying may exhibit symptoms such as difficulty sleeping, poor eating and bad dreams. Lee Salk, a professor of psychology and pediatrics at the New York Hospital-Cornell Medical Center, noted that straight talk about what really happens in armed conflict is critical (Salk, 1969). If children find out from a media source, without a parent to interpret and support them, fears may be increased.

A number of books are available in your local library that may inform and structure discussions in your home. Some are informational, with hard facts about tanks, artillery, terrorism and violence and the media. These are for older children and are in the juvenile collection. A particularly moving book, exploring causes for war, is *Some Reasons for War* by Sue Mansfield and Mary Bowen Hall, published by Thomas Y. Crowell (New York) in 1988. A number of books about the kinds of ideas, related to conflict, that younger children can understand are also available. They would be in the Easy Books section. Try *The Temper Tantrum Book* by Edna Mitchell Preston (Puffin Books,

1976) or *The Case of the Double Cross*, by Crosby Bonsall (Harper and Row, 1980) or *Over the Deep Blue Sea* (Knopf, 1993). A series of books called *Children's Problem Solving Books* from Parenting Press give social situations and ask children to make decisions about how to solve social conflicts. The books are very well done. Perhaps tomorrow's leaders raised with better problem-solving skills can avoid conflicts similar to the ones we face today.

A host of books about peace are also available at libraries and bookstores and should receive special emphasis. A wonderful collection of poems is called *Peace and War*, collected by Michael Harrison and Christopher Stuart-Clark. *The Lotus Seed* by Sherry Garland looks at the long-term effects of war. Another book, *The Big Book for Peace*, is a collection of works written by several renowned children's authors and illustrated by artists ranging from Teri Sloat to Maurice Sendak. It deals with peace among nations' peoples, brothers and sisters. The writing reflects true experiences, tales of peace from myriad cultures and letters from real children.

Despite the warning of Reverend Powell Davies—"The world is now too dangerous for anything but truth; too small for anything but brotherhood"— we often find ourselves and our country in a difficult conflict. For the sake of children, heed the words of Martin Luther: "If I knew that tomorrow would go to pieces, I would still plant my apple tree. Carry on." What choice do we have? Whining and worrying will only scare our children. Optimism can be learned; your children need to learn it from you.

TEACHING CHILDREN OPTIMISM

Teaching children to have hope and feel optimistic about the future is an important thing to give to the next generation, our children (Albrecht, 1996). Hopelessness, sometimes seems justified, given money problems, racism, bad traffic, drugs, etc., that influence daily living. However, hopelessness pulls children down and causes them to see no purpose in trying, no purpose in learning.

Children have to think they will be around in a few years to care about their futures. Children must see that their efforts mean something in order to continue making efforts. Children can learn to believe in their futures when the adults around them provide the model.

Optimism, thinking that good things can and sometimes do happen, is essential to hope. Children who live with adults who complain every day tend not to notice the good things that sometimes do happen. **Vow to complain less.**

Optimism requires that the good things that do happen receive a fair celebration. When you get that close parking space, find the last container of bargain laundry soap, get the rare chance to eat in a restaurant, these happenings should be celebrated. Children learn what they see. If only the bad things are spotlighted play and the adults look and talk in a depressed way, children learn to feel deprived.

When adults help children to celebrate even little things that go right, life is more tolerable. Life seems more worth living. Children begin to develop hope. **Vow to celebrate the little things.**

Children who have hope plan for the future. Children who have hope believe that they have chances and choices. Children who have hope see the point in trying to learn as much as they can; they see the point in trying to do things well. Children who do not have hope say "Whatever..." and mean it; anything will do because they have no expectation for anything good. **Vow to help your children want to learn, to see the point in living well and doing their best.**

In the famous *Little House on the Prairie* series of books, there were a number of times when events made life seem pretty bleak. But the parents in this real-life story made the best of their circumstances; they gave their children reason to hope. These parents did not share every grim worry with their children—they protected the children; they gave the children reason to hope. Despair does not help. **Vow to give your children reason to hope.**

TEACHING CHILDREN TO CARE

Faced with the decision of whether to have raised a child who is a good reader or a decent person, most parents would choose a good person. Fortunately, we can teach our children both. Learning to **care** is developed. For years, psychologists believed that children who showed concern for others when they were quite young must have just been born with that caring. Now it has been noted that children do have differences that can be partly explained by inborn traits. But it has also been demonstrated by research that children learn to care by living with adults who teach them that caring is good. If a child sees important adults help, the child learns to imitate that helping.

Adults who want to teach children to care must be able to put their own needs aside and meet the needs of the children first. Children who are compassionate are most often children who have their own needs met and, therefore, have the energy to invest in the well-being of someone else.

Adults must also watch what they show in front of children. Young children, under the age of two, often actually experience the emotional pain of the adults around them. They do not distinguish between their own pain and that of others. One study found that children of parents with mental illness felt their parents' anguish more deeply but then lashed out at playmates. This certainly suggests that adults should seek treatment for their own emotional problems. Treatment helps reduce the amount of pain and stress that their children will witness and take on as their own.

Children may also seek adult guidance on when and how to help. They may suggest bringing home stray animals. Perhaps they will want you to give your grocery money to a man begging on the street. Young children may need several explanations over their growing years to help them form good judgment about when to help and when it may not be safe to try to help someone.

Children learn "natural caring" from the kind of hope and love a parent feels for a child. Make sure that your child sees that hope and love on a daily basis. Sometimes parents work so hard for their children and think that the hard work shows the children that the parents care. But children also need physical and verbal expressions of parental love: hugs, arms around the shoulder, praise, kisses, and extended contact with the adults who care for them.

Children show their caring in their own ways. They may offer a toy or pat a hand for someone in distress. They try to help in ways that they would like to receive help. Parents who don't understand this might think that the child is insisting on being played with or demanding attention at a difficult time. It is very possible that the child is trying to help but couldn't possibly know the adult way of asking what is wrong or listening to a detailed list of what is bothering the adult.

Some children do respond to adults in distress by demanding attention. It's almost as if they are saying, "Get yourself together; I'm the child here—you're supposed to be taking care of me!" They are right. However, sometimes things are very difficult to handle, even for adults. It is a great idea to have a friend or relative who will listen. It's also good to concentrate on meeting the child's needs; take your mind off of your own problems until you have time, out of the child's sight, to have a good cry.

Some children become compassionate as a result of being hurt. They want to treat others differently than they were treated. However, most children treat others as they have been treated. And they will treat their own children in the same way that you treat them. The way you resolve problems, help others, settle differences, and deal with life's lows will become your child's inheritance. What attitudes and behaviors do you want to leave to them?

BULLIES

There are a number of things about school that are worth being excited about: seeing friends, meeting new friends, learning new things. For some students, though, thoughts turn to fear as they worry about taunting or worse from local **bullies.**

What causes some children to be bullies? Not all experts agree, but most research has pointed to learned behavior. Bullies are often children who have been bullied by their parents, older siblings, or others.

Bullies may taunt others for the very things they worry about in themselves. The overweight child may call other heavy children fat. The child who has trouble reading may be the first to point out someone else's error.

Punishing bullies may not work because, to their perceptions, punishment gives them an example of more bullying. Punishment may even serve to make the bullies angrier at their victims and more likely to seek revenge (Foltz-Gray, 1996).

From a parent's perspective, the plan of action may include making a contract with the bully. In the contract, the bully agrees not to victimize anyone else in order to earn some privilege. This relies on the adult to notice the bully's behavior closely or hope to get an accurate report from the bully.

Many bullies are slick enough to avoid observation of their behaviors by adults. They can even manage to face adults with a relatively calm face while hissing some threat to the children directly in front of them.

This may mean that parents have to suggest tactics of their own to the children who may be the victims. First, this is a situation that requires adult intervention. Sometimes, children aren't sure when to call on adults and when to handle it themselves. In cases of persistent bullying, adults should be alerted. Many bullies stop when directly confronted by an adult.

Strong words may also be required from the victim. "You can't talk to me that way" and walking briskly away may help. Ignoring sometimes works, but the bully often escalates the bullying behavior to get attention before he gives up, and most children can't live through the escalation patiently (Foltz-Gray, 1996).

The National School Safety Center (Seven steps, 1996) offers the following suggestions to parents:

1. Keep the lines of communication open.
2. Watch for symptoms, such as bruises, torn clothes, change in appetite, frequent need for additional money, etc., from children who may be afraid to tell you that they are being bullied (especially because they have been threatened by the bullies if they were to tell).
3. Take any complaints seriously; let your child know that you believe her.

4. Inform school officials immediately; it is the responsibility of the school to intervene with events that happen at school.

5. Teach your child to respond assertively, not aggressively.

6. Continue to boost your child's self-esteem.

7. Make sure that you don't bully your children.

If you suspect that your child IS a bully, spend some time talking about ways your child can connect socially without being "in power." Give your child some opening things to say to other children and let your child practice those things with you. Watch what you say to your child and in what tone of voice (especially when you are tired or angry). Try to make sure you are not a model for bullying.

If you worry about your child being bullied, let your child talk about it as often as needed. Give practical suggestions of what to say and do. Let your child practice these responses at home. It takes a while to build up the oomph to face a bully. Help your child avoid circumstances that lead to bullying (walking home from school by a certain route, etc.) so that your child gains more control over the situation (Fried & Fried, 1996).

With all this talk of bullying, you'd think that was the only kind of child out there. Certainly not! Fortunately, there are lots of great children for your child or teen to meet and connect with as friends. Having friends is also a way to avoid being bullied. There is strength in numbers!

Children's books about bullies may also help. A few good books include:

Alexander, M. (1981). *Move over, twerp!* New York: Dial. (gr. K-1)

Bottner, B. (1992). *Bootsie Barker bites.* New York: Putnam. (gr. K-1)

Cole, J. (1990). *Don't call me names.* New York: Random House. (gr. K-1)

Conford, E. (1983). *Lenny Kendall, smart aleck.* Boston: Little, Brown. (gr. 5-6)

Conford, E. (1980). *Revenge of the incredible Dr. Rancid and his youthful assistant,* Jeffrey. Boston: Little, Brown. (gr. 4-5)

Giff, P. R. (1990). *Matthew Jackson meets the wall.* New York: Delacourte. (gr. 2-3)

Kaufman, G., & Raphael, L. (1990). *Stick up for yourself! Every kid's guide to personal power and positive self-esteem.* Minneapolis, MN: Free Spirit Publishing.

Shreve, S. (1993). *Joshua T. Bates takes charge.* New York: Knopf. (gr. 3-4)

Stolz, M. (1985). *The bully of Barkham street.* New York: HarperCollins. (gr. 3-4)

Wardlaw, L. (1992). *Seventh-grade weirdo.* New York: Scholastic. (gr. 5-6)

SIBLING RIVALRY

Do the children at your house keep score cards? Do they record every compliment, snack, privilege, dime, attention, clothing, assistance, and book given to their siblings? The most common situation is that each scorekeeper finds herself dead last in the comparisons. Never mind that her brother thinks he too gets the short end of the stick. Such is the ritual of **sibling rivalry.**

Can't live with them; can't live without them. This familiar phrase aptly describes sibling relationships. Brothers and sisters often drive each other crazy. Joy Berry (in Every Kid's Guide to Handling Fights with Brothers or Sisters) identifies ten reasons for sibling rivalry.

Reasons for fighting with brothers or sisters include:
1. Wanting your parents' love;
2. Wanting to be the best;
3. Wanting to be respected;
4. Wanting to be treated fairly;
5. Not wanting to be teased;
6. No wanting to be embarrassed;
7. Not wanting your belongings abused;
8. Wanting privacy;
9. Being together too much; and
10. Feeling safe (Berry, 1987).

Berry also suggests four steps to follow to avoid fighting. She says that we should:

(1) think about it; (2) talk about it; (3) walk or run away; and (4) go get help. You can see that these steps would work in most circumstances, however, you can also see how children are not drawn to these steps instinctively. As with any other aspect of growing and learning, parents and caregivers must provide models and repeatedly encourage that these steps be taken (Berry, 1987).

In classical psychology, theorists talk about approach-avoidance. This is a tension that is created when we both do and don't want something. Having brothers and sisters is perhaps the classic approach-avoidance. Not only do we want siblings around sometimes and not others, but we also go back and forth in our responses to them. If we beat them up, call them names, tell on them, etc., this is to be expected. BUT, if someone else tries to do these same things, the tiger emerges and we fiercely defend our siblings. Weird!

Sometimes siblings have something extra special in common. That is, the same birth date! Twins, triplets, and more also raise the curiosity of others. This creates approach-avoidance too. In some ways, we like the extra attention. In other ways, living in a "fish bowl," drawing the constant scrutiny of others, is uncomfortable. Joanna Cole and Madeleine Edmondson capture some of these perks and challenges in their book, *Twins: The Story of Multiple Births*.

Another extra special ingredient in some sibling rivalries is the added dimension of one of the siblings having special needs, including special learning needs. Often, siblings have increased responsibility for care of the child with disabilities. At the same time that they are asked to be more responsible, siblings of a child with disabilities may be asked to do with less parental attention. They usually love their sibling with disabilities and are willing to help, but there can be intense approach-avoidance issues in this situation, too.

Actually, relationships with brothers and sisters prepare us for later relationships with marriage partners. Togetherness is good, too much togetherness is trouble. Some traits are endearing while some habits are irritating. Learning to love another person as well as tolerate differences is a good skill for living in a family with siblings and for living in a marriage relationship with another adult.

Sometimes people who are aggravated with their siblings are surprised to find that people who do not have brothers or sisters wish that they did. It's partly a case of the "grass being greener on the other side of the fence." It may also be that it is easier to see the "approach" aspect of something when you don't have to live with it. Only children report feeling lonely; children in larger families report feeling crowded. As with every situation there are good and bad sides.

Adults are sometimes surprised to think of their sibling rivalries continuing on through adulthood. Actually, this is the case more often than not. Who really takes care of the elderly parents when the chips are down? How is will money distributed? Whose offspring appear to be the favored grandchildren? Why does this persist? For the same ten reasons that Joy Berry identified for children! I guess grown-ups don't grow up all that much....

Eda LeShan (in her book *When Kids Drive Kids Crazy*) reports about a case in which Jennifer went away to camp. She received a postcard from her younger sister which was signed, "Love and Hate, Karen." Just about sums it up, huh? You can't live with them and you can't live without them. You can make it more manageable when you practice and teach your children the four steps from Ms. Berry. Smile!

Books that may help youngsters include:

Berry, J. (1987). *Every kid's guide to handling fights with brothers and sisters.* Chicago: Children's Press. (gr. 3-6)

Cole, J., & Edmondson, M. (1972). *Twins: The story of multiple births.* New York: William Morrow Company. (gr. 3-5)

LeShan, E. (1990). *When kids drive kids crazy: How to get along with your friends and* enemies. New York: Dial Books for Young Readers. (gr. 5-9)

Meyer, D. J., Vadasy, P. F., & Fewell, R. R. (1985). *Living with a brother or sister with special needs.* Seattle: University of Washington Press.

RAISING ADOLESCENTS

Raising **adolescents** presents some very challenging challenges! Despite the fact that these same individuals have typically been the same ones that you raised until they hit adolescence, the teenagers at your address may seem to have very little in common with the children who used to live there.

Adolescents experience an approach-avoidance relationship with parents as well as siblings. There are times when they may behave in a very juvenile, dependent way, seeming to want to return to early childhood, if not infancy! At other times, teens assert themselves and demand rights of an adult. They behave in these confusing ways because they feel pretty confused.

The life work of an adolescent is to determine who to be. In this search for identity, many different styles and behaviors are tried. This is what explains the hairdos (including odd colors, lengths and the absence of head hair at all). It also explains tattoos, piercings, and idiosyncratic clothing. All of these explanations are provided by Clarissa, the "Nickelodeon" teen who "explains it all." Perhaps pre-teens and teens like the show so much because Clarissa is on target so often.

Some of the experiments are also designed to raise the hackles of parents. One way to exert some power is to do something that will infuriate another person. Playing loud music, dressing in a garish way, or shaving one's head may infuriate parents, giving a sense of power to teens. Not all teens do such drastic things, but each one has to cope with the independence/dependence question in some way.

Teens are also up against heavy pressure from other teens. Glances take on new meaning. Adolescents know they are being judged harshly because they are probably doing some harsh judging themselves. Teens categorize each other and find it difficult to break out of the barriers those categories create. Maybe the song should be "GROWING up is hard to do." This reality may make acceptance at home more critical in adolescence than at any other time in your child's life. It's hard to believe that they pick the time that they're wearing "Mohawk" hairdos and wearing a nail polish color called Urban Decay to need acceptance, isn't it?!

It is also true, as perhaps you can recall in dim memory, that remarkable physical changes occur during adolescence. These changes are confusing in themselves and also cause teens to feel uncomfortable in physical ways. Moods may shift rapidly and result in unexpected and explosive interchanges between adolescents and their parents. Adolescence lasts even longer than the "terrible twos" and, thus, even greater patience is required of parents. In addition, you can no longer simply drag your belligerent or embarrassing child from the scene he is creating in the mall.

Most teens do grow up to be adults and time can heal a number of wounds. The most important thing is to continue to love your child and continue to show your child that love. Despite protests over "corny" expressions of love and having to chase your child around the kitchen for a simple hug, your teen requires that stability.

The second most important thing is to forgive. Adolescents will say some awful things when they feel awful. They may not really mean what's been said and that's why they need you to forgive them. Of course, sometimes you may say or do things that require forgiveness, too. That's what adolescents are for!

Books that may help parents include:

Caissy, G. (1994). *Early adolescence: Understanding the 10-15 year old.* New York: Insight Books.

Freeman, C. G. (1996). *Living with a work in progress: A parents' guide to surviving adolescence.* Columbus, OH: National Middle School Association.

Phelan, T. W. (1993). *Surviving your adolescents: How to manage and let go of your 13 to 18 year olds.* Glen Ellyn, IL: Child Management Inc.

Tracy, L. F. (1994). *Grounded for life?! Stop blowing your fuse and start communicating with your teenager.* Seattle, WA: Parenting Press, Inc.

Van Hoose, J., & Strahan, D. B. (1988). *Young adolescent development and school practices: Promoting harmony.* Columbus, OH: National Middle School Association.

THE BALANCING ACT

Another challenge of parenting is **effective balancing.** Balancing praise with constructive criticism. Balancing patience with real limits to behavior, demands and expectations. Balancing children's needs with your own energy level and your own needs.

Most parents become parents with a minimum of preparation. We all had parents who cared for us in a variety of ways. We've seen other parents in action: the parents of our friends when we were children, the parents of our friends and schoolmates when we were adolescents, parents of children in the grocery store or mall, parents on TV, our friends as parents.

We usually form judgments about ourselves as parents. However, if we have never had training to be effective parents and we observe this huge range of other parents, by what standard should our own parenting be judged?

Some guidelines, in the form of questions, follow.

1. Do I view being a parent as important as other work I do?
2. Do I take occasional opportunities to improve myself as a parent by reading, watching TV specials or sharing tips with other parents?
3. Do I spend time at least once per week reflecting on my parenting, congratulating myself and identifying areas for improvement?
4. Do I find time at least twice a week when I am with my children and not also "accomplishing something"—washing dishes, shopping, repairing the car, etc.
5. Do I compliment my spouse, baby-sitter or child care worker (anyone who shares in parenting) at least occasionally?
6. Do I occasionally do things that replenish my ability to give to my children (read a novel, go to lunch with a friend, see a movie with my spouse, do my nails, jog, etc.)?
7. Do I establish routines and patterns for family life from which my children may derive security?
8. Do I take pleasure in parenting, such as watching my children sleep, telling myself I'm lucky to have such great children or smiling to show how my children make me proud in a public place, at least once in a while?
9. Do I establish traditions for special events (choose your meals on your birthday, hang a St. Nicholas stocking, put your tooth under your pillow, etc.) so my children have things to look forward to and have memories of?
10. Can I honestly say that I love my children and that most of what I do with them and for them is out of love and not pride or fear on my part?

You will find that you have answered at least eight questions with a yes. You have a right to congratulate yourself for hard work and reasonable success considering we are "practicing without a license."

STAYING HEALTHY

Staying healthy is the key to enjoying life. Healthy children are also easier to take care of because they tend to be happier and less fussy than sick ones. Healthy children also cause their parents less worry. Parents can actually ease their burdens by paying more attention to children's health in the way of prevention.

Of course, encourage good eating habits. Fruit, vegetables, and whole grains are essential to good health. Fruit juices, milk, and plenty of water are important, too.

Make sure your children get their shots on time. This is not just for entry to school but beginning when they are babies. Below you'll find how many shots and vaccines doctors recommend before children ever start kindergarten. (These recommendations may change with new research, so be sure to check with your child's pediatrician or clinic doctor.)

Hepatitis B (HB) vaccine: birth, 1-2 months, 6-18 months
Diptheria, Pertussis, Tetanus (DPT): 2 months, 4 months, 6 months,
    15-18 months, 4-6 years
Oral polio (OP) vaccine: 2 months, 4 months, 6 months, 4-6 years
Haemophilus influenzae type B (Hbcv): 2 months, 4 months, 6 months*,
    15 months*
Measles, Mumps, Rubella (MMR): 12-18 months, 4-6 years
Diptheria Tetanus (dT): 14-16 years
Varicella Zoster (new vaccine for chicken pox): 12-18 months
      * depends on the product

Adequate washing of clothing, hair and body is also important to good health. Germs especially thrive in moist, warm, dirty places. Summer may automatically produce warm and moist places (due to rain and perspiration) on human bodies. It is important to reduce dirt and wash regularly to help resist disease.

Hand washing is a simple but effective way to reduce germs. Bathing the whole body should be done at least weekly. Hair should be washed thoroughly at least weekly as well. Bed clothes (sheets, pillow cases) can be cleaned so that newly cleaned bodies don't jump into soiled linens. Towels and sheets should be washed weekly too.

Heat in the kitchen provides ample opportunity for germs to multiply there. Foods with proteins (meats, cheese, fish) are the most vulnerable. Place foods into containers or plastic bags to refrigerate as soon as the meal is over. Do not leave these foods on a counter to "cool" before refrigerating.

Wash the kitchen counters and stove tops as well as tabletops after each meal or snack. Use bleach in the water for washing once in a while.

Wash bathroom areas with bleach as well. Bleach is a cheap and effective germ killer. Mix bleach with water to avoid damage to skin and irritation to eyes as you lean over your work.

Even young children can learn good habits of cleaning up after eating.

They can also learn to wash hands with soap after each bathroom use. Older children (including teens) will probably need to be reminded past the age when you may think that reminding should be necessary. Encourage healthy habits in your children!

KEEPING THEM SAFE

Beyond keeping children healthy is keeping them safe. Check each of these locations and review the safety tips.

Bedrooms. You are most likely to use an air conditioner in this room. Make sure that each air conditioner has been cleaned in the last year. Try to clean the filter of the air conditioner each week. It's easy; slide out the foam filter, wash it with water until all the lint is gone and dry for several minutes before replacing it. Check each electrical cord for missing insulation. Do not use a frayed cord. Cover all unused outlets if you have young children. Safety caps for this purpose are available in hardware stores and department stores. Check that you have a smoke alarm in each bedroom and that it has a working battery.

Kitchens. This room is the hottest in your home. Again, check for electrical cords on your fan, toaster, microwave and electric skillet. Discard or replace all frayed or worn cords. Check the placement of the fan. Be sure that its force cannot blow hot oil or grease out of the pan when you are cooking. Did you disconnect the smoke alarm in the hallway outside the kitchen the time you burned the catfish? Make sure it is reconnected and has a working battery in it. Move any poisons you use in the kitchen for insects and rodents well out of the reach of children. Check for poisons in cleaning supplies and move them out of reach too.

Bathrooms. Check for worn electrical cords. Replace or discard dangerous ones. Keep all electrical appliances well out of reach of young children and in places where contact with water is impossible. Cover unused outlets with safety caps. Remove all soaps, cleaners, hair products, etc., that contain chemicals that are not safe to eat or drink to a safe location. Children are often attracted by the pretty packages or "drinkable" look of bottles. All curling irons and crimping irons should be stored out of children's reach, especially when cooling after a recent use or heating up preparing for use. An adult should always adjust water temperature and check it before allowing a child to climb into a bath or shower. You may have to sound the "NO WATER" alert when someone is bathing if water use elsewhere in your home may lead to sudden changes in temperature in the shower or sink.

Basements or **Garages.** Clean these areas regularly. It is so easy to finish a job of painting or using a solvent and be so exhausted that you say to yourself that you will clean up "in a minute" as soon as you rest. Children need less than a minute to take fatal doses of chemicals. Clean up immediately or supervise the area. Check for rags and papers that could easily burn and remove them. Store items for recycling in plastic bags and out of doors whenever possible.

Out-of-Doors. Have your children wear safety helmets when biking, skate-boarding or skating. If you can't afford the helmet, you can't afford to let your child engage in these activities. It doesn't matter if no one else in your area wears helmets. Your precious child requires that protection. Require foot protection for your family when going outside. Broken glass, insects and even scalding hot pavements can be hazardous. So can bicycle spokes, for someone with bare feet who is a "passenger" on the back of a bike.

Cars. Use restraints every time you are in a car. Accidents can happen on your block. Use restraints even for the short trip to the grocery store. Do not allow young children to close car doors. They don't look for small fingers, including their own (!) carefully. Use restraints yourself. Your children would be lost without you!

Safety. More than 800 children die in the United States each year because they, their friends or siblings fire guns unintentionally. For a free copy of a brochure called "Steps to Prevent Firearms Injuries," send a self-addressed, stamped envelope to:

STOP brochure
Center to Prevent Handgun Violence
1225 Eye St., NW, Suite 1100
Washington, DC 20005

Water. Children should never be alone in the bathtub, in a family swimming pool, or in a hotel pool. Even expert swimmers who are older children should not swim alone. Young children, even under the supervision of an adult, should wear flotation devices unless they are able to swim independently in water over their heads. With regard to water at home, the water heater temperature should be set so that water can be no hotter than 120 degrees when it comes from the tap.

School. There are limitations to the actions that schools and day-care centers can take on behalf of your children. There are plenty of court cases that have caused schools and child care centers to be cautious and avoid certain kinds of assistance.

Even twenty years ago, when I was a preservice teacher, a parent of a second grader threatened to sue me and the school district because I had pulled a child's loose tooth that was rocking back and forth on its point and causing the child pain and bleeding on his schoolwork. The parents asserted that I was taking medical action, despite the fact that I was not trained medical personnel.

Limitations such as these mean that you should try to check your child for certain things before she leaves for school. Check for torn or ragged fingernails that may get snagged and tear further. Check for loose scabs or dry skin and cover with a Band-Aid or use a lotion. Check for loose shoelaces or dangling threads from clothing that might get entangled and trip your child.

School personnel in many states are not allowed to administer sunscreen to your child's skin. If your child is fair and will be outside for any extended period of time, sunscreen is certainly advisable. The pigment in the skin may be brought out by the sun and some people consider that color to be more attractive than fair skin. However, in order to get that color, skin must be exposed to the harmful rays of the sun's spectrum. Sunblock or sunscreen blocks the harmful rays from reaching the skin.

Many dermatologists actually recommend the use of a sunblock 365 days per year. With the concept that our children may live very long lives, they will need to protect their largest organ, their skin, to last perhaps up to a century. Even for children who "tan," the sun's rays may harm their skin and may have future results that are not desirable.

School personnel usually take good care of children in outdoor settings. They make sure that students are getting enough water to drink on hot days. Teachers have students rest more often on hot days and go to the shade to cool off. Teachers check for appropriate clothing for outdoor play on cold days; they may write to you or call you to suggest that your child wear boots or get a new pair of thicker or water-resistant gloves.

Still, teachers can only suggest; parents must provide. It is such a challenge to not only make sure that our children are on time for school but have a nutritious lunch, completed homework and book bags. Add to that the plan to check for hangnails, weather-appropriate clothing, and sunscreen, and you have a hectic morning. Is that why they say parenting is never easy?

Besides these challenges, perhaps you have a child or adolescent at your address who, shall we say, RESISTS your caring suggestions. This child wants to wear Bermuda shorts in January and woolen scarves in May. Battles over such issues may draw your attention away from other critical preparations. Perhaps a checklist near the door as your offspring leave for the day would help.

Just remember to give some attention to the care and safety of your children when they are out of your sight. Schools and day-care centers can only do so much, both by sheer numbers of children and by law. The real care of your children is in your hands.

SLEEP

SLEEP—It meant less to me when I got more of it. Now I long for it more than a Calgon bath, a chocolate bar with caramel, even, well, this is a family book. Anyway, you get the picture...and I wish I got the **sleep.**

What does sleep do for us and why is it necessary for human function? Sleep is important partly because we are not in motion and muscles and bones, as well as nerves and tendons, get the chance to realign and relax. Being relatively still during sleep allows the body to rest and rejuvenate.

In addition, during sleep that lasts usually longer than two hours, we experience rapid eye movement (R.E.M.). During R.E.M. sleep, the eyelids actually move as if the eyes underneath were rolling around. The eyelids even flutter, although they do not usually open. Some people do sleep without their eyes fully closed and it is easier to see what the eye is doing during R.E.M. sleep in these people.

During periods of R.E.M. sleep, the unconscious mind works on issues we experience during waking hours, even coming to conclusions or resolution at times. Scientists tell us that without R.E.M. sleep, we do not feel significantly rested. This may explain why "catnaps" (naps of about 20 minutes in duration) allow us to feel renewed physically—more "get up and go"—but often leave us without new cognitive or mental energy.

If R.E.M. sleep is so important, what can parents of young children who wake frequently during the night do to get enough true rest? What can families with adolescents do about noise and rest?

Of course, one solution is to sleep through anything. This may not be a good solution because important needs are not attended to and larger crises may develop, although some ignoring of children to allow them to get themselves back to sleep is healthy (Wolfson, 1992).

Another solution is to lie down as soon as the young child does or whenever the adolescent is gone for an extended period of time. In this way, the longest possible time period for sleep has begun, increasing the probability of getting R.E.M. sleep in the bargain. Parents often worry about "getting things done" during infant sleep times or adolescent away times. There will be plenty of time to get things done once the children wake you again. Remember that you often find it difficult to get back to sleep after a disturbance, even though you are very tired. Do the work then; you can't sleep anyway!

Still another solution for young children is to provide background or "white" noise when they sleep, perhaps enabling them—and YOU—to sleep a little longer. A simple box fan will do, but baby stores also sell machines specifically for this purpose. Waves lapping up on a beach or wind rustling leaves are among the choices of background noise.

Being a parent of teens may also put a crimp in your sleep patterns. As they stay up later and stay out later, parents sometimes experience worry at such levels that restful sleep is not possible. Parents may also feel less able to rest following a major blowup with an adolescent child. Even if there are no problems with raising teenage children, the challenge of helping children who do not drive yet or cannot commandeer the family car for long periods of time get where they plan to go, between extracurricular activities and employment, can be daunting. Picking up your adolescent from work at 10:30 p.m.when you have to get up at 5:00 a.m. may interfere with you getting enough sleep.

What about teens getting enough sleep? Cutting corners on daily sleep requirements may not be wise, but many teens do it at least occasionally. One way that teens may rejuvenate after several day of too little sleep is by "sleeping in." You usually don't have to worry that they've stopped breathing as you did when they were infants; sleeping for 12- or 15-hour stretches once in awhile is not uncommon for adolescents.

It is apparent to any parent of a baby or teen why the military has used sleep deprivation as a means of torture. When you don't get enough sleep, you are less resistant to illness, more irritable, find regular jobs more overwhelming, concentrate less fully, and generally feel less good. This is also true for children. Getting enough sleep is an important component of school success.

SELF-ESTEEM

One of the things that concerns parents (and should) is the self-concept that their children develop. There is an established link between behavior and **self-esteem,** although it is not certain which influences the other or whether they are just mutually influential. It is not difficult to see how self-esteem could relate to decisions children make and views they have of the world. Children who have high self-esteem believe that what happens to them happens through their own efforts. They also tend to have greater accomplishments. Children with low self-esteem view things that happen to them as due to fate, luck, or some other outside factor. Their accomplishments are fewer.

In order to have high self-esteem, individuals must feel capable. This means that the children need to view themselves as possessing skills and being able to achieve.

For high self-esteem, children must also feel significant. In other words, they must feel that what they do, say and think matters to those around them.

In addition, children must see themselves as powerful. They need to feel that they have some control over what happens to them and that they can make some choices and decisions (Owens, 1996).

Finally, children must feel worthy. It is important that they consider themselves to have value and be unique. They must further feel that their value is not just what they are able to accomplish.

These four components of self-esteem were proposed by Coopersmith (1967), a well-known researcher on the topic. Educators and psychologists who have built on his research have made a number of suggestions for activities and methods that are likely to enhance a child's self-esteem. A caution is that, unless children read praise or other congratulations from adults as sincere, they will not be influenced by the attention. If an adult praises everything, good or bad, the child concludes that the adult can't discriminate among levels of performance and begins to disregard the compliments.

Here are some self-esteem boosters. Choose the ones that seem to suit you and your children.

1. Celebrate the successes of your children. If they seem proud of some thing, join in the pride.

2. Preserve children's work. Most children produce too many papers, pictures, and tests to save them all. Display a few, as space permits.

3. Let students evaluate their own work and decide what they would like to have displayed. What they pick might surprise you. It is not always the perfect paper. Children know how much effort they expended on a particular assignment or creation. They may choose one with a less than perfect grade, but one which represents real effort.

4. Find something special about each child and spotlight it.

5. Teach your children a unique skill that they can teach others. This could include anything from mamba dancing or yodeling to sign language or karate.

6. Make a home suggestion box. Even if you feel that you cannot use the suggestions that the children make, just the idea that you value their opinions enough to create a place to collect them can be very positive.

7. Allow children to choose some of the topics the family talks about at meals.

8. Use contracts. When you want your child to accomplish a certain goal, try using a contract. It lets the child enter into an agreement with you, as an equal, and spells out the roles of both parties. They often take their "party of the first part" roles seriously. Be sure to include signing the document as part of the preparation.

9. When feasible, let children choose where to sit in the car or at the breakfast table, where to work, and with whom. Children may select their own clothing within limits, may make their own purchases within their own budgets from allowances, or decide which TV shows to watch within time and show limitations you have set.

10. Plan art projects that incorporate the children's pictures or names in some way.

11. Select reading materials (when there is a choice) with characters who have something in common with your child: race, gender, age, ethnicity, grade, hair colors, etc. Children get more from reading and learn more from the character's experiences if they believe themselves to be like the character.

12. Model self-praise. This is a tough suggestion to implement. What is suggested is that you learn to congratulate yourself aloud in the presence of your children. This is not bragging. If you have accomplished something difficult, praise yourself aloud.

    "How does she do it, night after night? All of the food groups represented, all the dishes hot at the same time, everything well seasoned and tasty! Wow!" or "I didn't think I would be able to figure out how to make the bookcases myself, but money was tight and I gave it a whirl. They look fantastic!"

    You show your children how to praise themselves when there has been a good effort, not to be dependent on the approval of others. The approval of others may not always be forthcoming, even when it is deserved.

13. Recognize birthdays or any other event unique to each child.

14. Share books that contain messages about the worth of each of us.

15. Find ways to let children know by words, signs, or gestures that every day is a new day—no grudges are held. This is also a difficult suggestion to implement. The human brain is a marvel for all that it can learn and remember. Sometimes it seems that we have forgotten some bad event...until it happens again. Children must be forgiven in order to learn to forgive themselves. Parents must keep trying to do this.

It's hard to talk about the self-esteem of youngsters for two reasons. One is that many adults were not raised using the suggestions that appear here. We tend to care for our own children in the same way that we were raised. The second reason is that the way we help others with their self-esteem gets back to how we feel about ourselves. It turns out that adults with poor self-esteem punish more, praise less, and are more rigid in their methods of parenting (Lesko, 1996).

It's also true that when people give advice about how to raise children they aren't always giving good advice. And when parents try new techniques, no one mentioned that new skills take practice just like a tennis backhand and good singing. So...when you try some new "moves" with your children, expect to feel awkward. It doesn't mean the ideas are bad, it's just that you may not be comfortable with the techniques. With that in mind, here are some additional ideas suggested by research with real parents and real children that may help enhance the self-esteem of children and adolescents.

1. Say something positive to each child each day.
2. Offer a variety of activities so that every child has a chance to shine. This makes a child feel capable.
3. Give each child recognition for the EFFORT she makes. Effort makes children feel powerful.
4. Listen to each child and look him in the eye when he is talking. This makes a child feel that he is worthy of your attention.
5. Answer each child's questions openly, honestly and immediately if possible. Again, the child learns that her concerns are important enough to warrant adult response.
6. Try not to embarrass a child, especially in front of others. This may make him question his worth.
7. Compliment the child when possible on neat work, improvements in her work, clothes or hair style, creative ideas, etc. These are all significant.
8. Do not set goals so high that the chance of failure prevents the child from trying.
9. Help set an atmosphere in which mistakes are understood and tolerated. Model tolerance for his mistakes and yours.
10. Use your child's name when speaking to her.
11. Use humor. Laugh with your children and at yourself. Humor can take the edge off of tense moments with your child. Laughter really can be the best medicine.
12. Let your child write a letter to you occasionally. Return it with a response. Children love to get letters and who better to get a special letter from than a loving parent? Besides, people sometimes say things in writing that they could not or might not say in words or actions.
13. Treat your child as you would like to be treated. This may be the hardest part of parenting, especially because parenting is exhausting! It's hard to be nice when you're tired. But most children give at least as

much as they're given. You'll get some replenishing and occasional boosts to your parental self-esteem as you build the self-esteem of your child.

A book about self-esteem for children is:

Hoffman, M. (1991). *Amazing Grace.* New York: Dial.

WHAT ABOUT TELEVISION?

What is the relationship of television to school learning? The news is bad, but not all bad. Let's examine some facts and ways to respond to the facts. There is an inverse relationship between the amount of time watching television and success in school (Walberg, 1985). That is, the more television watched, the poorer the performance in school. Part of this is due to the fact that too much of the child's waking time may be absorbed, so that homework remains undone.

Another larger part has to do with the passive nature of watching television. Children can just sit and "veg" out. Scientists conducted a recent study on the use of calories and concluded that children watching television burn fewer calories than children sitting and DOING NOTHING!

Watching television can almost place a child in a trance, causing all body functions to slow. Passivity does not lead to effective learning. Unless the learner exerts some effort, invests some energy, and builds on connections with prior knowledge and experience, learning is weak. Learning to "just sit by and watch" is not an effective school trait.

Finally, what children watch may have a negative impact on learning. We read that actors claim that the violence in television merely mirrors that violence in society. This claim is used to prove that television doesn't TEACH violence. In fact, however, many of our children do not see the level of violence depicted in many television programs as part of their everyday lives (fortunately). Therefore, they may be learning more violence by watching shootings, killings, poisonings, etc., on television. But aren't children naturally violent? Don't children who own no guns or other weapons create them out of Leggos, Tinkertoys, or other seemingly harmless objects? The answer to both questions is yes. But, do we really want to increase these tendencies or encourage more serious violence in children's play? Probably not.

Passively sitting, possibly learning that violence is a good, or at least satisfying, way to cope with the world, does not enhance your child's ability to succeed in school. We want children to build, not destroy. We want children to actively join in their learning, owning the knowledge they gain. We want children to grow up to be able to make decisions and control some of what happens to them.

Would a good parent eliminate television from a child's experiences? Probably not. Once in a while, a good trance may be very restful for a child! (And the child's parent!) It is also true that some television is entertaining, some educational, and some even fun. What experts in child development suggest is judicial use of television. The amount of time at any one sitting should be limited. The total amount of time watching television each day should also be limited.

If you created the costume box suggested at Christmastime, you might find that certain television programs stimulate your children to join in as members of the cast. Other programs result in children doing something other than being passive. For young children, *Mister Rogers* prompts speaking, dancing, and answering. For young children up to about five, *Barney and Lamb Chop's Sing-Along* may do the same. Older children may make projects under the direction of "Doc" Brown from *Back to the Future*. Future chefs can benefit from taping the *Frugal Gourmet* and then actually cooking while watching the tape, stopping as needed to coordinate materials, etc. Other television shows are good for starting conversations among family members, and many shows should be watched ONLY when parents are at least nearby to answer questions, explain vocabulary, and comment on the behavior of characters. Television may even be a starting point for instruction (Kelley & Gunter, 1996; Metheny, 1996; National Education Association, 1987c).

Many classics make their way to television. Using the television guide can be a good use of parent time, and it can help the family avoid keeping the television on all day and night and clicking endlessly "looking for something good." Just turn the television on when you already know what you are looking for and turn it off when that program is over.

What about seasonal specials? Just so much corn pone? Hogwash? To tell you the truth, they are a lot more real than the commercials that are interspersed, with increasing frequency toward the end of the story, throughout the shows.

You don't think you can stand another Charlie Brown Halloween saga or a hankie ringer with Dolly Parton? When was the last time you really watched these things?

Actually, the stories in the seasonal specials, while sometimes contrived to come out all right in the end, are quite wholesome and teach some of the values that parents most lament are unavailable on television.

Families support each other or rediscover the important links that hold us together. Neighbors know each other by name or learn to by the end of the show. People regularly find out how much more important human kindness is that giving lavish gifts (and owing huge amounts on the old credit card later).

These "corny" ideas have a place in the lives of children. I was proud to see that the first goal cited by two of my children for this academic year was "helping others." Maybe a few more holiday specials and a few less Mortal Kombats would do our children a world of good.

And what about us old folks? A little less cynicism and a lot less violence could do us some good, too. Our lives are so hectic; I wonder how often we talk to our friends about good deeds, community and caring? Without sharing these ideas with friends we may lose the sense that such things are important.

We need to feel supported in choices that we make. When you buy one less laundry detergent that is on sale so that you can buy seven cans of soup for your local food pantry, you need to know that others make those same choices. You need to have your choice affirmed.

If your life is too hectic to talk to others about such sacrifices, a TV show may offer you examples of "comrades" who choose to do as you do. It's not as good as talking with a friend, but at least we are provided with some sense that we do not act alone.

Christmas and other seasonal specials also serve as opportunities for family television watching. Watching the same show each year can be pretty amazing too, as you listen to what your children remember and what new things they understand because they are older and can see a more subtle point.

Many adults are wrecked by early evening. Numb clothes folding in front of the television or low level mail sorting may be all we can manage. Doing such mundane tasks in the presence of family members while you share television viewing can be uniting.

Finally, conversation and snacking during commercials can help reduce the impact of heavy advertising on bombarded brains. Thus, we can emphasize the "corny" messages of giving, learning to sacrifice, believing in something bigger and better than ourselves, and celebrating community over the messages of "shop 'til you drop" commercialization and "rush, rush, rush—there are only x days until Christmas."

Bake a plate of cookies, have a cup of tea and enjoy these holiday specials with friends and family who mean so much to you.

DAYTIME DRAMA

What is the role of **drama** in family life and children's learning? Considering that most of our life stories are in the running for soap opera plots, it is easy to see that drama has a central part in our lives.

Not only are there our own dramas as our lives play out, but there is also the drama that we observe on television. Consider how many hours per day you watch television? What about each child that lives at your address? How many televisions live at your address with you? On them, we observe the drama of police and doctor stories, the drama of live sports, and the drama of movies, comedies and series.

You probably find that your favorite preachers and singers are also those who are dramatic, really catching your attention and motivating you to stay attentive. Drama may take the form of a story that reaches into the heart or speaking with inflection (softly, loudly, using accents) or adding gestures.

If drama is such a natural interest of humans, why not use it to our advantage in parenting? A bit of inflection can command the attention of your off-spring, especially whispering. What child would not be interested in something that's supposed to be a secret? Unfortunately, our first inclination may be to **raise** our voices. While this may attract attention for a moment, if yelling is overused, children will just learn to tune it out. Varied volume, sometimes loud, sometimes soft, will bring the most consistent attention.

It's true that drama alone may not be sufficient. Sometimes we have to be sure that we are the only show in town. This means turning off the television when you want a child to hear you so that the child is not torn between a few of your words and many from the television. This results in the child not responding to you and also being angry that the meaning of the show was interrupted.

Turning off the television to communicate with your child doesn't have to be done rudely. It is important to be courteous to children as well as adults, especially because we want to teach courtesy. It's good to try, when you can, to wait until a commercial or for the show to be over before your turn off the television to chat with your child.

Drama also has a place in your affection for your child. As children get older, they sometimes balk at letting us cuddle, hug or kiss them. Making it dramatic, such as chasing them around for a hug, pretending you won a kiss at a game show and screaming with joy, or singing a silly song about your love for your child, may make the moment ridiculous and lead to laughing, but also display the undercurrent of continuous affection you have for your child.

Television can even be educational, especially if your child does not just sit like a couch potato. Let your children wear costumes or get props to match the characters they are watching. In this way, your children's television experience is more interactive and more likely to result in learning, instead of passive entertainment (National Education Association, 1987c).

Drama may also have a place in your child's education (Lindquist, 1996). Add a zeal and excitement to your study of math facts or geometry theorems by announcing their start in a radio announcer's voice. Adding melody, rap or choral reading (two or more voices at a time) may make repetition palatable and even useful.

Watching dramas or plays of any kind may also be educational. Look to community theaters, park district efforts, church plays, professional theater, and school dramas. Seeing a play is entirely different than seeing a television program or even a movie. These experiences with "up close and personal" theater inspire children to think of the motivations and behaviors of others; what makes people act as they do?

Live theater also demands more extended periods of listening comprehension. You can't rewind and it is not acceptable theater behavior to loudly check with the person next to you about what just happened. These parameters cause children to develop greater maturity and listening skills, both good goals for developing learners.

Performing on stage can also be a boost to children. Many children are born with exaggerated, theatrical behavior and may really enjoy portraying that on stage. Others may benefit in terms of self-esteem from their assessment of their ability to memorize lines, stand in the right place and "catch" the audience. Cautions and adult support are necessary when tryouts or limited character time are included (Bock, 1995); children need to be prepared for new experiences, particularly those in which they will be judged.

Add a little drama to your life! I'm not suggesting that you beat your children, burn your husband in his bed, etc. Those are types of drama we can do without. The drama I'm recommending will add to your ability to communicate with your children. You and your children can get more power out of study times as well as enjoy some live theater and the conversation that occurs based on plays and musicals. Be dramatic and spice up your life!

DISCIPLINE

Parents often struggle with discipline (Farner, 1996). What do children have a right to do? What is a mistake and what is misbehavior? If it is determined that there is misbehavior, how should a parent react? The following suggestions might be subtitled: *Who's the Boss? Home Management of Behavior in Children aged 3-12.*

1. **Set reasonable expectations.** Use a sensible book to get ideas. Listen to your child. Watch the results of limits and expectations you have set. Check misbehavior for the possibility that the child cannot behave under the conditions.

For instance, expecting children to be absolutely still and quiet during a long church service may be beyond what a young child can do. Bring heavy cardboard sewing cards. Buy a picture book of what happens during a church service in your faith, so that the child can match the unfolding events with the book. Bring books for children from a religious bookstore so that the pictures and words they are following at least have something in common with the theme of the service.

2. **Provide structure.** Provide structure in terms of TIME. Set and, for the most part, keep a consistent time for going to bed. Select at least one meal a day, and try to keep it at the same time and have every family member present. Choose a certain time for homework or study and use the same schedule Sunday through Thursday. Limit the amount of time at any one setting that children watch television.

Provide structure in terms of ROUTINE. Create and employ a routine for bedtime. For all ages of children, it is important to include books or stories. Read to children, let them read to you, exchange stories about the day and tell stories based just on the illustrations in books. Include singing, especially songs that tell stories. Don't worry about bad singing voices; it's the love and the lyrics that count!

Create a routine for setting the table, washing dishes, taking baths, doing homework, taking out the garbage, doing yard work, etc. The more consistent you are in delivery, the less balking you get each time you need to get things done.

Provide structure in terms of DISCIPLINE. Create a set of rules so that children know what is expected. Try to make the consequences "fit the crime," by deciding in advance so that you don't act in anger. Be willing to say no if you have decided in your adult judgment that what the child is asking is unreasonable. Children deserve choices, but adults should provide limits for those choices (Williams, 1987).

3. **Teach responsibility.** Model keeping commitments. Explain that sometimes you can't keep commitments and tell children how to explain to the person you are letting down.

4. **Encourage decision making.** Model thinking aloud. Propose logical consequences (what will happen if...) and use questions to get your child thinking about decisions.

5. **Follow through.** Be consistent. Employ logical consequences. Keep track; is there improvement? Make sure you say so!

6. **Use humor.** It is easier to back out of a tight spot or difficult moment with grace when humor is employed. Insisting that someone—even a child—do what you say while you stare them down as they do it creates a win-lose situation. Allow the child some dignity; look away for a moment after demanding or insisting on something. Praise work in the right direction and laugh about the conflict later.

7. **Use physical contact.** Often a hug, pat on the shoulder, kiss, or arm around a shoulder can defuse a standoff. Your love for your child can be expressed in a physical way and actually physically "break the ice" of conflict.

8. **Be forgiving.** Parenting is tough, so is growing up! Model forgiveness and self- forgiveness (Williams, 1987). Model self-praise and praise your child a lot.

REFERENCES

Albrecht, K. (1996). Reggio Emilia: Four key ideas. *Texas Child Care, 20*(2), 2-81.

Bauer, K. L. (1990). *Helping children deal with stress.* Washington, DC: National Education Association.

Becker, K. (1996). Halloween. *Saint Xavier University Parent Educator, 1*(9), 1.

Berger, M. (1984). *Space shots, shuttles and satellites.* New York: Putnam.

Bock, W. H. (1995). Tryouts without tears. *Learning, 24*(3), 62-63.

Butler, L. F. (1996). Gymnastics in the elementary school: What works. *Strategies, 9*(5), 5-7.

Coopersmith, S. (1967). *The antecedents of self-esteem.* San Francisco: W. H. Freeman.

Eysenck, M. (1994). *Individual differences: Normal and abnormal.* Hillsdale, NY: Erlbaum Associates.

Farner, C. D. (1996). Discipline alternatives: Mending the broken circle. *Learning, 25*(1), 27-29.

Fried, S., & Fried, P. (1996). *Bullies and victims: Helping your child through the school yard battlefield.* New York: Evans & Co.

Foltz-Gray, D. (1996). The bully trap: Young tormentors and their victims find ways out of anger and isolation. *Teaching Tolerance, 5*(2), 18-23.

Gardner, B. (1988). Chez les petits. *Instructor, 97*(5), 76-77.

Girard, S. (1996). *Partnerships for classroom learning: From reading buddies to pen pals to the community and the world beyond.* Markham, Ontario: Pembroke Publishers.

Hart, B. (1995). *Meaningful differences in the everyday experiences of young American Children.* Baltimore: P. H. Brooke.

Heyns, B. L. (1978). *Summer learning and the effects of schooling.* New York: Academic Press.

International Reading Association. (1980). *Your home is your child's first school.* Newark, DE: Author.

Kelley, P., & Gunter, B. (1996). Helping viewers learn from television: A new approach to increasing the impact of the medium. *Journal of Educational Media, 22*(1), 23-39.

Kronowitz, E. (1985). From customs to classroom. *Social Studies Review, 24*(3), 68-73.

Lambert, M. (1983). *50 facts about space.* New York: Warwick Press.

Landfried, S. E. (1989). *Ways to listen more effectively to your kids.* Washington, DC: National Education Association.

Lesko, D. S. (1996). Adolescent depressed mood and parental unhappiness. *Adolescence, 31*(121), 49-57.

Lindquist, T. (1996). Social studies now: Use simple puppets to connect to core subjects. *Instructor, 106*(1), 91-92.

Maslow, A. H. (1987). *Motivation and personality.* New York: Harper & Row.

McClure, L. (1977). *Experience-based learning: How to make the community your class-room.* Portland, OR: Northwest Regional Educational Laboratory.

McNamara, A. (1996). Response to "parenting for independence." *NAMTA Journal, 21*(2), 197-200.

Metheny, D. (1996). Investigations: Learning to "ad." *Teaching Children Mathematics, 2*(5), 284-288.

Nabors, M. L., & Edwards, L. C. (1996). Creativity and the child's social development. *Dimensions of Early Childhood, 23*(1), 14-16.

National Conference for Human Relations. (1994). *Appreciating differences: A resource manual.* Chicago, IL: The National Conference Chicago Northwest IL Region.

National Education Association. (1987a). *How to understand your child's development.* Washington, DC: Author.

National Education Association. (1987b). *Pressures on children and youth.* Washington, DC: Author.

National Education Association. (1987c). *TV, reading and writing.* Washington, DC: Author.

Owens, T. J. (1996). Self-determination as a source of self-esteem in adolescence. *Social Forces, 74*(4), 1377-1404.

Partridge, E. (1996). Cooking up mathematics in the kindergarten. *Teaching Children Mathematics, 2*(8), 492-95.

Phelan, T. W. (1989). *All about attention deficit disorder.* Glen Ellyn, IL: Child Management, Inc.

Salk, L. (1969). *How to raise a human being: A parents' guide to emotional health from infancy through adolescence.* New York: Random House.

Seven steps to help a child avert bullies. (1996, September). *Chicago Parent,* p. 27.

Stark, R. E. (1989). Early language intervention: When, why, how. *Infants and Young Children, 1*(4), 44-53.

Sylwester, R. (1995). *A celebration of neurons: An educator's guide to the human brain.* Alexandria, VA: Association for Supervision and Curriculum Development.

Texas Child Care. (1996). Puppets and stages: Tools of imaginative play. *Texas Child Care, 20*(1), 22-28.

Walberg, H.J., Paschal, R.A., & Weinstein, T. (1985). Homework's powerful effects on learning. *Educational Leadership, 42*(7).

White, B. (1995). *The new first three years of life.* New York: Fireside.

Williams, J. L. (1987). *Discipline that works.* Washington, DC: National Education Association.

Wolfson, A. (1992). Effects of parent training on infant sleeping patterns, parents' stress, and perceived parental competence. *Journal of Consulting and Clinical Psychology, 60*(1), 41-48.

Zaichkowsky, L. D., & Larson, G. A. (1995). Physical, motor, and fitness development in children and adolescents. *Journal of Education, 177*(2), 55-79.

Section Four

FAMILY LINKS WITH SCHOOL

Chapter 19

FUNDING SCHOOLS

You have been hearing a lot lately about the least appealing aspect of schooling in any community: **paying for schools.** First, it is most important for communities to realize that the education of their youth is not the sole responsibility of the parents of school age children. When school boards are comprised only of parents of children attending school, or when only parents of children in school speak up about education, we give the impression that schools belong only to current students. Youths do not live exclusively in their homes with their families. They spend time in the streets, playgrounds, businesses, churches, yards, and arcades of the community. Each person living in a community has contact with the products of the community's educational institutions. Some might believe that because their children are grown, they don't have to invest in the youth in the community, but that means they are ignoring their daily contact with children attending the community's schools.

It is not cheap to educate young people. Buildings must be built, maintained, cleaned, remodeled, and stocked with soap, toilet paper and paper towels. Cleaning supplies, construction paper, writing paper, typewriters, computers, books, basketballs, tambourines, markers, counting sticks, globes, tape recorders, and microscopes, to name a few supplies, must be purchased. Heat, phones, electricity and other utilities are necessary for each building. Teachers, principals, nurses, typists, secretaries, and other staff members must be paid salaries. Imagine if you had 30 children in your family, what your grocery and other bills would be! How many classes of 30 are there in your district?

What about the federal and state government? When the central government was formed at the beginning of the history of the United States, the states did not want to relinquish control over schools to the federal government. At that time, the states assumed responsibility for education. Over the centuries since then, the federal government has provided a portion of the

181

funding for education. The states have also continued to fund education, but at declining percentages of actual costs. That leaves individual districts to make up the balance of the funds necessary with local revenue sources.

Many districts use property taxes. Property taxes are thought to be fairer than some other forms of revenue because those who can afford larger, more expensive homes or properties pay more than those who can afford smaller homes or properties.   Some people assert that property taxes are unfair, however, because communities are often made up of similar housing stock. Therefore, all of the homes in a particular community may be relatively modest and bring in modest property tax revenues. All of the homes in another community may be spacious and expensive, bringing in a radically different type of revenue. Thus, richer communities have more money for education while poorer communities have less money.

Some states use primarily sales tax revenues. In this way, advocates say, taxes are proportionate to what you apparently have the money to buy. States then divide up the statewide sales tax revenues at some per child rate, making more equity across the state. Other states have tried lottery systems or combined with other states to make "big games." In some states, the state revenue from lotteries was to go exclusively to fund education. In other states, a portion of gambling money come to education coffers. In general, the problems of funding education and doing so equitably are large concerns for state legislatures.

Every reader is aware that costs for everything have gone up. Grocery bills, utility bills...the list is endless. We look for ways to conserve our personal revenues. Holding the line on property taxes or sales taxes may seem appealing. But it is unrealistic to expect a community's most important resource—its youth—to be educated on the same budget dollars from a decade or more ago when families cannot raise children or feed them on similar budget dollars.

Consider your individual responsibility to the schools of your community, whether you have children enrolled in those schools or not. Consider the real, not frivolous, costs associated with operating a quality school system. Consider raising your voice to improve the school system as a board member, concerned citizen, community volunteer in a local school, or taxpayer (National Education Association, 1987f).

Chapter 20

SCHOOL SELECTION

A re you facing the decision of schools for your kindergartner, first grader, or high school freshman? The high school entrance exams are often scheduled for private high schools in January and private elementary school registration begins in the spring. What about your local public schools? How does a parent choose?

The National Education Association (1987g) has prepared a pamphlet with many suggestions for helping you make a **school selection.** Some guidelines apply to all schools, others just to secondary schools, and others just to elementary schools. To obtain the information suggested in the guidelines, a school visit may be necessary. Contact the building principal to make arrangements.

ALL LEVELS: KINDERGARTEN THROUGH HIGH SCHOOL

The NEA (1987g) maintains, in general, that a good school provides:

1. One professional staff person for every 15 to 20 students. In addition, there should be a sufficient number of paraprofessional staff (aides, secretaries, custodial staff, etc.) to relieve teachers of non-teaching duties.

2. Individual attention in every classroom to the needs of individual students, including continuous assessment of individual potential and achievement (sampled in more than one way).

3. A broad curriculum to develop all aspects of students (intellectual, social, emotional, physical, and vocational competence). School programs should be reviewed by professional staff. Coordination of elementary and secondary programs should occur.

183

4. A staff of "enthusiastic, alert" teachers with a coordinated program for continuing training of teachers and faculty. The NEA suggests that all teachers meet state teacher certification requirements.

5. A written personnel policy including salary schedule and fringe benefit package.

6. A professionally staffed library with a balanced supply of good learning materials.

7. Teachers who nurture many kinds of skills.

8. A safe, efficient, pleasant building, kept in good condition, with enough space for all of the functions of the school.

9. Superior administrative leadership that encourages good teaching and open communication among faculty, parents, the public, and the leadership. The administration should be receptive to change, manage responsibilities well and encourage experimentation.

10. An atmosphere for intercultural understanding and use of instructional materials that portray women, men, and minorities realistically.

ELEMENTARY SCHOOLS

The National Education Association (1987g) states that good **elementary** schools:

1. Provide opportunities for each child to learn to read well, to communicate effectively orally and in writing, and to develop an understanding of elementary mathematics, science and social studies. They offer instruction and a chance for each child to express the self in fine arts and physical activity.

2. Respond to the fact that children learn at different rates by providing flexible organization, individualized instruction and opportunities for teachers to vary their methods and materials.

3. Relate learning to the real world of the child.

4. Provide learning experiences beyond the classroom and the school building.

5. Provide opportunities for children to practice and learn skills of effective group living and to develop a sense of values.

6. Are responsive to the needs of the child that arise from conditions in the the home, neighborhood and community.

7. Provide textbooks and other teaching materials free from racial and sexual stereotypes.

SECONDARY SCHOOLS

Finally, the National Education Association (1987g) maintains that good **secondary** schools:

1. Maintain optimum size. Junior high and middle schools should have about 500-800 students. The high school should be large enough to permit a comprehensive curriculum and broad activities.
2. Provide adequate guidance services with about one guidance specialist for every 250-300 students.
3. Set meaningful goals for the entire program.
4. Require all students to study English, social studies, mathematics, science, physical education, and fine arts. Students should have opportunities for rational discussion of controversial issues and social problems.
5. Provide for continuing relationships between teachers and students.
6. Employ flexible groups and scheduling methods.
7. Provide textbooks and other teaching materials free from racial and sexual stereotypes.
8. Make every effort to encourage students to continue their studies until they have completed high school and even higher levels of education so that they can achieve their goals and be responsible citizens.

The National Association of Secondary School Principals (1996) describes its recommendations for the best in high schools, based on extensive research in adolescent development and school design. A list of priorities (some quite revolutionary and perhaps implemented at very few high schools) emerges:

1. High schools should identify a set of essential learnings (particularly in literature and language, mathematics, social studies, science and the arts) in which students must demonstrate achievement in order to graduate. These curriculum areas should be integrated to the extent possible and emphasize depth of learning over breadth of coverage.
2. Teachers should design work to engage students, cause them to persist, and become successful. Assessment should be aligned with the curriculum. Each student should have a personal plan for progress. Cocurricular activities should be promoted (notice the emphasis on the equal value of non-academic with academic pursuits in the value of the experience to the adolescents by the shift away from "extracurricular" to COcurricular). High schools should reach out to the elementary and

middle schools that graduate students to the high school to form a connection for the successful transition of students from lower schools to
high school.

3. High school teachers should have a broad base of academic knowledge
    as well as depth in at least one subject. Teachers should know and use
    a number of instructional strategies. Teachers should help students
    become competent problem solvers, critical thinkers, and technology
    users. Teachers should convey caring, act as facilitators of learning, and
    integrate assessment into instruction.

4. High schools should be safe, clean, attractive, well-equipped places,
    where core values of a democratic society are practiced, students are
    encouraged in multiple talents, students participate in decision-making,
    and students each have a personal adult advocate (see teacher advisory
    model under Middle Schools).

5. High schools should create small units, within which students are not
    just anonymous numbers; teachers should be responsible for contact
    time with no more than 90 students in a term, in order to meet students'
    individual needs. The academic program should extend beyond the
    high school campus; high schools should use alternatives to ability
    tracking, and traditional discipline departments should be redefined in
    order to better accommodate integrated curricular study.

6. High schools should guarantee that graduates can meet performance
    standards in entry-level jobs, or those graduates should be allowed to
    return to school for additional studies. Schools will engage in ongoing
    supervision of personnel, and the highest standards should be used as
    criteria against which to evaluate teachers, principals, and all other staff
    members.

7. High schools should be communities of learners, where teachers have
    personal learning plans, where schools provide for the ongoing profes-
    sional growth of their teachers, and where support staff are encouraged
    and assisted in their career growth, too.

8. High school curriculums should expose students to a rich array of view
    points, experiences and perspectives, and high schools should employ
    practices, policies and decisions that recognize diversity, provide for
    diversity in staff, and offer professional development for staff to help
    them deal with issues of diversity.

9. High schools should have on-site advisory boards of persons who will
    make sure there is contact and communication with the community.
    Partnerships with institutions of higher education should be built.

You may choose a school that does not meet some of these requirements because you are willing to trade them for other things more important to your family or the child. Perhaps you want religious training or you want the school to be in the neighborhood. Once your child is enrolled, you may work with the school and support organizations, such as the Parent-Teacher Association or the school board, to improve the school to meet the standards most important to you.

PREKINDERGARTEN SCHOOLS

What about those of you who are faced with selecting a school for your **preschool** age child? These guidelines may be helpful for you.

When you choose a preschool, you may definitely want the school to be church affiliated or multiethnic. Or perhaps you are most interested in the location or the hours. If these factors do not influence you or they are not the most important considerations, you might be interested instead in the philosophy of the program that is offered.

One philosophy is **child centered.** In this model, children discover and learn on their own from interaction with other children, the teacher, and carefully selected materials. Children appear to be "playing" which some adults think means that they are not learning. This is not necessarily true. Children often learn well through the medium of play (Brenner, 1990).

Another philosophy is called **teacher directed.** The activities of each school day are planned and carried out by teachers. Routines and academic preparation are emphasized. Children in teacher-directed settings look very much like older children in regular classrooms, just younger (Brenner, 1990).

A third type of preschool is often termed **developmental** or **developmental interactionist.** Teachers and children form a learn/play partnership. Teachers plan some activities and provide a routine schedule. For blocks of time, students choose their own activities and initiate learning and play under teacher supervision (Brenner, 1990).

Philosophy is not the only issue to consider when looking for a match between your child and a school. You probably also want to consider your child's tolerance level. Your own observation and instincts about your child may help you determine whether a full-day program or some form of part-time attendance is more appropriate.

Cost may also influence your decision. Many parents would choose not to work if all of the earnings go only to support the cost of preschool. Community preschools (operated by the park district, church groups, etc.) have low fees or sliding-scale fees (matched to family income). There may even be a scholarship fund. Cooperative preschools could he staffed with a small professional staff plus parents on regular volunteer schedules to keep costs down.

Parents sometimes have very strong value systems that they want reflected in the teachings of a school. Most public and non-church-affiliated schools teach what might be called secular humanism values. These include sharing, playing fair, following rules set for the greater good, cooperation over competition, to name a few. The types of books read aloud to children and classroom rules are based on these values. Parents who do not agree with these values sometimes choose to **home school** (families apply to county boards of education to assume responsibility for the academic instruction of their children) or create schools with friends or relatives who hold values similar to those of the family.

The time of school may also be important for coordinating with the family. One of my brothers worked on a 10:00 a.m. to 8:00 p.m. away-from-home schedule. The family ate dinner after he came home and then spent some time together. A 7:45 a.m. school day start (necessitating that the family get up at 6:00 or so) was not the best for a family getting to bed well after 10:00 p.m. School should enrich a child's experiences, not result in family chaos. Fortunately, an afternoon kindergarten was an option. For this family, this choice made the most sense in light of the other parameters of their lives.

The qualifications of teachers may also be of interest to parents. Credentials such as college degrees, years of experience, etc., may be considered. In addition, parents should probably observe at the school to see if they like what goes on, and the way children are valued and treated.

Good luck in your search for a good education for your child!

Books that may help you choose schools include:

Brenner, B. (1990). *The preschool handbook: Making the most of your child's education.* New York: Pantheon Books.
National Association of Secondary School Principals. (1996). *Breaking ranks: Changing an American institution.* Reston, VA: Author.

Chapter 21

PARENT INVOLVEMENT IN SCHOOLS

There are any number of roles that parents can play with regard to the learning their children do in school (NEA, 1987a). The continuum should include "passive" and "supportive" as well as "active" participation strategies to accommodate every family and parent type, and to meet a variety of family needs and times frames (Carroll & Smith, 1990).

PASSIVE PARENT INVOLVEMENT

Choose from this list the **passive parent involvement** in schools that makes you feel comfortable:

1. Read and discuss school newsletters and announcements with your child (Clark, 1996; Jones, R., 1996).
2. Receive school phone calls and notes; respond as appropriate.
3. Review your child's home-school folder and return it to school with comments (Sui-Chu & Willms, 1996). (A home-school folder is a neat way of making sure both teachers and parents expect some papers back and forth at least once a week.)
4. Attend school open houses and children's productions, such as plays, art exhibits, and concerts (Sanders, 1996).
5. Observe in classrooms.
6. Listen to your child read at home (Butler, 1988).
7. Help your child get started and follow through on homework.
8. Proofread your child's written assignments.
9. Assist your child in finding materials at the library, learning to type, or learning any other skill that will aid school learning.

10. Engage your child in conversation about school. Isn't it hard to believe that every child sits in school all day every day after the age of five and does "nothing" (by their own report)? Use humor to get your child to give you a more complete response to your questions about what happened in school.

As you can see, there is nothing passive about these activities. They require time and effort from parents who have numerous other responsibilities. The strategies are merely called passive because they do not require excessive interaction with school or teachers during school days. That may make these strategies somewhat easier to implement for parents who work during school hours or who have had negative experiences in school themselves.

Research on parent involvement in the learning of children suggests that a little consistent effort makes a tremendous difference in the success of the child in the classroom (Dalton, 1996; Sui-Chu & Willms, 1996). Fortunately, helping children learn is the gift that keeps on giving!

SUPPORTIVE PARENT INVOLVEMENT

Supportive involvement strategies often include participation in activities that influence the learning of children without taking on a leadership role. However, many supportive involvement activities take place at the school and some occur during school hours. Choose from among the following:

1. Participate in parent-teacher conferences.
2. Help organize parent meetings, school shows or academic fairs (for examples, science fairs).
3. Write reports for the school newsletter (Clark, 1996; Jones, R., 1996).
4. Serve as a classroom resource person or a field trip guide (Fehlig, 1996).
5. Participate in parent education programs.
6. Assist in the classroom or library.
7. Host a student club or parent club in your home.
8. Create a parent information center or bulletin board in the school, where parents picking up children or conducting other school-related business are able to see it.

ACTIVE PARTICIPATION STRATEGIES

The last type of parent involvement in the education of children can be termed active participation strategies. These involve parents taking a teaching role with their children or a leadership role in helping other parents become involved in education (Ellis, 1996; Epstein & Hollifield, 1996; Young Children, 1996). The following is a partial list of strategies:

1. Organize a policymaking group, such as a cultural pluralism, environmental awareness or community action council.
2. Serve as an officer in the parent-teacher organization or the home-school council.
3. Serve on a district curriculum committee or program and textbook review committee.
4. Lead a parent special-interest group.
5. Seek election to the school board.
6. Serve on a parent advisory committee to provide representative input to school or district officials.
7. Plan and lead classes for children, in collaboration with the teacher (NEA, 1987a).
8. Help organize special events, such as a career awareness fair.
9. Act as an auxiliary teacher in your child's classroom (NEA, 1987a).
10. Set up a parent center.
11. Act as a tutor to individual students or to a small group of students.
12. Create learning materials for the teachers at your school. For example, create questions that go with the specific computer encyclopedia the school has instead of using generic worksheets of questions that result in so much frustration for novice computing students. They don't know if they can't find the answer because it isn't there or because they have not looked in the right place!

Once you see a list like this, it is likely you will think of other strategies or activities along these lines that may suit you as an individual. The list is designed merely to stimulate your thinking.

Each school and district is quite individual. It may take a little research to find out which school person to go to when you want to get involved. In some schools, teachers are very autonomous; approaching them individually to work out a plan is the best. In other districts, formal arrangements are made through the superintendent's or principal's office (NEA, 1987a).

Setting up a parent center can empower other parents to get involved in school or the learning of their children too (McDonald, 1996). A parent center might be a place to store support materials for parenting. These materials could include reference books on topics of interest to parents: books on learning, motivation, homework, child development, discipline, special learning needs, etc. Issues of magazines related to parent interests (Parents, Exceptional Parent, Psychology Today, etc.) could he housed in the center as well.

Media of various types could also find a home in a parent center. Videotapes on parenting, child development, home health issues, child safety, etc., could be made available on a short-term loan basis, similar to a library. Audiotapes on similar topics could also be borrowed for use in family tape machines or car tape players. A parent center might serve as a clearinghouse for families. Parents could "register" in a ring binder to list areas of their expertise which they would be willing to provide to others, to trade services with another family or to ask for assistance. Users could quickly scan the list for another person with the appropriate need or skill. For instance, one parent might need a math tutor for his seventh grade daughter and trade services with another parent who could tutor in math but needed some prepared dinners two nights a week.

A parent center would need volunteers to sort and file information as well as to determine needs and order materials. Volunteers would also be needed to raise funds or to tap local parent-teacher organizations for funds to pay for purchases. With a sufficient number of volunteers, it also might be possible to schedule various speakers and consultants to provide professional services to parents who use the center.

It is critical for parents to see the ongoing nature of their relationship with schools on behalf of their children. It is also important once parents have gotten involved (by coming to a parent-teacher conference or attending a parent training session, etc.) to foster that involvement and provide support for continued involvement. A parent center, coordinated and staffed primarily by parents, might do just that.

Chapter 22

ACADEMIC FAIRS AND
PARENT INVOLVEMENT

Participation in **academic fairs** is sometimes a real challenge for parents. The focus should be on learning, independence and follow-through, rather than on competitiveness. The most common kind of academic fair is the science fair. Here are a few tips, many of which may easily be applied to any other areas of academic study (e.g., history fairs, math fairs, etc.).

SCIENCE FAIRS

Getting started on a project for a **science fair** is the hardest part. Be sure to let your child know that you value and support school work. Be sure NOT to do the work of the project. Who is supposed to benefit from the learning anyway?

In general, steer children away from dioramas and reports. Good science experiments require children to solve problems. Consider creating learning centers at which children can explore scientific questions. This means using a table in the playroom or a shelf on a bookshelf and making a particular set of materials available for perhaps a week at a time. Having children use a jelly roll pan or the cardboard supporter for 24 cans of pop (that most generic varieties of pop usually come in covered by shrink plastic) under their scientific works may preserve your floor and table from destruction.

Here are two learning centers you could set up at home to "get things started":

1. **Magnet center:** two bar magnets, a horseshoe magnet, iron filings, a variety of metal and non-metal objects.

Q. How will two bar magnets react to each other?
   (Similarly charged ends will repel, opposites attract.)

193

Q. What will a magnet attract? (Steel and iron are best)

Q. Will a horseshoe magnet attract iron filings through a hand?
   (Yes, it has a strong enough pull.)

2. **Paper airplane center:** paper, paper clips, tape, scissors, measuring tape.

Q. What makes paper airplanes fly?
   (The shape of the plane causes air to move faster over the top so air pressure above the plane drops. This means more air pressure above the plane which keeps the plane aloft.)

Q. Does wing shape matter to distance flown?
   (The more streamlined, the more efficient. But there also must be enough wing to get enough air pressure under the plane to keep it up.)

Q. Will weight help?
   (If placed at the nose.)

Put a chart up on the center to record flight distance by various children. Encourage students to dig out facts. For experiments, encourage children to: (a) Use a control; (b) Keep careful records; and (c) Repeat test. If an experiment fails, encourage children to persist and find out why. This may result in the most learning.

Remind them that ordinary materials make fine displays. It is better to spend time on thinking and building rather than on nagging parents to procure hard-to-find materials. Avoid fancy lettering, borders or elaborate drawings. Concentrate on neat, clear and accurate charts and graphs. Use construction paper strips with words to glue onto poster board. If your child makes a mistake, remove that strip and replace. This doesn't waste the whole poster board.

If you are having trouble finding a topic, Markle and Cichowski (1983) suggest these questions that even professionals are pursuing as bases for experiments.

1. How can we generate electricity from solar energy?

2. How can we heat buildings with solar energy?

3. How can we forecast weather and natural disasters?

4. How do you build a bridge so it doesn't collapse?

5. What are pesticides? Can we grow food without them?

6. How can more food be raised on less land?

7. Where does water come from when you turn on a faucet? How can we save water?

8. How does the type of soil affect plant growth?

9. What can be done to slow rusting?

10. How do you teach a computer to solve problems?

11. What is a computer language?

12. How do you make a video game?

13. How does a robot work?

14. What are integrated circuits?

15. How does a computer compute?

16. How can we teach animals to behave in certain ways?

17. Why are there different kinds of dogs?

18. How can we prevent endangered animals from becoming extinct?

19. In what shape will water support the most weight?

20. How can cars be made safer?

21. How can cars be made to cause less air pollution?

22. How does overcrowding affect life in a terrarium?

23. What will stop soil erosion?

24. What will prevent mold growth?

25. How can we make light bend?

26. What can be done to protect a stream from becoming polluted?

27. What happens when an oil spill occurs in the ocean?

28. How does a pulley work?

29. What determines how fast water will evaporate?

30. What can be done to reduce friction? (p. 70).

How you interact and react when your child has a larger project, instead of individual assignments, is important. Setting aside time is difficult. Knowing how best to spend the time you have set aside is another challenge. Perhaps the suggestions above will be useful!

HISTORY FAIRS

History fairs are another area of academic exhibit that is growing. In the Chicago metropolitan area, for instance, the Metro History Fair has been held for decades. To participate in this fair, high school students conduct their own research on a topic dealing with family or community history. Many have chosen to do research on local businesses, architectural sites, locally famous persons, etc. The students, under the direction of their social studies teachers, determine ways to demonstrate what they have learned, through exhibits, essays, or performances. Judging takes place, beginning at the local level, much like traditional science fairs.

The use of history fairs encourages students to think of themselves as capable of primary research. Often the students learn more about aspects of their communities which encourages community pride and connectedness. Students practice social and oral language skills as they interview sources. They practice written language and organizational skills as they write up their reports and structure their demonstrations and exhibits. Fostering such a range of skill development contributes to the development of good self-esteem.

History fairs may also be constructed so that historical periods are recreated. In this design, students work together with faculty to engage in intensive study of a historical period. In one multidisciplinary unit, students in third through fifth grade experienced U.S. history at a five-day fair where different periods of history had been recreated (Deaton, 1990).

INVENTION CONVENTIONS

Invention conventions are another way for students to conduct their own research and engage in multiple skills development. These are usually designed so that students work alone or in pairs for a period of several weeks, with some time in school devoted to it and some time outside of school expected. Students as young as grade three dream up a product that may solve some problem they have observed in the world (how to reach the top of the van to wash your own car, how to make a sundae with a compact machine). The children collect materials and try to construct the invention.

The inventions are rounded up for an "Invention Convention" at which students display their inventions, explain to judges or alternatively parents and guests what they attempted to do, and sometimes demonstrate the working of their inventions (Robb, 1993). Often, students are asked to keep logs or journals indicating what they tried, how they came up with ideas, what things they discarded and why—just the kinds of things real scientists and inventors might do. The inventions do not necessarily have to work. The learning experience and following an experimental model is paramount.

Sometimes hassles arise. Children may have difficulty getting together outside of school time. Without serious parent commitment, children may get too frustrated or give up easily. Time and space must be given up from the curriculum and in the school for the convention itself. Awards may put undue emphasis on competition. In some cases, parents may do too much (all?!) of the work and a few students are unfairly awarded prizes. Solutions include partnerships with community organizations and businesses which may add motivation and interest for students (Robb, 1993). There is great learning potential in these kinds of experiences; if parents cannot devote enough supervisory time, perhaps students could work on the projects exclusively in school, relying on home only for the raw materials needed to build the inventions.

Another version of invention conventions is the **future fair,** which includes inventions that might be useful in the future, as students imagine the future to be. Critical thinking skills, use of current knowledge, and extrapolation of knowledge to take educated guesses about the future are fostered. Models, inventions, photo essays, and creative writing focused on art, fashions, space travel, future schools, and future life-styles were the projects developed by students in a future fair in South Carolina (Weatherly, 1992).

Chapter 23

PARENT-TEACHER CONFERENCES

Parent-teacher conferences are significant because they are the most commonly used opportunity for parents and teachers to collaborate. Communication is the key to their success (Vickers & Minke, 1995). The things you may choose to communicate about include your child's ability level, progress in each subject area of study, titles of books being used, social interactions and achievements, special interests and abilities demonstrated by your child in school, and discipline concerns (NEA, 1987c). Here are some suggestions for parents to follow. Parents, be sure to:

1. Treat the teacher as another adult, with respect.

2. Mention the strengths of the teacher as well as possible concerns that you have.

3. Be a good listener; your child's teacher sees a side of your child that you may not see. People behave differently with peers and in large groups.

4. Come to the conference without younger children or other people if possible (NEA, 1987c). If the "other people" have some role in raising the child, this is a different case and that person should be present. Be open to suggestions and activities; teachers and parents are excellent collaborators for the welfare of children.

5. Make a list of any specific questions you have about curriculum, text books, homework, or other aspects of school life. The few minutes allotted to a conference should be used efficiently (NEA, 1987d).

6. Call ahead to see about making an appointment with auxiliary personnel. Will the guidance counselor, PTA president or other support person with whom you would like to meet be available at the time of the conference, or will you have to make another appointment to see that person?

7. Be ready to roll up your shirt sleeves and do some work to improve

198

your child's learning–parents are still the persons primarily responsible for making sure that their children become educated.

8. Bring an interpreter (friend, relative) if there is a possibility that the teacher you will visit does not speak your native language and you are "limited English proficient" or unable to benefit from communication in English.

9. Take the opportunity to congratulate the teachers who have taught your children well.

10. Take a least one positive message from the teacher home to your child!

In addition, be cautious and DO NOT:

1. Tell the teacher that he or she is wrong.

2. Raise your voice.

3. Try to make the teacher responsible for any learning problems the child may be experiencing.

4. Take the blame for any problems in the child's learning yourself; focus on what can be done now to help the child, not to assign blame.

5. Refer to or compare your child to other children; this child is an individual. Besides, confidentiality is important–the teacher cannot discuss another child with you. If the "other child" is another of your children, separate the conference into two parts: one for Child A and one for Child B.

6. Belittle the personality or teaching style of the teacher. The miracle of school is that our children have access to diverse teaching styles, contents, personalities, and strengths. This varied experience is part of the richness of learning.

7. Try to get all of your needs met in the conference. Teachers are not social workers or therapists.

8. Do all of the talking; be sure to listen.

You hold a significant key to the education of your youngsters in the partnership you form with teachers. Have a good conference!

Chapter 24

GOING TO SCHOOL

STARTING SCHOOL

Time to **start school**? For the first time? For a new academic year? Truth be told, there are at least a few students looking forward to school. And they are not all "A" students. What factors cause children to like or dislike school? Are there any of those factors that parents can influence to the good?

One thing that makes school appeal to most children is the ready assortment of children of the same age. On your block or even in the few blocks in any direction from your home, there may be few children of the right age for your child. And, what with people moving in and out, a "good block" for your child at one age can become a dismal place for your child at another age. School, however, offers a whole class full of students within a year or two of your child's age. Relationships can be forged and after-school plans made.

For children with poor social skills, however, the promise of new friendships doesn't always pan out. Make time to talk with your child about school and making friends. If your child is struggling, you may detect a pattern as your child describe attempts to reach out. Do you suspect that you child is too bossy, insists on her own way too much, is too shy to initiate a conversation, or forgets to listen enough? Talk over ways to improve. Model good social interaction. Practice new ways of communicating by role playing with your child.

School may also appeal to your child because of the schedule and the structure. Children are not usually comfortable with lots of surprises. They make them feel off guard and insecure. (Of course, a few surprises—birthday presents, relatives who haven't visited in awhile—keeps life thrilling!)

Because schools have to coordinate the movements of large numbers of people, schools use routines. Many children find these routines comfortable and empowering. Even young children love to tell "what comes next" in a typical school day. Older children "psych themselves up" for fourth period math or a spelling test because they hold the information to predict such things.

That's why summer, although it's fun, can also be stressful to some children. The routine is less apparent, so children don't feel control over their experiences. Begin to build toward the school routine in August, by starting to be consistent about bedtime, perhaps moving it gradually to an earlier, more school-appropriate hour. Get school supplies and records together over the summer; avoid the last-minute flurry that can make children anxious and get them worrying about school.

Worrying about school is something that all children do at least a little. One kind of worry grows out of what other children say at school. If your child is starting kindergarten, taking a bus for the first time, or going to a new building, he is especially susceptible to reports from others about what to expect—and what other children say is rarely encouraging.

It is human nature to tell about the most unusual features of our experiences. Adults don't come home from work and say, "I opened the mail, I emptied the garbage can, I placed 50 return calls, and I engaged in small talk at the water cooler" if those things happen every day. Instead, adults will tell about the "crazy" customer, the machine that went out of control or the weird encounter with a coworker. Children do the same selective reporting, and they are more prone to embellish their stories. So other children hear only about the "dragon" teacher, the pink slips, the fire drills, and the "impossible assignments." Help your child check for reality amount the wild stories. Some reassurance by adults can assuage child anxieties.

Another appealing aspect of school is the opportunity to complain. "I have to go to school and slave at hard labor for six hours!" No less than adults, children enjoy work and its productive results in the school world. But they also love to complain. Be alert to real pain in the complaining. There are sometimes things that require adult intervention; however, much complaining is just letting off steam or feeling important or both.

School is terrific, too, because, as it stands now, there is a beginning middle and end. A school year is over, there's the respite of summer vacation, and then it starts again. Closure is very satisfying to children, as it is to adults. The most important thing parents can do is work to increase the satisfaction by helping the child do well in school. Showing an interest in school topics as well as an interest in good performance is critical. Actually have conversations about what your children are studying. Help your child have the time, space and materials needed to complete homework and school projects. Make the effort to communicate with the child's teachers. Read and respond to what is sent home from school.

The life work of children is learning. Lots of that learning can be done in school. Nip in the bud negative comments from other adults about school—"Gearing up for another year of the same old grind?" or "Summer vacation is almost over; what a shame!" Adults must provide lots of positive talk about school and learning in order to facilitate another great year.

FAMILY CHAOS AND SCHOOL READINESS

Who invented this whole school thing anyway? Is your house a place of **chaos** on school mornings, afternoons and evenings? Do lost headbands, unmatched socks, and jumpy tummies characterize your mornings? Do homework tantrums and snack battles consume your afternoons? Are evenings of quiet book reading or TV a thing of the past? Does text anxiety dominate your home in March and April? Then you must have children in school.

School is probably a great place to learn useful things such as how to withstand an unkind word from a peer. School is also the place where most children learn to read and work math problems. But getting ready for, recovering from, and getting back and forth to school can pose some real challenges for families.

Let's start with the mornings, because most days do. Actually, this leads us to evenings. Remember how quaint it was to get out your clothes for school the night before? It's time to resurrect quaint. Get the children in he habit of choosing clothes and finding matching headbands, socks or whatever before going to bed. Always lay things out in the same place or you defeat the purpose of saving time and hassles in the morning.

Right after toothbrushing before bed, some families find that putting on toothpaste for the next morning saves another step in the groggy A.M. The toothpaste gets a kind of film over it, but once you wet it again, it works just fine.

Prepacking book bags is also a good idea. Whatever homework hasn't gotten done by bedtime probably isn't going to get done in the morning either, so pack up homework, supplies for the next day, etc., and put the book bag in the same place each day.

Mornings may not be the time to have gourmet meals. Breakfast cereals that lack full nutrition but get eaten by the "picky troops" may be worth it. A healthy bowl of oatmeal that remains uneaten provides no nutrition. Jumpy stomachs may benefit from a cup of tea. Mint tea may be especially good for soothing mild cramps of anxiety. Ask each eater to bring dishes to the sink; at least it won't look so bad after work or after school.

If you find yourself chronically cutting it too close, and the wear and tear on your nerves is not worth it, try getting up ten minutes earlier. The pain may be endurable because the start to your day isn't so grim with that little time cushion. Have you seen the video *Alexander and the Terrible Horrible No Good Very Bad Day*? Watch the morning "get it together" scene as a family. A little humor couldn't hurt.

Okay, let's say they get to school. It's a foregone conclusion that they will eventually return home too. Afternoon homework tantrums can be reduced by using the same time each day. For some families, right after school is perfect because the homework can be "gotten over with." For other families, homework must wait until parents are home from work to insist and supervise. The important thing is to establish routines. Use a stopwatch and prove how little time homework can really take. By the amount of moaning and whining, you would be convinced that homework will consume no less than 30 or 40 grueling months! The stopwatch may also create some competition against the clock and add fun to homework for some children.

Snack battles may be resolved by involving children in the planning. Let them choose from two things or take them to the store and have them help select things in the first place or have children take turns planning and preparing snacks.

Ah! Evening! Plenty of rest and relaxation as soon as the dishes, grass, homework, preparing for morning, dinner, baths, nail clipping, hair curling, washing, shopping, bill paying, etc., are done. Can it be 9:00 already? Today, as long as you're not going to get any rest anyway, make sure to ask that your child tell you one thing about the bus ride or walk to school and one thing that happened at school. All of the other trials can be borne if your relationship with your children is good. Keep the lines of communication open and hang in there. School only lasts for nine months!

SCHOOL SUPPLIES–AND TIME!

In the last weeks of August, I see thousands of children with their hundreds of parents swarming from Venture to Wal-Mart to K-Mart, shopping for school supplies. Watching the credit cards and cash pass hands, I began to think about what it really takes for a child to succeed in school. All of the parents who were buying crayons, scissors, Gitano knap-sacks, pencils and glue certainly had the right idea. They were simultaneously providing two things important to school success to their children: **time** and **things.**

It seems that we are more comfortable providing the things because it is easier for us to know which things will be right. Occasionally, we might accidentally get the wrong designer label on the book bag or the wrong character on the lunch box or even the wrong kind of markers. But at least we have a hint of the kind of supplies necessary to make it in school. Fortunately, many of us went to school so we know what things they use there.

The other factor, so critical to the learning of children, is TIME. But here we are less sure. Do we spend the time nagging that homework should be done or do we spend the time nagging that breakfast should be eaten? Do we spend time conducting interviews about what happened at school or do we spend time taking children to the zoo and museums? Actually, the answer is yes to all of the above.

Yes, plan with children every day how to approach homework. This is tough after about the first week of school because we burn out. But if we burn out, so do they. Consistency of parent interest and attention is the single biggest factor in children's school success. So plug on. Set aside a place and time for homework and set a minimum amount of time to do it. If no formal homework has been assigned, spend the time having the children read books, listen to learning tapes, read the newspaper, etc.

Yes, nag the children about eating decent food at decent intervals. Engines do not run without fuel, and brains do not function well without nutritious food and beverages.

Yes, ask your children lots of questions about what happens in school. Refuse to accept "nothing" as a response. Find out the names of their teachers and the topics of their classes. Try to ask every day about each one and the homework that might have been assigned for each. You will probably find that the children will probably balk—our oldest often complained about the Spanish Inquisition and suggested that we simply put bright lights on him and beat him with a rubber hose, thinking that would be preferable to our "conversations" about school. After three months of such complaints, I left him alone one day, only to be asked at 10:00 p.m., "Doesn't anybody care what happened to me at school today?" Children don't always know what they need, and sometimes we must give them what they need despite their protests. If you miss your children some days because of work hours, use a notepad or tape recorder system for communication. Waiting until the next day to "chat" may simply be too late.

Yes, be informed about school. Most of your information will come from your child, from your daily talks about school and from letters sent home from school. Don't hesitate to follow up by phone either. There is no rule that you must wait until report card time to meet or contact your child's teacher(s). Teachers cannot come to the phone when you call because they are in the classroom, but you can leave a message and most will readily return your calls.

Yes, engage your children in activities that help them learn about the world around them. Zoos and museums, libraries and gyms, beaches and concerts are all fine places for families to interact and learn. One of my children told me to get off the highway at the green sign one day. I had never explained to them that green signs signal exits but they have seen me get off the highway at such signs often enough to figure out that that is the rule. And this child was two! Some researchers estimate that we learn 90%-95 percent of what we know incidentally, that is, not by means of intended instruction. The more exposure children have, the more likely they are to make such connections.

You matter a great deal to your child's success in school. You demonstrate that you think learning is important in all of the activities described here, even by buying the things they need. But don't stop at investing the kind of time that buying school supplies takes. Keep investing that kind of time for every week of the school year and you will be delighted with the results in the gains made by the most important reason for school—your child(ren).

Chapter 25

FAMILIES AND ACADEMIC SUBJECTS

Sometimes parents think of school learning as something that happens only at school. That is probably just a fond hope. Besides there's always homework...and conversations about school. You get the picture. It is the responsibility of a parent to make sure the children become educated. Part of that responsibility means making sure that children are enrolled in a school where they can learn, part of that responsibility is monitoring the progress of children at school, and part of that responsibility is to stimulate learning in every facet of a child's life. Some of those facets actually intersect with school subjects. In the following sections, there will be many suggestions which you can use to strengthen **your child's learning in the traditional academic disciplines.**

READING SKILLS

Let's think of learning to read as a six-step language ladder. First, babies experience the world with their **senses:** touch, taste, hearing, sight, smell. Then, they begin to form **concepts** about what they have experienced. As babies get older, they begin to realize that people around them say the same sounds every time they point at the same object. Eventually, babies begin to realize that these sounds must name the object, and the words spoken and understood are termed **receptive language.** Babies then try to produce those words (**expressive language**). The last two steps of the language ladder are **reading** and **writing.** These cannot be climbed until there has been considerable practice on the first four rungs (McMahon, 1996). Reading and writing development is enhanced in homes where literate family members read and write for their own purposes (Purcell-Gates, 1996).

Research has demonstrated that a child does not meaningfully grasp the name for something until the concept for that object is solidly in the mind of the child. Even as adults, we do not add words to our listening and speaking vocabularies until we have the concepts behind them. So it remains important for children in all grades to have varied and numerous experiences, still using the five senses, to form the basis for new concepts and growing vocabularies.

As children gain new concepts and build listening/speaking vocabularies upon those concepts, they develop the base for reading and writing vocabularies. In fact, until about the end of elementary school, listening/speaking vocabularies are the best predictors of reading/writing vocabularies. This shows us that sense experiences are actually part of reading instruction.

Reading asks children not only to represent their ideas in spoken words but to take another step and recognize symbols that stand for the spoken word that stands for their ideas. No wonder it takes six years of preparation to learn to read!

In fact, the best research says that most children learn to read when they are six, unless there is a serious impediment. Therefore, we should not be worrying about whether children can read until they are six! You would not expect a baby of one month to walk, because you know that one-month-old babies do not have the skills (balance, spinal control, etc.) necessary to do so. We should not expect children younger than six to read, because they do not have the necessary skills to do so.

So why do some children younger than six read? For the same reason that some children walk at eight months of age and others walk at eighteen months. There is a great variety among individuals. However, we do not expect children younger than eight months to walk and we should not be impatient when children younger than six do not read. Instead, it is the role of teachers and families to continue to surround children with experiences that build concepts and words to describe those concepts. Slowly we add letters and their sounds.

We must also remember that it is at six that we expect children to **begin** to read. Most children will not be picking up novels or the newspaper and reading as fluently or with the same ease as they speak. We should applaud their efforts all along the way just as we laughed, clapped, and repeated their early spoken words. Only six years old and on the second to last rung of the ladder!

There are things that families can do to help children learn to read (Exceptional Children, 1996). Here are some family reading activities. Please notice that most of these are activities that any family can use. Don't worry if you work; a number of studies (Parcel, 1996) have indicated that parental work does not have a strong direct effect on reading achievement; put your time and effort when you can into the following types of activities:

1. Model reading for your child (Butler, 1988; Purcell-Gates, 1996). Show that you enjoy reading newspapers, books and magazines. Share pictures, stories and anecdotes from these sources.

2. Read the newspaper with your child. Introduce children to regular sections and special features. Discuss front-page headlines and political cartoons. Complete children's quizzes, puzzles or contest applications. Plan family outings from the cultural and special events listing. Collect articles and pictures for a school paper, discussion, bulletin board or debate. Clip favorite headlines, pictures, cartoons or stories to share with the family on your bulletin board or refrigerator.

3. Encourage summer reading. Compile summer reading lists for leisure, recreation and vacation reading. Make reading a relaxed activity and spend fifteen minutes reading in a hammock, in a tree, on a beach, or on the front porch. Encourage your child to join a summer reading program to explore new book themes or old favorites.

4. Engage in a variety of family reading formats. Read before you go on a car trip, start a new hobby or begin holiday preparations (Wayman, 1995). Read to find recipes, tour a museum, or find out about a play from its program. Engage in parallel reading; family members can all read at the same time or on the same topic at their own reading level. Have older children read to younger children.

5. Encourage adolescents to read. Suggest materials dealing with their special interests: sports, relationships, musical groups, careers, science fiction, the supernatural, adventures.

6. Read to your child and have your child read to you (Butler, 1988; Instructor, 1996).

7. Conduct a variety of library trips to challenge family reading interests.

8. Incorporate reading into home and community activities (Instructor, 1996). Demonstrate the practical uses of reading: finding telephone numbers, following cookbook directions, making home repairs, planning and caring for gardens, clothing and pets. Play family games which require reading.

9. Read at home to support school learning. Read about topics that your children are studying in school when you read your news weekly, newspaper or other books.

As you read **to** and **with** your child, you will discover your areas of common interest as well as your child's unique interests. You will strengthen your child's academic skills, broaden the scope of leisure-time activities and develop a bond that will enrich your family life.

WRITING SKILLS

Donald Graves, of the University of New Hampshire, thinks that in terms of **writing,** we should be "taking students off of teacher welfare," that is, topics for writing do not have to come from the teacher. Children have their own experiences and ideas and should write about them. In addition, teachers and parents should also write with their children (Graves, 1978).

It is always important to have a reason to write. Writing "just for practice" when they were young may be one of the reasons that some adults now avoid writing. When a person is really motivated to write, writing meets a need. Some reasons for writing include: thank-you notes for relatives and friends who have given a gift or done something nice; letters to legislators, media (editorial, questions about programming), companies (send me more, I need a part, we are dissatisfied with our purchase, etc.), and entertainers (you are my favorite, when is your next movie?, etc.; stories for younger siblings, baby-sitting clients, school assignments, friends, and local and national publications; poems to express a deep feeling, play around with words and rhyming, complete an assignment in an unusual way; and news items for church bulletins, school newspapers, local newspapers, and publicity pieces.

The list is endless. These ideas may just get the family thinking of some ways to write **for a purpose.**

Once a child or a family sets a purpose and it is time to write, it might help to know that writing is not a one-step activity (Dodd, 1996). The writing process is one that takes several steps and improves with practice. Writing down thoughts is not just talking aloud and writing down what you hear yourself say. But that is not a bad start. Talk into a tape recorder to tell a story, "write" a letter, or make a statement. Then play it back, starting and stopping to allow time to write down what is heard. This helps avoid "'writer's block."

Writing is different than printed speech because it is often necessary to be more formal in written English. What sounds perfectly natural when you talk may look less than perfect on paper (Holmes, 1993). Learning to write (and writing well) takes four basic steps (Dailey, 1991).

The first step is prewriting. In this step, the stage is set. The second step in the process is writing the actual words on paper. The third step is editing and the fourth is publishing or sharing.

Each of these steps can include a number of fun and helpful activities. As usual, there are a few books that may help you: *How to Write a Composition* by Bertha Davis (1985), published by Franklin Watts and *Help Is On The Way For: Writing Skills* by Marilyn Berry (1986), published by Children's Press of Chicago.

Writing is important as a means of communication and as a way to clarify thoughts. Writing things down, even if no one else ever reads them, can be therapeutic. You can write down gripes and "get them off your chest." You can write down lists in the middle of the night when too many responsibilities keep you awake. Making the list can relieve the worry and let you get to sleep. Children may use writing for the same purposes. Keeping journals or diaries, jotting down concerns or worries can be helpful for the spirit.

Formal writing for school is another form of writing. It is not as simple as just jotting down ideas. For school writing, attention must often be paid to details like punctuation and capitalization. For this kind of writing, a number of steps are necessary. The steps are prewriting, writing, editing and publishing.

Prewriting

In order to get the stage set or get ideas to write about, you can brainstorm. Have a discussion of ideas, words, story lines, characters, settings, etc. (Awbrey, 1989). Make lists, words that might be used, vocabulary for the topic. Make a list of what you want to be sure to include in the writing. You can have a shared experience so that every person in the family has the same thing to write about. Shared experiences might include taking a trip; seeing a movie or TV show; going to hear a speaker or listening to the stories of a relative you visit; eating something new together, or trying a new recipe; observing an exhibit or going to a museum together; playing a game; engaging in a physical activity or sport; taking a walk; going shopping; going to the park; or reading a book. When you get down to the writing, everyone should have ideas to express.

Writing

Perhaps you are writing to complain about a product you bought or to state your opinion. To help with this and any other type of writing, you might use some of the following tips.

Make a list of helpful words: introductory words (once upon a time, in the beginning, first); transitional words (in order to, then, secondly); connecting words (and,. but, therefore, nevertheless, because); or summarizing words, (finally, in conclusion). Perhaps you could use a checklist of what should be in the story if that is the type of writing you are doing: setting, characters, plot, crisis, and resolution. You could also use a checklist of what should be in a letter: heading, greeting, body, and closing. Use a formula to be sure you've included everything you want to say. Try reporting questions: who, what, when, where, why and how.

Be creative in choosing writing topics. Here are some suggestions: When My Parents Were Little, My Family, Crazy Creatures, My Best Friends, and Just Before I Go to Sleep....

Editing

Editing and revising is another step in the writing process. Revising uses feedback to alter the written words. The idea here is to be comfortable with and approve of your writing. You also want to communicate with your readers. Using correct spelling, for instance, is a courtesy to the reader, so that the reader can recognize the word.

Try these ideas when revising. When you use self-evaluation, read what has been written aloud. Use a resource to check spelling, grammar, and punctuation. Pose questions: What did I leave out? What would someone else need to know? What do I like best? Especially in a family, group evaluation or editing is very helpful (DeBaryshe, 1996; Howard, 1996). When you use group evaluation, read aloud to family members. Pose questions: What didn't you understand? What do you want to know more about? What did you like best? The writer should make notes on the original paper as improvements are suggested.

Publishing

Publishing or sharing is the last step in the process. Now the letter or story is rewritten to include the improvements that were suggested in the editing phase. The final product may be neater, clearer, look more formal or be presented to a larger group. Read the writing aloud to the whole family or some other group. Rewrite the work on good paper and display it somewhere in the home. Prepare copies to distribute. Mail the letter. Record the story on a tape recorder with dramatic reading. Act out the play, poem, story or dialogue.

Publish for fun; publish with flair! What about 'binding" the book with decorated cardboard? Lace the pages together with ribbon, yarn or shoelaces. Put your family poems on construction paper and laminate them as placements. Spend some time illustrating your stories and make a children's book for younger readers. Check publications for the possibility of sending in children's work for evaluation.

Highlights Magazine, Children's Digest, and others publish work by children.

Books for children include:

Make your own book: A complete kit. (1993). Philadelphia, PA: Running Press.

Nixon, J. L. (1988). *If you were a writer.* New York: Simon and Schuster.

Stevens, J. (1995). *From pictures to words: A book about making a book.* New York: Holiday.

Swain, G. (1995). *Bookworks: Making books by hand.* Minneapolis, MN: Carolrhoda.

Books by children (as models) include:

Leigh, N. K. (1993). *Learning to swim in Swaziland: A child's eye view of a southern African country.* New York: Scholastic. (gr. 1-4)

Temple, T. (1993). *Dear world: How children around the world feel about our environment.* New York: Random House. (gr. 2-6)

SPELLING SKILLS

An important aspect of editing is **spelling.** Once you have an idea for writing, spelling can be a stumbling block. The following information may help (NEA, 1987b).

Why bother with spelling? Basically, it's a courtesy to the reader. What seems like a logical spelling to you may not seem so to your reader. We agree on arbitrary rules so that we all know what to expect and can recognize what word is meant when we see it.

How will children learn to spell? Learning to spell is developmental, like most other things we learn. Developmental spelling is also called invented spelling. Most of the errors children make when they invent their own spellings follow some systematic pattern (Green, 1990; Topping, 1995). The pattern might be due to an error in remembering the visual shape of a word or an error in hearing the sounds of the word. The more children are exposed to correct print in books, signs, and by role models, the more often they will attempt to imitate that correct spelling (Holmes, 1993).

Should parents spend a lot of time correcting spelling? In kindergarten and first grade, and perhaps in second grade, probably not. Parents can, however, help with repeated exposures to correct spelling in books. Read, Read, Read! Call attention to the way words are spelled. "Isn't that weird? That word starts with an 'n' sound but the first letter is 'g'."

There are guidelines to follow in teaching spelling.

1. Do not confine spelling to formal instruction; children can look up words as the need arises.

2. Provide children with occasions to write.

3. Provide children with lots of exposure to print, even if they are not

reading yet (looking at the printed page while parents read to them, posters in children's rooms, etc.)

4. Encourage invented spellings at first.

5. Encourage the use of phonics; "the letter 'b' makes a 'buh' sound."

6. Make allowances for inexperience with print. Every writing experience should not be subjected to criticism.

7. Provide intense language experiences and word study.

8. Teach children to look at the length of a word, and look at what's inside a word (a smaller word). Make up memory tricks. (Say silent letter sounds aloud just for the purposes of spelling.)

9. Practice with spelling. Write a word several times when rehearsing. Say the word aloud or the letter names when writing them. Write on a chalkboard. Practice with individual syllables of a word. Practice moving letters around or touching the shapes: write in sand or use Scrabble tiles.

10. Help children with homonyms (pear, pair).

11. Be careful with words that many people mispronounce (jewelry, nuclear, similar).

12. Teach your children to check words through the strongest sense: Does it look right? Do I see a letter for every sound I say?

13. Reduce the size of the spelling list. There is no rule that says you must study 10 or 20 words every night. Spread out the work; study most nights but review only some of the words.

14. Be sure to teach the method or principle behind words of a certain type. You will never be able to teach a large enough word bank so that children can manage independently in all settings. Strategies and principles that will help them with new words are important.

15. Remember that learning to spell is problem solving that can be learned from modeling (the parent thinking aloud: "i before e, except after c").

16. Check out this K-2 book: Zalben, J. B. (1981). *Oh, simple!* Greenville, SC: Farrar, in which one child derides another's inability to spell.

17. Improve your own spelling!

SOCIAL STUDIES SKILLS

Social studies is the part of the school curriculum that deals with human relationships. Family, school and community life are rich with experiences that give children opportunities to study people and their interactions. The social studies include economics, history, geography, urban studies, political science, anthropology, and sociology. Other special topics might revolve around global education or international studies, legal studies, women's studies, future studies, and racial or ethnic issues. These areas of study help children develop the following skills: Entering into group discussion, reading and casting a ballot, reading a map, applying for a job, opening a bank account, valuing human life and dignity, articulating one's own viewpoint, choosing an occupation, listening and responding to the view of others, seeking out new information, and making decisions.

It is readily observable that numerous activities at home, at school and in the community facilitate the development of social studies skills (Hennessey, 1994; Hurst, 1996; Klefstad, 1995; Kronowitz, 1985). Here are some activities that might be suggested to parents:

1. Read various sources for information on the same topic.
2. Go to the library as a family; allow children to make their own selections.
3. Watch television shows, films or plays together and discuss them.
4. Read the daily newspaper, or parts of it, aloud. Watch a newscast together and discuss it.
5. Have a map and globe available in the home. Use them to identify locations that come up in family experiences.
6. Listen to recordings and radio. Go to hear various speakers. React to what has been heard.
7. Carry out experiments. For example, find out if using polite words (thanks, please, etc.) encourages more cooperative behavior among family members.
8. Take field trips to gather information. Go to ethnic restaurants, museums, exhibits, or fairs, or meet people of different ethnic groups and just talk. Visit local historical places, choose historical sites for vacation spots or form a history league of your own neighbors to learn about the area in which you live. Go to the city hall or village center in your community. Attend court sessions or stop into offices that have significance for your family.
9. Look for good places to find inexpensive objects around a theme for a "home museum" display.
10. Write letters to get information. Write to legislators, public officials, companies, organizations, television stations, etc., whenever a family discussion leads to the need for more information.

11. Give children opportunities to make choices within the constraints of limits set by adults. (You must clean your room. Would you rather start under the bed, in the closet, or on the floor around the bed?)

12. Interview people. We had a great chance to interview a Norwegian man in full native dress at a local zoo. He was on hand to supervise the moving of a long ship that had been on exhibit in a city park to a warehouse for restoration. He had swords and GREAT axes (the boys were thrilled!), as well as a beautiful hat with decorative studs and reindeer boots. We learned so much!

13. Get family histories. Interview relatives, particularly those in other generations. Check how their experiences differ by when they were born, where they were raised, their genders, etc.

14. Encourage children to express opinions. Solicit their opinions when it is appropriate for children to participate in family decisions.

15. Study pictures, drawings, charts, tables, graphs, and public statues. It is surprising how many examples of these are in the local newspaper, in home towns, and in books, once the search begins.

16. Make charts, graphs, drawings and tables to represent family activities and other data.

17. Participate in school events and encourage your children to do likewise. Community involvement begins there.

18. Look for geographic information (elevation signs, mile markers, historical markers, etc.). Discuss what these pieces of information mean to the people who live near them.

19. Ask children to voice their reasoning processes. Why did Arthur select this present? When will Maria have to get up in the morning to coordinate her use of the bathroom with the time needs of others in the family?

20. Encourage your children to have and actively pursue hobbies or other areas of interest.

21. Have a good reference library at home if possible. Include reference encyclopedias (for most topics, a current set is not necessary), an atlas, and an almanac (paperback copies are less than $10). Borrow these things or use them periodically at the library if that suits your family better.

22. Model democracy; treat all children within the family fairly and equally. Participate in democratic family meetings. Establish rules and assume leadership and "followership" roles in helping govern the family and carrying out its plans.

23. Designate each family member as a media expert on a topic of their choice. That person acts as a magnet for information on the topic and then as a clearinghouse for information about the topic to others.

24. Vote in elections and model the kinds of behaviors you want your child to engage in within the community.

25. Participate with others in their ethnic, cultural and religious celebrations when invited. Look up information about the event before or after attending to gain even more insight and knowledge. Investigate why these groups value their customs.

26. Allow children to help keep family banking records, fill out applications, etc., when it is appropriate.

27. Educate the whole family about politicians that represent your community. Be sure every member of the family knows the president, mayor, and important legislators. Contact these persons by letter when necessary.

28. Read and discuss stories about famous Americans in government.

29. Use a sample voter registration form and have the child fill it out. Bring political party posters, handouts, buttons, and information home and make a display for a local or national election.

30. Take your children when you vote on Election Day. Get a sample ballot during your visit.

31. Display the American flag on national holidays.

Because social studies involves all of the social skills used in group living, opportunities for practical application abound, beginning in the family and extending into the community.

Books that may pique the interest of children in the social studies include:

Ackerman, K. (1990). *Araminta's paint box.* New York: Atheneum.
Edwards, M. (1990). *Dora's book.* Minneapolis, MN: Carolrhoda.
Spier, P. (1973). *The star spangled banner.* New York: Doubleday.
Winnick, K. B. (1996). *Mr. Lincoln's whiskers.* Honesdale, PA: Boyds Mills Press.

MATHEMATICS SKILLS

Literacy. What is it? Probably most people know that literacy refers to the ability to read, comprehend what is read and use reading for everyday living and leisure. What about numeracy? Some use this word to mean the ability to use numbers, understand their meanings, compute, and work with number concepts in everyday living and leisure.

Many parents help their children gain literacy skills. Parents help by talking and singing to very young children, encouraging children to handle books (even chewing on the cardboard ones!), and reading in front of children so that they see that adults read too.

How can parents help their children gain numeracy skills? It's so easy! You can start today.

1. Refer to numbers around you as you talk with your children. Counting fingers, toes, ears, noses, and other body parts is a beginning with very young children. Over time, babies learn the names of the body parts and begin to gain familiarity with the numbers, too. Count stairs, plates to set the table, number of persons in line at the movie, etc.

2. Mention time and money numbers as you use them. We aren't sure when children are able to grasp these concepts. Using the words and referring to the concepts regularly allows children to understand them when they are ready. "It's 3:00." "I have $2.00." "I need 40 cents for the toll."

3. Let your children cook with you. There are plenty of numbers in cooking, from ounces and quarts to numbers of potatoes or apples to measuring spoons and cups. Even pans have measurements (13" by 9"). Pots are rated in size by the quart. Older children can also understand volume and area as well as linear measurement.

4. Build with your children. Kits, models, birdhouses, Tinker Toys, Leggos, blocks, K-Nex. It doesn't matter what you build. How things connect, how their spaces fit together, and even sometimes numbers to refer to their measurements help children learn about numbers.

5. Street signs that refer to numbers or the use of numbers in their names are great: 159th Street, 47th Place, etc. House numbers are useful for finding places you need to go, and practice with those numbers builds toward numeracy. Learning that a certain street is 4000 west will help children navigate as they get older, too.

6. Using travel time on the bus or car, using "wait" time at the doctor's or dentist's office, making use of the minutes as you wait for a train...these are perfect times for practicing basic facts from memory. Children often struggle with more advanced concepts because they have to put so much mental power into figuring out the basic facts. Having memorized basic facts, gaining "automaticity"–recalling the facts without much cognitive effort, frees up the brain to concentrate on new concepts, such as multiplying by two digits or adding mixed numerals.

7. There is good evidence that practice with patterns enhances the brain's ability to acquire and use mathematics concepts. Any visual patterns

in logos, billboards, floor tiles, etc., can be studied and identified. Patterns in music, order of presentation, room construction, etc., are identifiable, too.

8. Schedules, menus, meters (for gas, electricity, water), scales, bills, invoices, business brochures, labels, packaging, the list is endless! Each of these has a numerical, measurement or rating component. Learning math skills with these "authentic" items makes learning relevant and more innately motivating to youngsters.

Books about math may include those with a number of topics. Money books include the following:

Anno, M. (1991). *Anno's math games III.* New York: Philomel. (gr. 5-9)
Axelrod, A. (1994). *Pigs will be pigs.* Portland, OR: Four Winds. (gr. 1-2)
Brandrath, G. (1984). *Numberplay.* New York: Barnes and Noble. (gr. 5-9)
Byars, B. (1993). *McMummy.* New York: Viking. (gr. 4-5)
Herman, C. (1991). *Max Malone makes a million.* New York: Henry Holt.

Counting books include these:

Anno, M. (1995). *Anno's magic seeds.* New York: Philomel.
Baker, A. (1994). *Gray rabbit's 1, 2, 3.* New York: Kingfisher Books.
Bang, M. (1983). *Ten, nine, eight.* New York: Greenwillow Books.
O'Keefe, S. H. (1989). *One hungry monster.* Boston: Joy Street Books.
von Noorden, D. (Ed.). (1994). *The life size animal counting book.* London: Dorling Kindersley.

SCIENCE SKILLS

The most important question that can be asked in science is "WHY?" Children are naturally interested in science kinds of things when they are young. Why does it rain? Where do the stars go? Why do some people have freckles? Why do planes stay up? Curiosity, developed through active participation, is what children need to get them interested in science (Hagerott, 1997).

Not knowing enough science yourself is a reason that parents give for not doing science with their children. You don't have to know it or teach it. You just have to do it. You just have to watch your children do it and talk about what happened. If you want to learn things you never learned when you were a child, children's books about science in the library are the best source. Forget trying to learn from sophisticated adult or college-level books; the authors of children's science books, particularly those with illustrations, photographs, and experiment descriptions, make science clear and even fun.

Sometimes a parent is an expert on one aspect of science. This may not only help the child of that parent but the parent may provide a service to the school or at least one class. Parent volunteers may lead students through a hands-on science activity. This may help the parents become positive and enthusiastic advocates for the cause of good science education (Fehlig, 1996).

In one case, a sixth grade science teacher called on parents of the three classes that she taught to join a "Science Club." Of approximately 75 sets of parents of the students in her classroom, three parents came to the first meeting. Not discouraged, the teacher explained that she would like to have parent input and assistance in any way that went along with the curriculum. After some open discussion, one of the parents, who worked at a large fruit and vegetable market in a transportation hub city that furnished a huge metropolitan region with their produce, volunteered to make weekly visits to the three classes. Each week, the parent would come with a different fruit or vegetable. The parent provided an explanation of where and how the produce grew and what part of the plant it was. He also served the students a small taste of whatever produce was featured that week. At the end of twelve weeks of study, the parent coordinated (with the help of the teacher) a field trip to the open market at the time of fresh produce delivery at around 4:00 a.m.! Everyone had a great time and the principal had the good grace to call the school day over when the group arrived back at school at 8:00.

Parents have the most interest in their own children, and their interest and concern may overcome any inadvertent or even deliberate lack of attention or expectation for science achievement at school. M. Jones (1996) described a national program designed to promote equity in mathematics, science and technology. Parents were encouraged via this program to conduct science investigations together. This kind of "learn together" idea may work best for busy families with just a half hour or hour to share together.

Parents may even be in the best position (compared to teachers) to help children learn science. No matter how tightly classroom behavior is controlled and guided by teachers and curriculum materials, students always retain personal control over their attention and effort (Anderson & Lee, 1997). So, effective science instruction has something to do with understanding students, their personal agendas and their other commitments. Parents often know their children and their children's lives intimately; this edge can help us decide which science ideas to explore when. Interest in makeup is a sign to discuss skin care and reaction to chemicals and sun. Baseball season prompts discussions of force and distance. Encouraging children to ask why and to continue to experiment and read to find the answers is the most important thing parents of students can do with regard to science.

Books that can help children love science include:

Pfeffer, W. (1995). *Marta's magnets*. Silver Burdett.
Sis, P. (1996). *Starry messenger*. New York: Farrar, Straus & Giroux.

MAKING MUSIC

Music is sounds and silence put together in a special way. Music may be written down. The written form of music using marks and symbols is called a score. The marks and symbols are called notation. Music is meant to be heard, but some people have more fun writing music or playing it than just listening. Your family can choose the way(s) you want to enjoy music.

Music education may have several goals: composing music and creating scores; performing music by playing an instrument or singing; listening and understanding what the composer or musician is "saying" to you; listening and identifying which instruments or voices are creating what you hear; changing or adding something new, such as singing a harmony or speeding up the beat or adding another instrument. Children learn self-discipline from practicing an instrument or singing and achieve a sense of accomplishment that comes with mastering something that takes work (Marsalis, 1995).

Musicians agree that several things make up music. These things are melody, rhythm, tempo and tone. **Melody** is a group of sounds that are strung together. **Rhythm** has to do with how long or short the notes or sounds are. **Tempo** has to do with how quickly or slowly the sounds are played or sung. **Tone** is harder to understand. Tone is the difference between different instruments and voices even when they are playing or singing the same notes. A violin has a different tone than a tuba. A soprano (higher female voice) has a different tone than a tenor (higher male voice). People who write music (composers) and people who perform music use these aspects of music to make their messages clear to the listener (Green, 1983).

Even in the same family, different members seem to have more or less interest in listening to music, different tastes in type of music and different talents for writing or performing music. Sometimes all members of the family like to sing, such as the Pointer Sisters, the Jacksons, the Mandrells, and the Osmonds. Whatever way your family chooses to enjoy music is just fine. But you may want some ideas on how to use music for family activities and learning. Here are several:

1. Take the whole family on a music outing, to a concert at a hall or in a park, or to a school program. Check for music events in your town.

2. Provide lots of opportunities for children to hear all kinds of music, from jazz to classical, from rock to gospel.

3. Sing along with tapes, CD's or the radio together.

4. Sing along at public events such as church services.

5. Enjoy songs on car trips, some you might even make up, using a melody you know but making up your own words.

6. Bring different tapes along on family outings including those you borrow from your library. Experiment with voting on which family members like which kinds of music.

7. Tune into a variety of radio stations in order to experiment with different types of music. If the songs are in a language you don't know, guess by the sound of the song what the words might be.

8. Participate in any programs that might be offered through school (NEA, 1987e). Some programs allow children to rent or lease instruments.

9. Expose children to music lessons whenever possible or when they show interest. Taking lessons does not mean a child will become a musician but broadens exposure to interesting things. Learning another symbol system (musical notation) can also aid in reading development (NEA, 1987e).

10. Play rhythm and tapping games at home. One person taps out a rhythm and someone else tries to repeat it, or family members take turns "drumming" to records, tapes or radio programs.

11. Watch MTV and other music channels together.

12. Watch public television broadcasts of various musical artists together.

13. Enjoy silly activities such as communicating during a meal only by singing the things that need to be said.

14. Parents can make up songs for their young children with the child's name and facts about the child in the song.

Music is something that is a part of every person's life to some degree. Often, however, we do not recognize its meaning or contribution. Parents who become consciously aware of music in their lives and expose their children to listening, creating, and performing music, add a new dimension to the learning of their children (NEA, 1987e).

Books about music for children include:

Fiarotta, N., & Fiarotta, P. (19--). *Music crafts for kids: The how-to-book of music discovery*. New York: Sterling.
Haseley, D. (1983). *The old banjo*. New York: Macmillan.

ART SKILLS

Art is a powerful expression of emotions and feelings. It allows children and adults to express themselves. Art gives pleasure, enjoyment, entertainment and fun and helps us communicate in new ways. Art is also non-threatening because the child is free to search for information, skills, and techniques without the need for one correct answer.

Art also facilitates the development of small muscle coordination by manipulation. Art activities help to develop use of the senses as vehicles for learning.

The reference to art really includes numerous forms of expression. Just seeing these forms listed may give your family ideas for art experiences.

Photography
Filmmaking
Sculpting (with clay, wire, stone, etc.)
Drawing (with crayon, marker, pencil, chalk, etc.)
Weaving (with cotton, wool, synthetics, lanyard, paper, reeds, etc.)
Illustrating (cartoons, ads, etc.)
Architecture (including drawing and building models)
Printmaking (from fingerpainting to lithography)
Painting (with oils, acrylics, tempera, watercolors, food-dyed
    liquids, pudding, etc.)

Like music, art can be enjoyed in the making or in the appreciation of someone else's production. Families may experience art at an art museum, arts and crafts show, local school or library display of art, local college or university gallery, business or bank that may have a temporary exhibit or display.

Read about and look at pictures in books or on the computer about art. Some libraries and museums even lend slide collections of famous works of art. Produce your own "books" of art with photographs taken by family members.

Art displays in homes often take the form of pictures or other projects held to the refrigerator with magnets. Another possibility is to install self-adhesive cork strips along a hallway or on the wall of a child's room. Pushpins can be used to easily change this temporary exhibit.

Crafts may serve not only to beautify your home but may have functional roles, too. How great to curl up under a lovely afghan for a rainy day movie! Make the afghan or other craft on a rainy day, too. Crafts are closely related to art and may have some of the same benefits. Excellent sources of family learning, crafts may include rug-hooking; bead work; origami; macramé; paper mache; dried and silk flower design; painting small wood objects; leather-working; making dioramas, shadow boxes, collages, or decoupage; needlework; metal-working; and woodworking.

There is no limit to the kinds of materials or experiences families can share in creative arts and crafts. The important thing is to have fun and allow a great deal of room for creative expression.

Books about art for children include:

Agee, J. (1988). *The incredible painting of Felix Clousseau.* Greenville, SC: Farrar.

Jonas, A. (1983). *Round trip.* New York: Greenwillow.

Tucker, J. S. (1994). *Come look with me: Discovering photographs with children.* Charolottesville, VA: Thomasson Grant.

REFERENCES

Awbrey, M. J. (1989). A teacher's action research study of writing in the kindergarten: Accepting the natural expression of children. *Peabody Journal of Education, 64*(2), 33-64.

Brenner, B. (1990). *The preschool handbook: Making the most of your child's education.* New York: Pantheon Books.

Butler, A. (1988). *The elements of a whole language program.* Crystal Lake, IL: Rigby.

Carroll, M. K., & Smith, K. M. (1990). *The home as learning center: The family as educator.* Dubuque, IA: Kendall/Hunt.

Clark, J. (1996). Involving parents in middle school. *Teaching PreK-8, 27*(3), 52-53.

Dailey, K. A. (1991). Writing in kindergarten: Helping parents understand the process. *Childhood Education, 67*(3), 170-75.

Dalton, D. (1996). The parents as educational partners program at Atenville Elementary School. *Journal of Education for Students Placed at Risk, 1*(3), 233-47.

Deaton, C. D. (1990). History and community resources: Teaching children about our national heritage. *Social Studies and the Young Learner, 3*(1), 6-8,11.

DeBaryshe, B. D. (1996). What a parent brings to the table: Young children writing with and without parental assistance. *Journal of Literacy Research, 28*(1), 71-90.

Dodd, A. W. (1996). What do parents mean when they talk about writing "basics" and what should English teachers do about it. *English Journal, 85*(1), 58-61.

Ellis, S. S. (1996). Principals as staff developers: "Putting theory into practice": A profile of Anna Steffin. *Journal of Staff Development, 17*(3), 51-52.

Epstein, J. L., & Hollifield, J. H. (1996). Title I and school-family-community partnerships: Using research to realize the potential. *Journal of Education for Students Placed at Risk, 1*(3), 263-78.

Fehlig, J. C. (1996). Parents' science lab. *Science and Children, 34*(2), 17-19.

Graves, D. (1978). *Balance the basics: Let them write.* New York: Ford Foundation.

Green, C. (1983). *Music.* Chicago: Children's Press.

Green, C. (1990). Assessing kindergarten children's writing. *Dimensions, 18*(2), 14-18.

Hagerott, S. G. (1997). Physics for first graders. *Phi Delta Kappan, 78*(9), 717-720.

Hennessey, G. S. (1994). Reliving colonial days in your classroom: Curriculum boosters. *Learning, 23*(3), 66-68.

Holmes, J. G. (1993). Teachers, parents, and children as writing role models. *Dimensions of Early Childhood, 21*(3), 12-14.

Howard, K. (1996). When parents serve as writing critics. *Teaching PreK-8, 27*(2), 58, 61-62.

Hurst, C. O. (1996). Mini-learning centers. *Teaching PreK-8, 26*(8), 62-64.

Instructor. (1996). The primary theme club: Home and family. *Instructor, 106*(1), 77-84.

Jones, M. G. (1996). Family science: A celebration of diversity. *Science and Children, 34*(2), 26-30.

Jones, R. (1996). Producing a school newsletter parents will read. *Child Care Information Exchange, 107,* 91-93.

Klefstad, J. (1995). Cooking in the kindergarten. *Young Children, 50*(6), 32-33.

Kronowitz, E. (1985). From customs to classroom. *Social Studies Review, 24*(1), 68-73.

Markle, S., & Cichowski, R. (1983). Science expo '83. *Instructor, 92*(8), 68-71, 78.

Marsalis, W. (1995). We all need time in the woodshed. *Our Children, 21*(2), 28-29.

McDonald, L. (1996). The Hazeldean Project: Strategies for improving parent information sessions. *Teaching Exceptional Children, 29*(2), 28-32.

McMahon, R. (1996). Introducing infants to the joy of reading. *Dimensions of Early Childhood, 24*(3), 26-29.

National Association of Secondary School Principals. (1996). *Breaking ranks: Changing an American institution.* Reston, VA: Author.

National Education Association. (1987a). *Get involved in your child's school.* Washington, DC: Author.

National Education Association. (1987b). *Good spellers: Born or made?* Washington, DC: Author.

National Education Association. (1987c). *Let's have a conference: You and your child's teacher.* Washington, DC: Author.

National Education Association. (1987d). *Making parent-teacher conferences WORK for your child.* Washington, DC: Author.

National Education Assocation. (1987e). *Music in the schools.* Washington, DC: Author.

National Education Association. (1987f). *The schools are yours: Help take care of them.* Washington, DC: Author.

National Education Association. (1987g). *What to look for when visiting your child's school.* Washington, DC: Author.

Parcel, T. L. (1996). The effects of parental work and maternal nonemployment on children's reading and math achievement. *Work and Occupation: An International Sociological Journal, 23*(4), 461-83.

Purcell-Gates, V. (1996). Stories, coupons, and the "TV Guide": Relationships between home literacy experiences and emergent literacy knowledge. *Reading Research Quarterly, 31*(4), 406-28.

Robb, J. (1993). Young inventors ask what if. *Roeper Review, 15*(4), 243-245.

Sanders, M. G. (1996). Action teams in action: Interviews and observations in three schools in the Baltimore School-Family-Community Partnership Program. *Journal of Education for Students Placed at Risk, 1*(3), 249-262.

Sui-Chu, E. H., & Willms, J. D. (1996). Effects of parental involvement on eighth-grade achievement. *Sociology of Education, 69*(2), 126-141.

Topping, K. J. (1995). Cued spelling: A powerful technique for parent and peer tutoring. *Reading Teacher, 48*(5), 374-83.

Vickers, H. S., & Minke, K. M. (1995). Exploring parent-teacher relationships: Joining and communication to others. *School Psychology Quarterly, 10*(2), 133-150.

Wayman, M. (1995). Quick starts. *Instructor, 105*(3), 14-18, 20-23.

Weatherly, M. S. (1992). A future fair: Building tomorrow today. *Gifted Child Today, 15*(5), 27-28.

Young Children. (1996). Using NAEYC's code of ethics. *Young Children, 52*(1), 66-67.

CONCLUSION: WHAT DID YOU LEARN ABOUT SCHOOL TODAY?

Scientific and psychological information on how humans learn, what affects memory and how to facilitate learning: what to do about homework; research data about learning styles and how to acquire study skills—all that in just the first section!

Inclusion, cooperative learning, whole language, middle schools, multi-disciplinary study, bilingual education, school testing, and parents' rights; now you have the vocabulary and conceptual basis for interpreting what goes on at school and what it means to you and your children.

You didn't need to be told what the challenges of parenting are, especially those that relate to school learning. But perhaps now you have some ideas of what to do about those challenges. You have tips for child development, learning wherever you and your children are, and learning in every season.

Finally, you've brought what you know about school funding and selection into conscious awareness and you have suggestions for how to use the knowledge you have. A variety of types of parent involvement in schools is available to you, and everything from starting school to parent-teacher conferences to family learning in each academic subject has received review.

You've expended effort and come away with a likely answer for the question you've often posed to your children: What did you do at school today?

EPILOGUE

As you finish this book, you now have some of the answers to the question the title poses about your child: What did you do at school today? However, you still may not know exactly what your child did at school this particular day. Please consider the following suggestions for keeping up with you child's current school experiences:

1. Spend at least three minutes every day in conversation with your child about school. This can include what happened at school, what homework there might be, and who sat with whom at lunch.

2. Memorize your child's schedule and teachers names. Use this information in specific questions regarding the day's events.

3. Use information from this book so that you can speak the "lingo" of the school and gain access to your child's school experience.

4. Show you care by finding the time and space for your child's school "stuff."

5. Demonstrate that you continue to learn, even as an adult. Observed lessons are stronger and more easily learned than spoken ones.

6. Love your child as a whole person, whose main responsibility right now happens to be going to school. Good luck!

INDEX

229